P9-CJX-423

Secret Missions of the Civil War

SECRET MISSIONS
of
the Civil War

First-hand Accounts by Men and Women
Who risked their Lives in Underground Activities
for the North and the South

woven into a continuous narrative by

PHILIP VAN DOREN STERN

―――――

WINGS BOOKS • NEW YORK / AVENEL, NEW JERSEY

Copyright © 1959, 1987 by Philip Van Doren Stern.
Copyright 1959 under International Copyright Union
by Philip Van Doren Stern.
All rights reserved.

This 1990 edition is published by Wings Books,
distributed by Outlet Book Company, Inc., a Random
House Company, 40 Engelhard Avenue, Avenel, New
Jersey 07001, by arrangement with Philip Van Doren
Stern.

Printed and Bound in the United States of America

Library of Congress Cataloging-in-Publication Data

Stern, Philip Van Doren, 1900-1984
    Secret missions of the Civil War : first-hand
accounts by men and women who risked their lives in
underground activities for the North and the South /
woven into a continuous narrative by Philip Van Doren
Stern.
        c.   cm
    Reprint. Originally published: Chicago : Rand
McNally, 1959.
    ISBN 0-517-00002-4
    1. United States—History—Civil War, 1861-1865—
Secret service.   2. Spies—United States—History—
19th Century.   3. United States—History—Civil War,
1861-1865—Personal narratives. I. Title.
E608.S8   1990
973.7'852—dc19   88-39636
                                            CIP

14 13 12 11 10

CONTENTS

CONTENTS

CONTENTS

Contents

INTRODUCTION

I FIRST BECAME INTERESTED IN THE CONSPIRATORIAL ASPECTS OF THE
Civil War in 1937 while doing research for a book on the assassination of Abraham Lincoln. At that time certain documents relat-
ing to Civil War history were still restricted. The Government felt
that some of the people involved—or their immediate descendants
—might be living and that their reputations might be harmed by
letting the public examine material that had to do with disloyalty,
treason, court martials, espionage, or the other clandestine activities that are characteristic of the kind of warfare which goes on
behind the lines in any period of armed conflict.

Americans, perhaps more than any other people, seem to
believe that spying is a wicked practice indulged in only by the
enemy, and that we, as honest, forthright citizens of a free nation,
do not ordinarily engage in such underhanded work. This attitude
has cost us heavily in the past and may again in the future. George
Fort Milton, in his fine book, *Abraham Lincoln and the Fifth*

9

Column, summed up this attitude: "There seems something insidiously debasing about the business of being a spy. Such men play a two-faced game of false representation and connivance. They employ the general principle that the end to be served—the service of their country—is so important . . . that they are justified in almost any sort of conduct to carry out their task. Yet there is something inevitably corrupting and cankering attached to evil, whether the evil lie in the means or in the ends. Character can seldom stand up against these unseen assailants. Perhaps this is why many spies come to betray both masters. Moreover, the profession seems to have the almost inevitable accompaniment of the money itch. . . . Almost never do these men become great heroes in the public mind, either during the war itself or in . . . history . . . but this does not mean that they are free from hazard. . . . At any moment the spy may be suspected, or detected and rushed to a firing squad. The danger . . . differs from that of combat on the battlefield only in that . . . it hangs forever over the secret agent's head. The fear is not of the bayonet, or the bullet, or the chance of capture by raid. It is that of sudden suspicion, secret betrayal, or chance blunder."

In 1953 the last of these long-suppressed secret service files of the Civil War were finally released *in toto:* today any qualified person can examine them in the National Archives.

I was allowed to go through the Lincoln Assassination files in 1937 when they were still in the custody of the Judge Advocate General. I have been through them many times since. They make fascinating reading, for one always feels that perhaps the very next document will cast new light on the many mysterious aspects of the Lincoln Conspiracy that still remain unsolved.

To go through all the Union and Confederate secret service records is quite a chore, since they are numerous, largely unsorted, difficult to read, often fragmentary, and in many cases exceedingly dull. Yet in them and in the allied records of the Union and Confederate Armies and Navies, the State and Treasury departments in the National Archives are literally thousands of dramatic and thrilling accounts, any one of which could be the starting place for a full-length book. Unfortunately, though, the material is all too often incomplete, so you may stumble across something that seems interesting but for which you can find no beginning or end.

You may discover, for instance, the record of a dispute about repaying $28.50 to a Federal woman spy, Mrs. Frank Abel of Baltimore, for buying men's clothing to use as a disguise. But that is all there is. Why this otherwise forgotten woman was prowling around the United States in wartime disguised as a man is not revealed. You will also find many references to the record book of Sheridan's scouts, but the volume itself cannot be found. This is a great pity, because the free-ranging Union cavalrymen led by Sheridan's chief of scouts, Harry H. Young, habitually entered the Confederate lines wearing Confederate uniforms, and their adventures and escapes would make lively reading. Perhaps the record book will turn up some day.

The Union secret service records take up many feet of shelf space. Many of them, especially the section with the eye-catching title "Scouts, Guides, Spies, and Detectives," are still kept in the clumsy Woodruff file holders into which they were put in the nineteenth century. The Baker-Turner papers are so numerous that they have their own contemporary index. And then there are all kinds of miscellaneous documents. The accounting records for secret service funds disbursed in some parts of the country are very complete; they are missing entirely for other sections. Some of the correspondence of the Confederate commissioners stationed in Canada still exists. So do documents written in cipher or code. But despite the fact that these records are so voluminous, they represent only a small part of what was originally confided to paper by spies and undercover agents. And what was recorded was only a very small fraction of the secret information that was gathered

11

on both sides. Most of it—and probably the most interesting part —was never committed to paper at all, but was reported verbally. Much of what was written was immediately and purposely destroyed, or was burned up accidentally during the great conflagrations that devastated Richmond, Atlanta, Columbia, and other Southern cities during the war. Later, still more went up in flames when private individuals decided to destroy anything they thought might be embarrassing or incriminating.

After you have spent day after day examining such data in the National Archives, the Manuscript Division of the Library of Congress, and the other libraries which preserve documents of the Civil War period, you finally come to the conclusion that you have touched only the outer edges of a vast, murky area which must always remain largely unexplored.

Yet going through the records is absorbing work. The agents who turned in this information scooped up everything that came their way. Stored with the manuscripts is the brass seal of the secret filibustering organization known as the Knights of the Golden Circle, which the mysterious Dr. George W. L. Bickley organized before the Civil War began; this later became the Order of American Knights (OAK), the symbol for which was an ordinary oak leaf pinned to the lapel or passed on concealed in a closed fist in what seemed to be an ordinary handshake. All kinds of odd physical objects are scattered through the papers, including small copper stars of approximately the same size and shape as those worn on the shoulders of American generals to indicate their rank. These were probably used by members of the Order of the Star, a local Copperhead group centering in Ohio. Plans of fortifications made by spies are there; so are small packages of chemicals to be used for invisible writing.

The files are a strange hodepodge; in some cases the true meaning of the material is still hidden, as is the case of a large sheet of yellow paper which reads in part: ". . . horses is own

France England his and family at he of for and earnestly lived
use a a hen . . ." and so on in the same vein of seeming non-
sense. This is a coded message, of course, but a code—especially
an old one—is even harder to break than a cipher, for to translate
a code requires finding or reconstructing the agreed-upon set of
word substitutions that was originally used. No modern cryptanalysis expert is likely to want to waste his valuable time trying
to unravel the meaning of a long-obsolete bit of military information.

The raw material of history is there in the Archives, but it is
in such chaotic form that it seems unlikely that much sense can
ever be made out of much of it. It is most useful when a well-
trained person goes through it and is lucky to dig out valuable
nuggets of information which shed some new light on a subject
about which he already knows a good deal. James Horan, combin-
ing odds and ends from the Archives with the Hines Papers in
the Margaret I. King Library of the University of Kentucky, was
able to bring to life that strange and daring conspiratorial figure,
Captain Thomas H. Hines, in his pioneering book *Confederate
Agent*. Yet Horan only touched upon the enormous and widespread plot against the United States Government in Civil War
times. Wood Gray's *The Hidden Civil War* deals only with the
Copperheads; so does George Fort Milton's *Abraham Lincoln and
the Fifth Column*. But Union and Confederate secret missions
went far beyond those covered in these modern authors' books.
They were world-wide in extent. James D. Bulloch, who headed
the Confederate secret commissioners overseas, told of their activities in England and on the Continent in his *Secret Service of the
Confederacy in Europe*. The Canadian aspect was at least outlined
by another Confederate agent, John W. Headley in *Confederate
Operations in Canada and New York*. And other Confederate
agents, such as John B. Castleman, Basil W. Duke, Adam R.
Johnson, and Bennett H. Young, wrote books about their various

activities. Unfortunately, in many cases these soldiers told more about their exploits on the battlefield than they did about their work as secret agents.

There were more Confederate than Union secret missions for the simple reason that the Southern states, which lacked manpower and natural resources, had to resort to stratagem and deception more often than the North. The North, with its much greater strength, could afford to be more reckless in its expenditure of soldiers' lives and military material, knowing that there were always more men and weapons to be had.

Many of the personal accounts written by the Union and Confederate civilian agents and military personnel who went on secret missions are of dubious literary quality. Relatively few people were well educated in those days, and even among those who were, the style of writing varies widely from the cut-and-dried, factual wording of a formal military report to the overblown elegance of Victorian prose. In some cases, the participant used the services of a ghost writer—often with disastrous results. Pauline Cushman, a Union actress-spy, is practically lost to history because she entrusted her story to F. L. Sarmiento, a pretentious hack who wrote her biography in so lush a style that the modern reader can hardly get through it.

Another Union spy had the record of his really important activities spoiled by an utterly incompetent printer. Felix G. Stidger, whose *Treason History of the Order of Sons of Liberty* tells the inside story of how this remarkable agent broke up the Copperhead conspiracy in Indiana, had the misfortune of having his not very well-written text printed on very bad paper in a type face which is so grotesque that it is practically impossible to read.

The books and pamphlets which tell the personal stories of the men and women who went on secret missions for the North or the South form an interesting body of literature, but most of them were issued in very small editions by local printers or publishers and have become very scarce. Some few exploits, like the Andrews Locomotive Raid, have been so widely publicized that I have purposely omitted them. I have included William B. Cushing's rather well-known account of blowing up the Confederate ram, the *Albemarle*, because I consider it one of the finest of all Civil War personal adventure stories. (The original manuscript, incidentally, is in the Old Navy records in the National Archives.)

Generally speaking, the personal narratives written for publication offer more interesting reading than the raw material found in manuscript collections. These accounts are better integrated, more consecutive in action, more understandable, and are much better in their characterizations than the contemporary documents. The writers of the contemporary records took it for granted that the person receiving his message or report would be acquainted with the antecedent action, the terrain, and the people concerned. As a result such documents are of interest only to scholars who must bring to them a vast amount of previously assimilated Civil War history. In order to make the eyewitness accounts printed here more understandable to the modern reader I have introduced each piece with an explanatory note which sets the background, and, where circumstances warrant, have also provided a terminal note to tell the reader what happened afterward. Then, in order to place everything within the general scheme of things during a war that involved nearly thirty-two million people, I have written brief summaries which give the backgrounds of military and political events for each year from 1861 to 1865.

In this way I have attempted to trace the evolution of underground activity for the entire Civil War. Oddly enough, this has never been done before. No one has tried to show how military actions were often tied in with secret missions undertaken by civilians who may seem far removed from what the Union and Confederate Armies and Navies were doing. Nor has anyone endeavored to demonstrate how various secret missions were often interconnected, how one grew out of another, or how a group of men who had gained experience and proved their courage and daring in one field of action would be sent to work in another. The hard core of Confederate agents who came from John Hunt Morgan's Kentucky raiders to operate in Canada, New York, Chicago, and other places is a prime example of this.

Words used during the Civil War do not always mean now what they did then. Then an army intelligence office was a bureau which tried to answer questions asked by families and friends about the probable whereabouts of soldiers who had been reported killed, wounded, or missing. There was nothing secret about its activities; its purpose was kindly, its intentions humane. Its work sometimes called for friendly contact with the enemy in order to claim the bodies of the dead and arrange for the exchange of prisoners of war.

The term "secret service" as used in America has also undergone a great transformation of meaning since the Civil War when "special service" or "detached service" meant practically the same thing.

The United States Secret Service was founded on June 23, 1860, as a bureau of the Treasury Department to suppress counterfeiting. It did not have an officially appointed chief until July 5, 1865, after the war had ended. The present United States Secret Service is still a bureau of the Treasury Department. One of its two functions is to suppress counterfeiting and to guard the money, securities, obligations, and other fiscal activities of the Government. Its other function is to maintain the White House Police Force and to protect "the person of the President of the United States and members of his immediate family, the President-elect, and the Vice President at his request." And those are the only two functions of the modern bureau as defined by law.

During the Civil War all kinds of detective and counterespionage activities were loosely called "secret service." Allan Pinkerton, who is sometimes said to be the first head of the United States Secret Service, was actually in charge of such work specifically for the Army and then only while McClellan was in command. And Lafayette C. Baker, who wrote *History of the United States Secret Service* and acted as if he were in charge of all detective, police, espionage, and counter-espionage activities for the Federal Government, was careful to sign his official communications as "Agent of the War Department" or "Provost-Marshal, War Department." He was sometimes referred to in the press as "Chief of the Government Detectives."

The State Department under Seward largely directed secret service work for the Government during the first year of the war. After January 13, 1862, when the strange, dictatorial Edward Masters Stanton took over the War Department, Baker carried out his orders. Together, they arrogated to themselves practically all national secret service activities, and made and executed their own laws. During their regime, the "Secret Service" was all powerful; even the mighty were afraid when they were visited by its representatives; its star-chamber proceedings often outraged lawyers, judges, and the public, but once a person was arrested and incarcerated in one of the jails set apart for political prisoners, he sometimes had to remain there for months without even being able to find out what charges were to be brought against him.

Yet, despite the highhanded methods used by its officials, the Secret Service probably did a fairly good job during the Civil War if one considers the adverse circumstances under which it had to work. It was very new and had had no time to build an organization. There was no precedent for what it might do or might not do. It had to operate during a national emergency of such a nature that it was often impossible to determine who was friend and who was foe. Its agents were often charged with being corrupt, but it must be remembered that this was a time when high military and governmental officials were working with respected business-men on deals that often bordered on treason.

But if secret service in the North was slow in getting under way its Southern counterpart was even slower. The North had a regular Army and a skeleton organization on which various governmental activities could be based. The Confederacy did not establish an official secret service bureau until November 30, 1864, when the war was nearly over. It may have been prodded into doing so then by George P. Kane,* who appealed to Jefferson Davis on October 8, 1864, to establish a secret service corps. In his letter to the president of the Confederacy, Kane suggested that such an organization might work with the Signal Corps. Because of its experience in using codes and ciphers, the Signal Corps was then often closely connected with secret service activities.

Both sides were absurdly unprepared at the beginning of the war, because neither had truly believed that sectional antagonism would ever flare into armed conflict. Except for the minor Mexican War in 1846-48, neither the people of the North or of the South had had much experience in military affairs. They knew even less about gaining information by stealth, influencing the enemy's mind by propaganda, or destroying property by sabotage.

With one aspect of underground warfare, however, both sides had already had a great deal of firsthand experience. Secret raids into hostile territory had been carried out in Kansas in 1856 by border ruffians bent on spreading slavery there. New England's Emigrant Aid Society had armed the antislavery settlers by shipping in Sharps rifles packed in crates marked "Bibles." (These were the famous "Beecher's Bibles," named after the abolitionist minister, Henry Ward Beecher.) When proslavery men from Missouri and Southern states sacked Kansas towns, John Brown and his sons immediately retaliated with a night raid in which the slaughter was swift and merciless. Their attempt to seize the Government arsenal at Harpers Ferry on October 16, 1859, can be called

---

*Probably Marshal of Police in Baltimore. He was arrested and then fled to the South.

18

the first important secret mission of the Civil War—even though the armies had not yet begun to march. Brown failed to free a single slave, but he succeeded brilliantly on the propaganda front, for his deed was celebrated in song and story long after he and most of his men had been killed.

The modern reader, whose life has been spent in an era of gigantic professional wars waged on a world-wide scale and who is so used to elaborate security measures that he takes them for granted, will probably be amazed and perhaps amused at the amateurishness of most Civil War secret missions. At the beginning particularly, both armies were so incredibly naïve that they ignored people who were gathering information right under their noses. And both armies were remarkably gallant in trying to preserve the amenities of civilian life in wartime. Since no one would then think of executing a woman for espionage, female spies could come and go almost without hindrance. Such weapons as land and naval mines were adopted with great reluctance because they were regarded as infernal devices unfit for civilized warfare. Even the repeating rifle was slow to be adopted, for it was felt that its superior firepower gave its users an unfair advantage over their opponents.

As the war progressed and hostilities became bitterer and bloodier, these pleasant amenities were gradually dropped. By 1864 the Confederacy was in such desperate straits that underground warfare seemed to be the only way out. This was the time of the incredible Northwestern Conspiracy by which the Confederates hoped to stir up armed insurrection in Indiana, Illinois, and half a dozen surrounding states. Acts of sabotage, armed robbery of trains and banks, attempts to seize ships by stealth, and plots to burn Northern cities became common during the last terror-ridden months of that year. The Confederates, whose homes and cities had been destroyed by Sherman and Sheridan, believed that they were justified in using such extreme violence.

19

Unfortunately, none of the Confederate secret agents who were at work in 1864 left a complete, well-written, or fully integrated account of the vast conspiracy they were planning against the North. But they did write about certain aspects of it. Two of the leading figures in the plot began a detailed history which started to appear serially in *The Southern Bivouac* late in 1886. These were Thomas H. Hines and John B. Castleman, who had access to the papers of the Canadian commissioners. Their history started out bravely; then it became more general in tone; finally it petered out altogether without revealing much that was new or interesting. Forty years later, when Castleman's equally fragmentary book *Active Service* was published, he said that Jefferson Davis had advised them to be cautious. As a result, they were so guarded in their statements that they were criticized even in the South.

Since the intricate plot against the North was not told in full by any of the men who participated in it, I have gone to some length in my introductory note to the year 1864 to clarify the complexities of this widespread conspiracy which would have broken up the United States into a number of small, independent nations if it had been successful.

During the winter of 1864-65, it became increasingly evident to thinking men that the Confederacy could not hold out once Grant's armies began moving in the spring. On January 15, 1865, when Fort Fisher, the Confederate key to Wilmington, North Carolina, fell before a Federal amphibious assault, the South lost her last port of any consequence and was practically cut off from the outside world. Nevertheless, two men set out on secret missions to seek last-minute support in Europe.

Duncan F. Kenner, a Louisiana sugar planter who owned many slaves, boldly entered the Northern states to take a steamer from New York to London, where he arrived late in February to find that James Mason and John Slidell, the Confederate diplomatic commissioners to England and France, were in Paris. He went there to meet them and to convey a message from Richmond that the Confederacy might be willing to give up slavery in exchange for European recognition. An interview was arranged with the French Minister of Foreign Affairs, and everything momentarily looked hopeful.

In March, another Louisianian, C. J. Polignac, went to Paris without authorization from Richmond, and was granted an audience with Napoleon III. Both missions were doomed because Sherman and Grant were bringing the war to a close so rapidly that no foreign country would dare to come to the aid of the falling Confederacy at that late date. Although Polignac afterwards denied that his privately organized mission was in any way connected with a project for setting up a Southwestern Confederacy, there is no doubt that such an idea was being considered during the last stages of the war. Texas, Louisiana, Mississippi, and Arkansas, were to be united into a new slaveholding confederacy that would also absorb as much adjacent Mexican territory as could be obtained. An emissary had been sent to Emperor Maximilian, the puppet of the French, some time before, and that ill-fated ruler was reported to have listened favorably to the scheme. It seems very possible that he would have been glad to exchange land peopled by unruly peasants far from his base in Mexico City for the support of battle-trained Confederate soldiers to hold his shaky empire together. The whole plan, of course, came to nothing on April 9, 1865, when Lee entered the McLean house at Appomattox to surrender the Army of Northern Virginia to Grant.

On April 14, only five days after the surrender at Appomattox, a young, handsome, and well-known actor named John Wilkes Booth stepped into a box in Ford's Theatre and assassinated the President of the United States. In the wild hysteria that followed, charges were repeatedly made that Booth's senseless act was part of a vast Confederate plot to eliminate the chief officers of the

United States Government. Since a nearly successful attempt at assassination was made simultaneously on Secretary of State Seward by one of Booth's fellow-conspirators, and evidence brought out later showed that attacks may also have been planned that same evening on the lives of Vice President Andrew Johnson, General Grant, and perhaps still others, the people of the North felt that they had good reason to believe that the Confederate government and its leaders may have been implicated in a widespread murder plot.

When the conspirators associated with Booth were brought to trial before a military commission, the Federal Government charged that Jefferson Davis and certain Confederate commissioners stationed in Canada had "incited and encouraged" those who were being tried for murder. The trial was so mismanaged by the Government, which made use of notorious perjurers to try to implicate the Confederates in everything from planning assassination to poisoning reservoirs and shipping clothing "infected" with yellow fever into the cities of the North, that the absurdity of some of the charges and the dubious character of some of the witnesses caused the Government's case against the Confederates to collapse.

Ever since then, constant debate has gone on as to who—if anyone—was behind the Booth assassination plot besides the conspirators known to have been connected with him. There is every reason to believe that unseen backers were aiding Booth, but their identity has always remained shrouded in mystery. Were they people connected with the Confederate Government, as was then believed? This has never been proved and is still indignantly denied. Or were they Northern Radicals acting through Secretary of War Edwin M. Stanton to put Lincoln out of the way so they could punish the rebellious South? Otto Eisenschimil, in his book *Why Was Lincoln Murdered?* examined the evidence on this with great care and had to deliver the verdict that "an indictment against Stanton cannot be sustained for lack of material evidence."

One thing is certain, however. Booth's violent act was a secret mission. Whether it was authorized by the Confederate government or was treasonably sponsored by Northern people cannot be proved one way or the other. I have spent years examining the documents in the case, and although I have discovered many new, strange, and interesting clues I cannot arrive at any definite conclusion. The mystery remains unsolved and must continue to be so unless important new material is discovered. Such material may not exist, for there was a general holocaust of anything having to do with John Wilkes Booth during the frenzied days immediately following the assassination.

The whole body of documentary evidence dealing with all the secret missions of the Civil War is extensive, but it is not impossibly large. Every scrap of evidence in printed or manuscript form could be summarized on not too many thousands of IBM punch cards and organized in various interesting ways. If this were done it might then be very revealing to set the indicators of the sorting machine to drop out what was wanted and see what cards, all related to each other, would come tumbling down. Suppose, for instance, that one were to call for all the cards referring to that ever-puzzling figure, John V. Andrews, who appears in history only for a day or two in connection with the New York Draft Riots in July, 1863. With what other secret missions might he have been connected? He may, of course, have used a series of aliases. This was common practice; therefore certain agents might have to be traced through a maze of a dozen different names. Yet some of the different aliases used by some of the agents are known; perhaps still others could be found. Booth, too, would be well worth trying to track down. His sister, Asia Booth Clarke, in a book that was not released to the public until 1938, said that her brother had told her how he had traveled in Texas and Kansas using a pass signed by U.S. Grant. Her admission that Booth was acting as a spy and a blockade runner for the Confederacy can be corroborated from other sources. But how did he get a pass from General Grant?

This brings up the most interesting question of all those concerned with secret missions. Who was working for whom? And to what cause, if any, were some of the secret agents really loyal? There were many double spies; there may have been more of them than anyone has ever suspected.

In this book I can only sketch the outlines of this most fascinating and baffling of all areas of Civil War history—the secret missions, civilian, military, and diplomatic. The field still remains largely unexplored. For decades after the end of the war, scores of men who had taken part in it wrote what they knew about the military operations. Government historians worked from 1864 to 1927 to compile the 128 volumes which contain the Official Records of the Union and Confederate Armies and the 31 volumes which print similar accounts for the two Navies. Captured Confederate records dealing with underground activities were published rather freely in this Government publication, but except for military missions, the Union side of the story was cautiously withheld from the public. Only within the past two decades has enough material from many sources been released to make it possible for the serious historian even to attempt to explore this uncertain field. As yet very few have taken advantage of the fact that the seals have at last been broken.

It will take many years of patient research by a number of people to sort out and make the new material freely available; it will then take more years to piece their findings together so they make some kind of sense. From all this work worthwhile new evidence may emerge. People whose loyalty to one cause or the other has always been taken for granted may prove to have been secretly disloyal.

In certain cases the clues may lead to high places and involve people who have thus far seemed remote from any charge of perfidy. During the past twenty-five years the release of more and more material has already shown us that some of the Civil War figures who once appeared to be of heroic stature have since been proved to be decidedly less than lifesize. However, no charge of actual disloyalty to their own cause has yet been successfully proved against any of the major figures of either the North or the South.

The long dispute as to whether or not Robert Todd Lincoln destroyed some of his father's papers that may have "contained the documentary evidence of the treason of a member of Lincoln's Cabinet" was not settled on July 26, 1947, when the eighteen thousand individual documents comprising his collection were made public. No such evidence was found. Does this mean that there was no such treasonous Cabinet member? Or does it mean that Lincoln's son burned any compromising documents as several people close to him said he did?

More light has been brought to bear on the lesser figures. It has recently been shown, for instance, that Senator William Sprague of Rhode Island, who married Secretary of the Treasury Salmon P. Chase's daughter Kate, was engaged in treasonable deals that might have brought him to the gallows in a sterner civilization. Orville H. Browning and "General" James W. Singleton, fellow-attorneys of Lincoln in Illinois, were not the staunch friends of the President they long were believed to be, for they were both engaged in profiteering in contraband cotton and tobacco. Even Ward Hill Lamon and Leonard Swett, who were really close to Lincoln, were also using their connection with the White House to profit personally by trading in the spoils of war. None of these men is likely to have been an agent of the Confederacy, but their loyalty and usefulness to the Union cause was certainly vitiated by their willingness to be corrupted for pecuniary gain.

It is even more difficult to find proof of perfidy or treason among the leading figures of the Confederacy than it is among their counterparts in the North. This does not necessarily mean that these men were of a purer breed. The shipowners who profited by bringing in luxury goods through the blockade were as morally culpable as the Northern businessmen who dealt in contraband goods. It is merely that documentation of the Union side of the war is far more complete than the Confederate, so more is known about its peoples' activities. This is especially true about secret service activities, for most of the really vital Confederate secret records were destroyed when the fleeing Confederate government abandoned Richmond to the flames.

Yet enough remains to be worth trying to piece together. When Union and Confederate accounts are thoroughly explored and cross-indexed, a fresh appraisal of certain aspects of Civil War history may be required. Then the fading documents in a dozen different collections may give us enough information to make it imperative to revise our ideas of what really went on behind the military fronts of the Civil War. Ordinarily it takes just about a hundred years for all the participants in any action to die off. Centennials are based on something stronger than sentiment; they have a factual reason for being celebrated as well. The period between now and 1965 should reveal many things that have long been concealed and correct others that have intentionally been distorted. Civil War history is far from being exhausted. It should reach its fullest flowering in the years to come.

P.V.D.S.

Secret Missions of the Civil War

1861

As the decisive year 1860 drew to a close, the controversial Lincoln election, which had upset the precarious balance of power between the Southern and the Northern states, brought on secession. The slaveholding states had been threatening to secede ever since Calhoun's time, nearly a generation before, and were now making good their threat. Eleven states, with South Carolina leading the exodus, began to leave the Union. It was evident that war was at hand, but almost everyone believed that if it came it would be short. The North, with a population of twenty-two million and most of the country's factories, railroads, telegraph lines, ships, mineral and monetary wealth, could afford to feel secure when opposed by a small group of Southern states with a total population of only nine million, of which more than a third were Negro slaves. And the South could not believe that it would actually be invaded and held by force of arms to a compact it wanted to abrogate. Even if Federal troops did enter its territory, it felt quite sure that the despised "Yankee shopkeepers" would easily be repelled. Despite all the menacing gestures and pompous boasts, neither side was ready for war. The Confederacy had no standing army and no armed vessels. There were only 16,000 men in the United States Army, nearly all of whom were stationed in the West to guard frontier posts against Indian raids. Its commander, Lieutenant General Winfield Scott, was seventy-four years old and so fat from indulgence in rich food that he could not mount a horse. The Navy, too, was weak. Its fleet consisted of less than seventy serviceable ships, of which about forty were in commission, and of these only four steam-powered vessels were on the east coast. The rest were scattered all over the world, and, with communications as slow as they were then, it would take many months to bring them home. All these ships, of course, were built of wood; the day of the armored vessel was just about to dawn.

"Civil Wars," says the Army's official record of its own past (American Military History 1607–1953, Washington, D.C., 1956), "are almost impossible to plan for. . . . Further, it is unlikely that the Army could have prepared plans to coerce dissident states even if machinery had existed. When the Southern states began seceding, President Buchanan showed that he had no policy by doing nothing. Moreover, the men who served as Secretaries of War from 1853 until the end of 1860 not only opposed the Federal Government's right to coerce a state but joined the Confederacy themselves."

Some strange things had been happening while these pro-Southern Secretaries of War were in office. In December, 1859, just after the scare caused by the John Brown raid at Harpers Ferry, John B. Floyd, Buchanan's Secretary of War, ordered 115,-000 old-type percussion muskets and rifles to be shipped to five Southern arsenals. This, however, was not illegal, nor did it do the South much good, for the weapons were semi-obsolete and the Northern arsenals needed the space they took. But on December

20, 1860 (the day South Carolina seceded), Floyd gave verbal orders to ship 124 heavy guns from Pittsburgh to two uncompleted forts on the Gulf. Floyd was in trouble at the time because of improper financial dealings with contractors (from which he, however, did not benefit personally). On December 29, President Buchanan asked Floyd to resign and appointed Joseph Holt as his successor. Holt promptly cancelled the order for transferring the cannon.

On January 5, 1861, Senators from Mississippi, Alabama, Florida, Georgia, Louisiana, Texas, and Arkansas met in a committee room of the Capitol of the United States and passed a resolution urging their states to secede from the Union. They also recommended that a convention of the seceding states meet in Montgomery, Alabama, not later than February 15.

Early in February, representatives from the rebellious states organized a provisional government at Montgomery, where they elected Jefferson Davis president of the new Confederate States of America, authorized the raising of a volunteer military force of 100,000 troops, and appointed a three-man commission to go to Europe to seek recognition for their new government and make the treaties needed for dealing with foreign countries.

On February 11, Lincoln left Springfield, Illinois, for a slow journey east. Ten days later, he was warned that he might be assassinated when he changed trains in pro-Southern Baltimore. Accompanied by Allan Pinkerton, the professional detective who was to play an important part in the secret service activities of the first year of the war, the President-elect traveled in great secrecy from Harrisburg to Washington, where he arrived early in the morning of February 23. He stayed quietly in Willard's Hotel until he was inaugurated on March 4.

He had to face his first major issue early in April, when Fort Sumter in Charleston Harbor had to be supplied with provisions. The Confederates fired on the island fort on April 12; two days later the garrison evacuated their untenable position, and a full-scale war began.

On April 17, Jefferson Davis issued a proclamation announcing that he was ready to receive applications for letters of marque authorizing shipowners to operate their vessels as privateers. Some twenty-five of these hastily equipped privateers are known to have gone out searching for their prey during 1861, but most of them were small and poorly armed so they were not very effective. The threat they offered, however, was very real. New York merchants, frightened lest the richly laden steamers bearing gold from the mines of California be captured, protested loudly to Washington.

President Lincoln, galvanized into action after weeks of indecision, proclaimed a blockade of the ports in the rebellious states on April 19. His inadequate navy could not hope to enforce a blockade along 3,600 miles of hostile seacoast at that time, but all kinds of sailing ships, river steamers, ferry boats, and almost anything that would float, were being pressed into service. Lincoln had called for 75,000 militia volunteers on April 15; on May 3 he called for 42,000 more, and also authorized increasing the regular army to 22,714 officers and men. In the same proclamation he asked for the three-year enlistment of 18,000 additional seamen to enforce the blockade.

The troops were called up to repossess the forts, arsenals, navy yards, ships, and other Government property which the Confederates had seized. On the day after the proclamation of blockade, the important Gosport Navy Yard near Norfolk was destroyed by Union officers to prevent its ships, ordnance, and supplies from falling into the hands of the Confederates who had already carried off 2,800 barrels of gunpowder which had been stored in a magazine outside the yard. And the Government arsenal at Harpers Ferry, in which nearly 20,000 rifles and pistols were stored, was also burned by its Union garrison for the same reason.

Both sides now needed a respite during which raw recruits could be trained and arms and ammunition be obtained.

During this breathing spell there was relatively little action. The Confederate Congress met in special session on April 29 to raise money by issuing bonds, and to instruct its citizens to pay into the Confederate Treasury all debts owed in the Northern states. It then adjourned to meet again in Richmond on July 20.

On May 20, at exactly three o'clock in the afternoon, Federal agents descended upon every telegraph office in the North to confiscate copies of all the dispatches that had been sent during the previous year. These were carefully examined "to discover what persons had corresponded with the rebels." This overt move, of course, simply warned Confederate sympathizers in the Northern states to be more careful. The use of codes and ciphers became more widespread, and messages were often sent verbally instead of in writing. Want ads in newspapers also became a means of secret communication.

Washington had always been more Southern than Northern in its sympathies. During the time between the election of Lincoln on November 6, 1860, and his inauguration on March 4, 1861, the highly vulnerable capital of the United States was torn by dissension and uncertainty. People did not know where their neighbors stood, and Army and Navy officers of Southern origin began to resign in order to join the fighting forces of the Confederacy. Enlisted men were not allowed to resign; they could only desert. Yet very few in the regular Army or Navy deserted. They were professionals who had come to look upon the services as their permanent homes, so they nearly all remained at their posts throughout the war. Those suspected of being pro-Southern were kept at isolated places far from the scene of action.

The first major military action of the war took place on July 21 at Bull Run (First Manassas) with disastrous results for the

Union. General George B. McClellan was called to Washington a few days later, placed in charge of what was then called "The Division of the Potomac," and given orders to make soldiers out of the untrained recruits who had broken ranks and fled when they first encountered the Confederates.

The Federal Government made an abortive effort to put a stop to privateering by threatening to hang captured privateersmen as pirates on the theory that the Confederacy was not a real nation and that it therefore had no legal right to issue letters of marque. But when the Confederates met this threat by having Union officers who were being held at Richmond as prisoners of war draw lots to be hanged in retaliation, the Union backed down. The prisoners in question were then exchanged.

As the Federal blockade became more effective, Confederate privateers found it unprofitable to operate. By the end of 1861, practically all the smaller vessels, which Union Navy men contemptuously called the "mosquitoes of ocean warfare," had either been captured, destroyed, or driven back to port. A much more serious menace to Northern commerce were the Confederate cruisers. These were professionally operated warships with official belligerent status. J. R. Soley, the scholarly naval historian who was Assistant Secretary of the Navy during the administration of Benjamin Harrison, defined privateers and cruisers: "The essence of a privateer lies in its private ownership; its officers are persons in private employment; and the authority under which it acts is a letter-of-marque. To call the cruisers pirates is merely to make use of invective. Most of them answered all the legal requirements of ships-of-war; they were owned by the Government, and they were commanded by naval officers acting under a genuine commission. Some of them were put in commission at sea or in foreign waters, and never saw the country of their adoption; but their commission could not thereby be invalidated. There is no rule of law which prescribes the place where a Government shall commission its ships, or which requires the ceremony to take place, like the sessions of prize-courts, within the belligerent territory. . . . Neither the privateers, like the Petrel and the Savannah, nor the commissioned cruisers, like the Alabama and the Florida, were guilty of any practices . . . contrary to the laws of war."

The first Confederate cruiser was the Sumter, a former packet steamer which had been in service between New Orleans and Havana. Raphael Semmes, who was later to achieve world-wide fame for his exploits on the Alabama, was placed in command of her. She was not really suited for naval warfare, but he hurriedly had her rebuilt and armed. Late in June he descended the Mississippi only to find its mouths guarded by Federal warships. How he escaped is told here.

Although the Federal blockading fleet quickly drove the privateers off the seas, the owners of fast blockade runners operated by hard-driving masters, found the situation to be an exceedingly profitable one. Faster and faster ships, which were more and more heavily armed, ran contraband cargoes into Southern ports where they brought out cotton, a commodity that kept rising in price as the blockade made it scarce. Most blockade runners were privately owned and operated, but in the fall of 1861, the Confederacy's first government-owned blockade runner, the Fingal, sailed from Scotland to Savannah with a cargo of arms and ammunition.

The great sensation of 1861 was the seizing of two Confederate commissioners, James M. Mason and John Slidell, who were being sent to Europe to seek recognition for their new government. Captain Charles Wilkes, commander of the U.S. frigate San Jacinto, took them off a British steamer, the Trent, on November 8 and created an international incident which almost brought on a war with England. After much protest from the Confederacy and the British Foreign Office, the two men were allowed to go on their way on January 1, 1862.

The year 1861 proved to be an encouraging one for the South, but their early victories made the Confederates too confident. The Confederacy, however, did not do so well in Europe; there the new government was treated as a belligerent, but it could not gain full recognition as an independent nation.

Washington on the Eve of the War

by CHARLES P. STONE
from Century Magazine, July, 1883

[In 1860 the nation's capital was still a leisurely place with a small-town atmosphere. There were 3,200 slaves in the city, which had long been a slave-trading center where Negroes were sold to be shipped farther south. More than a third of the 66 Senators and 237 members of the House of Representatives were avowedly pro-slavery men. They, their families, relatives, and employees, made a large group of disaffected—and sometimes actively disloyal—citizens who had great influence in the country's seat of government at a time when the nation was rapidly drifting toward war.

Colonel Charles P. Stone, Massachusetts-born and a graduate from West Point in 1845, had served with distinction in the Mexican War. He tells how Washington almost became a Confederate city even before Lincoln was inaugurated.]

THE COUNTRY at this time (December, 1860) was in a curious and alarming condition; one state (South Carolina) had already passed an ordinance of secession from the Union and other states were preparing to follow her lead. The only regular troops near the capital of the country were three hundred or four hundred marines at the marine barracks, and perhaps a hundred enlisted men of ordinance at the Washington arsenal. The old militia system had been abandoned (without being legally abolished), and Congress had passed no law establishing a new one. The only armed volunteer organizations in the District of Columbia were: One company of riflemen at Georgetown (the Potomac Light Infantry), one company of riflemen in Washington (the National Rifles), a skeleton battalion of infantry (the Washington Light Infantry) of about one hundred sixty men, and another small organization called the National Guard Battalion.

It was evident that, on its assembling in December, Congress would have far different work to consider than the organization of the District of Columbia militia; and also, that it would not be the policy of the President [Buchanan], at the very outset of the session, in the delicate position of affairs, to propose the military organization of the Federal district. It was also evident that, should he be so disposed, the Senators and Representatives of the Southern States would oppose and denounce the project.

What force, then, would the Government have at its disposal in the Federal district for the simple maintenance of order in case of need? Evidently but a handful; and as to calling thither promptly any regular troops, that was out of the question, since they had already been distributed by the Southern sympathizers to the distant frontiers of the Indian country—Texas, Utah, New Mexico, Oregon, and Washington Territory—and winter was rapidly approaching. It must be remembered that in those days there were no railways reaching out into those distant regions, and months would have been necessary to concentrate at Washington, in that season, a force of three thousand regular troops. Even had President Buchanan been desirous of bringing troops to the capital, the feverish condition of the public mind would, as the executive believed, have been badly affected by any movement of the kind, and the approaching crisis might have been precipitated.

I saw at once that the only force which could be readily made of service was a volunteer force raised from among the well disposed men of the District, and that this must be organized, if at all, under the old law of 1799. . . .

On the 31st of December, 1860, Lieutenant-General Winfield Scott, commander-in-chief of the army (who had his headquarters in New York), was in Washington. The President, at last thoroughly alarmed at the results of continued concessions to secession, had called him for consultation on the situation.

On the evening of that day I went to pay my respects to my old commander, and was received by him at Wormley's Hotel. I found the General alone at the dinner table, just finishing his evening meal. He chatted pleasantly with me for a few minutes, recalling past service in the Mexican war, etc.; and when the occasion presented itself, I remarked that I was glad to see him in good spirits, for that proved to me that he took a more cheerful view of the state of public affairs than he had on his arrival—more cheerful than those who resided in Washington had dared to take during the past few days.

"Yes, my young friend," said the General, "I feel more cheerful about the affairs of the country than I did this morning; for I believe that a safer policy than has hitherto been followed will now be adopted. The policy of entire conciliation, which has so far been pursued, would soon have led to ruin. We are now in such a state that a policy of pure force would precipitate a crisis for which we are not prepared. A mixed policy of force and conciliation is now necessary, and I believe it will be adopted and carried out." He then looked at his watch, rose, and said: "I must be with the President in a quarter of an hour," and ordered his carriage. He walked up and down the dining-room, but suddenly stopped and faced me, saying: "How is the feeling in the District of Columbia? What proportion of the population would sustain the Government by force, if necessary?"

I replied:

"General, it is my belief that two-thirds of the fighting stock of this population would sustain the Government in defending itself, if called upon. But they are uncertain as to what can be done or what the Government desires to have done, and they have no rallying point."

The General walked the room again in silence. The carriage came to the door, and I accompanied him toward it. As he was leaving the room, he turned suddenly, looked me in the face, placed his hand on my shoulder, and said:

"These people have no rallying point. Make yourself that rallying point!"

The next day I was commissioned by the President colonel in the staff and Inspector-General of the District of Columbia. I was mustered into the service of the United States from the 2d day of January, 1861, on the special requisition of the General-in-Chief, and thus became the first one of the million citizens called into the military service of the Government to defend it against secession.

I immediately entered upon my duties, commencing by inspections in detail of the existing organizations of volunteers. The Potomac Light Infantry company, of Georgetown, I found fairly drilled, well armed, and, from careful information, it seemed to me certain that the majority of its members could be depended upon in case of need, but not all of them.

On the 2d of January, I met, at the entrance of the Metropolitan Hotel, Captain Schaeffer, of the "National Rifles" of Washington, and I spoke to him about his company, which was remarkable for its accurate and rapid drill and full ranks. Schaeffer had been a lieutenant in the First Regiment of United States Artillery, and was an excellent drill-master. He had evidently not yet heard of my appointment as Inspector-General, and he replied to my complimentary remarks on his company: "Yes, it is a good company, and I suppose I shall soon have to lead it to the banks of the Susquehanna!"

"Why so?" I asked.

"Why! To guard the frontier of Maryland and help to keep

the Yankees from coming down to coerce the South!"

I said to him quietly that I thought it very imprudent in him, an employee of the Department of the Interior and captain of a company of District of Columbia volunteers, to use such expressions. He replied that most of his men were Marylanders, and would have to defend Maryland. I told him that he would soon learn that he had been imprudent, and advised him to think more seriously of his position, but did not inform him of my appointment, which he would be certain to learn the following morning from the newspapers.

It must be admitted that this was not a very cheerful beginning.

On inspecting the "National Rifles," I found that Schaeffer had more than one hundred men on his rolls, and was almost daily adding to the number, and that he had a full supply of rifles with two hundred rounds of ball cartridges, two mountain howitzers with harness and carriages, a supply of sabers and of revolvers and ammunition, all drawn from the United States arsenal. I went to the Chief of Ordnance, to learn how it was that this company of riflemen happened to be so unusually armed; and I found at the Ordnance office that an order had been given by the late Secretary of War (Floyd) directing the Chief of Ordnance to cause to be issued to Captain Schaeffer "all the ordnance and ordnance stores that he might require for his company!" I ascertained also that Floyd had nominated Captain Schaeffer to the President for the commission of Major in the District of Columbia militia, and that the commission had already been sent to the President for his signature.

I immediately presented the matter to the new Secretary of War (Holt), and procured from him two orders: one, an order to the Chief of Ordnance to issue no arms to any militia or volunteers in the District of Columbia unless the requisition should be countersigned by the Inspector-General; the other, an order that all commissions issued to officers of the District of Columbia should be sent to the Inspector-General for delivery.

An office was assigned me in the War Department, convenient to the army-registers and near the Secretary of War, who kindly gave orders that I should at all times be admitted to his cabinet without waiting, and room was made for me in the office of Major-General Weightman, the senior major-general of the District, where each day I passed several hours to confer with him, and to be able promptly to obtain his authority for any necessary order to the District forces. . . .

The National Rifles company (Captain Schaeffer's) was carefully observed, and it was found that its ranks received constant accessions, including the most openly declared secessionists and even members of Congress from the States proposing to secede. This company was very frequently drilled in its armory, and its recruits were drilled nearly every night.

Having, as Inspector-General, a secret service force at my disposition, I placed a detective in the company, and had regular reports of the proceedings of its captain. He was evidently pushing for an independent command of infantry, artillery and cavalry, having his rifles, cannon, sabers, and revolvers stored in his armory. He also began to prepare for action, ordering his men to take their rifles and equipment home with them, with a supply of ammunition, so that even should his armory be occupied, they could assemble on short notice, ready for action. Meantime, his commission as major was signed by the President and sent to me.

I reported these matters to General Scott, who ordered me to watch these proceedings carefully, and to be ready to suppress any attempt at violence; but to avoid, if possible, any shock, for, said he, "We are now in such a state that a dog-fight might cause the gutters of the capital to run with blood."

While the volunteer force for the support of the Government was organizing, another force with exactly the opposite purpose was in the course of formation. I learned that the great hall over Beach's livery stable was nightly filled with men, who were actively drilled. Doctor B_____, of well-known secession tendencies, was the moving spirit of these men, and he was assisted by other citizens of high standing, among whom was a connection of the Governor of Virginia. The numbers of these occupants of Beach's hall increased rapidly, and I found it well to have a skillful New York detective officer, who had been placed at my disposition, enrolled among them. These men called themselves "National Volunteers," and openly discussed, in their meetings, the seizure of the national capital at the proper moment. They drilled industriously, and had regular business meetings, full reports of which were regularly laid before me every following morning by "the New York member."

In the meeting at which the uniform to be adopted was discussed, the vote was for gray Kentucky jeans, with the Maryland button. A cautious member suggested that they must remember that, in order to procure arms, it would be "necessary to get the requisition signed by 'Old Stone,' and if he saw that they had adopted the Maryland button, and not that of the United States, he might suspect them and refuse the issue of arms!" Doctor B_____ supported the idea of the Maryland button, and said that, if Stone refused the arms, his connection, the Governor of Virginia, would see them furnished, etc. These gentlemen probably little thought that a full report of their remarks would be read the next morning by "Old Stone" to the General-in-Chief.

The procuring of arms was a difficult matter for them, for it required the election of officers, the regular enrolling of the men, the certificate of elections, and the muster-rolls, all to be reported to the Inspector General. The matter was long discussed by them, and it was finally arranged that, out of the three hundred and sixty men in their midst, a pretended company should be organized, officers elected, and the demand for arms made. This project was carried out, and my member brought to me early the next morning the report of the proceedings, informing me that Doctor B___ had been elected captain, and would call on the Inspector-General for arms. Sure enough, Doctor B___ presented himself in my office and informed me that he had raised a company of volunteers, and desired an order for arms. He produced a certificate of election in due form. I received him courteously, and informed him that I could not give an order for arms without having a muster-roll of his men, proving that a full one hundred had signed the rolls. It was, of course, very desirable to have the names of men holding their known sentiments and nursing such projects as were known to be theirs.

He returned, I think, on the following day, with a muster-roll in due form, containing the names of one hundred men. This was all that I wanted. I looked him full in the face, smiled, and locked the muster-roll in a drawer of my desk, saying:

"Doctor B___, I am very happy to have obtained this list, and I wish you good morning."

The gallant doctor evidently understood me. He smiled, bowed, and left the office, to which he never returned. He subsequently proved the sincerity of his principles by abandoning his pleasant home in Washington, his large and valuable property, and giving his earnest service to the Confederate cause. The "National Volunteer" organization broke up without further trouble.

Next came the turn of Captain Schaeffer. He entered my office one day with the air of an injured man, holding in his hand a requisition for arms and ammunition, and saying, that, on presenting it at the Ordnance office, he had been informed that no arms could be issued to him without my approval. I informed him that that was certainly so, and that the order of the Secretary of War was general. I told him that he had already in his possession more rifles than were required for a company and that he could have no more. He then said, sulkily, that he could easily, with his company, take the arms he wanted.

I asked him, Where? and he replied:

"You have only four soldiers guarding the Columbian armory, where there are plenty of arms, and those four men could not prevent my taking them."

"Ah!" I replied, "In what part of the armory are those arms kept?" He said they were on the upper floor, which was true.

"Well," said I, "you seem to be well informed. If you think it best, just try taking the arms by force. I assure you that if you do you shall be fired on by one hundred and fifty soldiers as you come out of the armory."

The fact was, that only two enlisted men of ordnance were on duty at the Columbian armory, so feeble was the military force at the time. But Barry's battery had just arrived at the Washington arsenal, and on my application General Scott had ordered the company of sappers and miners at West Point to come to Washington to guard the Columbian armory; but they had not yet arrived. The precautions taken in ordering them were thus clearly proved advisable.

The time had evidently come to disarm Captain Schaeffer; and when he reached his office after leaving mine, he found there an order directing him to deposit in the Columbian armory, before sunset on that day, the two howitzers with their carriages which he had in his possession, as well as the sabers and revolvers, as these weapons formed no part of the proper armament of a company of riflemen. He was taken by surprise, and had not time to call together men enough to resist; so that nothing was left to him but to comply with the order. He obeyed it, well knowing that if he did not I was prepared to take the guns from his armory by means of other troops.

Having obeyed, he presented himself again in my office, and before he had time to speak I informed him that I had a commission of major for his name. He was much pleased, and said: "Yes, I heard that I had been appointed." I then handed him a slip of paper on which I had written out the form of oath which the old law required to be taken by officers, that law never having been repealed, and said to him: "Here is the form of oath you are to take. You will find a justice of the peace on the next floor. Please qualify, sign the form in duplicate, and bring both to me. One will be filed with your letter of acceptance, the other will be filed in the clerk's office of the Circuit Court of the District."

He took the paper with a sober look, and stood near my table several minutes, looking at the form of oath and turning the paper in his hand, while I, apparently very busy with my papers, was observing him closely. I then said:

"Ah, Schaeffer, have you already taken the oath?"

"No," said he.

"Well, please be quick about it, as I have no time to spare."

He hesitated, and said slowly:

"In ordinary times I would not mind taking it, but in these times—"

"Ah!" said I, "you decline to accept your commission of major. Very well!" and I returned his commission to the drawer and locked it in.

"Oh no," said Schaeffer, "I want the commission."

"But, sir, you cannot have it. Do you suppose that, in these times, which are not, as you say, 'ordinary times,' I would think of delivering a commission of field-officer to a man who hesitates about taking the oath of office? Do you think that the Government of the United States is stupid enough to allow a man to march armed men about the federal district under its authority, when that man hesitates to take the simple oath of office? No, sir, you cannot have this commission; and more than that, I now inform you that you hold no office in the District of Columbia volunteers."

"Yes, I do; I am captain, and have my commission as such, signed by the President and delivered to me by the Major-General."

"I am aware that such a paper was delivered to you, but you failed legally to accept it."

"I wrote a letter of acceptance to the Adjutant-General, and forwarded it through the Major-General."

"Yes, I am aware that you did; but I know also that you failed to inclose in that letter, according to law, the form of oath required to accompany all letters of acceptance, and on the register of the War Department, while the issuance of your commission is recorded, the acceptance is not recorded. You have never legally accepted your commission, and it is now too late. The oath of a man who hesitates to take it will not now be accepted."

So Captain Schaeffer left the "National Rifles," and with him left the secession members of the company. . . .

If my information was correct, the plan had been formed for seizing the public departments at the proper moment and obtaining possession of the seals of the Government. Schaeffer's part, with the battalion he was to form, was to take possession of the Treasury Department for the benefit of the new provisional government. Whatever may have been the project, it was effectually foiled. With the breaking up of the "National Volunteers"; with the transformation of the secession company of "National Rifles" into a thoroughly faithful and admirably drilled company ready for the service of the Government; with the arrival from West Point of the company of sappers and miners, and, later, the arrival of the Military Academy battery under Griffin; and with the formation in the district of thirty new companies of infantry and riflemen from among the good citizens of Washington and Georgetown—the face of things in the national capital had much changed before the 4th of March, 1861. . . .

One day, after the official declaration of the election of Mr. Lincoln, my duties called me to the House of Representatives; and while standing in the lobby waiting for the member with whom I had business, I conversed with a distinguished officer from New York. We were leaning against the sill of a window which overlooked the steps of the Capitol, where the President-elect usually stands to take the oath of office. The gentleman grew excited as we discussed the election of Mr. Lincoln, and pointing to the portico he exclaimed:

"He shall never be inaugurated on those steps!"

"Mr. Lincoln," I replied, "has been constitutionally elected President of the United States. You may be sure that, if he lives until the 4th day of March, he will be inaugurated on those steps."

As I spoke, I noticed for the first time how perfectly the wings of the Capitol flanked the steps in question; and on the morning of the 4th of March I saw to it that each window of the two wings was occupied by two riflemen.

I received daily numerous communications from various parts of the country, informing me of plots to prevent the arrival of the President-elect at the capital. These warnings came from St. Louis, from Chicago, from Cincinnati, from Pittsburgh, from New York, from Philadelphia, and, especially, from Baltimore. Every morning I reported to General Scott on the occurrences of the night and the information received by the morning's mail; and every evening I rendered an account of the day's work and received instructions for the night. General Scott also received numerous warnings of danger to the President-elect, which he would give me to study and compare. Many of the communications were anonymous and vague. But on the other hand many were from calm and wise men, one of whom became, shortly afterward, a cabinet minister; one was a railway president, another a distinguished ex-Governor of a State, etc., etc. In every case where the indications were distinct, they were followed up to learn if real danger existed.

48

So many clear indications pointed to Baltimore, that three good detectives of the New York police force were constantly employed there. These men reported frequently to me, and their statements were constantly compared with the information received from independent sources.

Doubtless, Mr. Lincoln, at his home in Springfield, received many and contradictory reports from the capital, for he took his own way of obtaining information. One night, between eleven o'clock and midnight, while I was busy in my study over the papers of the day and evening, a card was brought me, bearing the name "Mr. Leonard Swett," and upon it was written, in the well-known hand of General Scott, "Colonel Stone, Inspector-General, may converse freely with Mr. Swett. . . ." I quickly found . . . that Mr. Swett had come directly from Mr. Lincoln, having his full confidence, to see for him the state of affairs in Washington, and report back to him in person.

Mr. Swett remained several days in the capital, had frequent and long conversations with General Scott and myself. . . . As he drove with me to the railway station on the evening of his departure, Mr. Swett said: "Mr. Lincoln, and in fact everybody almost, is ignorant of the vast amount of careful work which has been done here this winter, by General Scott and yourself, to insure the existence of the Government and to render certain and safe the inauguration of Mr. Lincoln. He will be very grateful to both." I replied, with more sincerity than tact: "Mr. Lincoln has no cause to be grateful to me. I was opposed to his election, and believed in advance that it would bring on what is evidently coming, a fearful war. The work which I have done has not been done for him, and he need feel under no obligations to me. I have done my best toward saving the Government of the country and to insure the regular inauguration of the constitutionally elected President, on the 4th of next month."

As President Lincoln approached the capital, it became certain that desperate attempts would be made to prevent his arriving there. To be thoroughly informed as to what might be expected in Baltimore, I directed a detective to be constantly near the chief of police and to keep up relations with him; while two others were instructed to watch independent and without the knowledge of the chief of police. The officer who was near the chief of police reported regularly, until near the last, that there was no danger in Baltimore; but the others discovered a band of desperate men plotting for the destruction of Mr. Lincoln during his passage through the city, and by affiliating with them, these detectives got at the details of the plot.

Mr. Lincoln passed through Baltimore in advance of the time announced for the journey (in accordance with advice given by me to Mr. Seward and which was carried by Mr. Frederick Seward to Mr. Lincoln), and arrived safely at Washington on the morning of the day he was to have passed through Baltimore. But the plotting to prevent his inauguration continued; and there was only too good reason to fear that an attempt would be made against his life during the passage of the inaugural procession from Willard's Hotel, where Mr. Lincoln lodged, to the Capitol.

On the afternoon of the 3rd of March, General Scott held a conference at his headquarters, there being present his staff, General Sumner, and myself, and then was arranged the programme of the procession. President Buchanan was to drive to Willard's Hotel, and call upon the President-elect. The two were to ride in the same carriage, between double files of a squadron of the District of Columbia cavalry. The company of sappers and miners were to march in front of the Presidential carriage, and the infantry and riflemen of the District of Columbia were to follow it. Riflemen in squads were to be placed on the roofs of certain commanding houses which I had selected, along Pennsylvania Avenue, with orders to watch the windows on the opposite side and to fire upon them in case any attempt should be made to fire from those

50

windows on the Presidential carriage. The small force of regular cavalry which had arrived was to guard the side-street crossings of Pennsylvania Avenue, and to move from one to another during the passage of the procession. A battalion of District of Columbia troops were to be placed near the steps of the Capitol, and rifle-men in the windows of the wings of the Capitol. On the arrival of the Presidential party at the Capitol, the troops were to be sta-tioned so as to return in the same order after the ceremony.

To illustrate the state of uncertainty in which we were at that time concerning men, I may here state that the Lieutenant-Colonel, military secretary of the General-in-chief, who that after-noon recorded the conclusions of the General in conference, and who afterward wrote out for me the instructions regarding the dis-position of troops, resigned his commission that very night, and departed for the South, where he joined the Confederate army.

During the night of the 3rd of March, notice was brought me that an attempt would be made to blow up the platform on which the President would stand to take the oath of office. I im-mediately placed men under the steps, and at daybreak a trusted battalion of District troops . . . formed in a semicircle at the foot of the great stairway, and prevented all entrance from without. When the crowd began to assemble in front of the portico, a large number of policemen in plain clothes were scattered through the mass to observe closely, to place themselves near any individual who might act suspiciously, and to strike down any hand which might raise a weapon.

At the appointed hour, Mr. Buchanan was escorted to Willard's Hotel, which he entered. There I found a number of mounted marshals of the day, and posted them around the car-riage, within the cavalry guard. The two Presidents were saluted by the troops as they came out of the hotel and took their places in the carriage. The procession started. During the march to the Capitol I rode near the carriage, and by an apparently clumsy use of my spurs managed to keep the horses of the cavalry in an uneasy state, so that it would have been very difficult for even a very good rifle shot to get an aim at one of the inmates of the carriage between the dancing horses.

After the inaugural ceremony, the President and the ex-President were escorted in the same order to the White House. Arrived there, Mr. Buchanan walked to the door with Mr. Lincoln, and there bade him welcome to the House and good morning. The infantry escort formed in line from the gate of the White House to the house of Mr. Ould, whither Mr. Buchanan drove, and the cavalry escorted his carriage. The infantry line presented arms to the ex-President as he passed, and the cavalry escort saluted as he left the carriage and entered the house. Mr. Buchanan turned on the steps, gracefully acknowledged the salute, and disappeared. The District of Columbia volunteers had given to President Lincoln his first military salute and to Mr. Buchanan his last.

[Colonel Stone, who has so graphically described conditions in the nation's capital here, was made a brigadier general of volunteers in August.

Bull Run was a major disaster for the Union. Just three months later, on October 21, 1861, an ill-conceived and badly executed attempt to cross the Potomac at Ball's Bluff in too few boats became another Union disaster, although on a smaller scale. Colonel Edward D. Baker, a former Senator and a lifelong friend of President Lincoln, was killed in action there.

The public and the press were tired of disasters; they demanded a victim. The dreaded Joint Committee on the Conduct of the War was formed; it quickly concentrated its attention on Stone. During its investigation, it "heard many witnesses, but refused their names to Stone, refused him their testimony, refused to tell him what acts were charged against him." (Perhaps someone had informed the Committee that the outspoken but loyal

52

general freely admitted that he had opposed Lincoln's election.) He was arrested on February 8, 1862, on a trumped-up charge of treason and imprisoned in Fort Lafayette, the small brick-walled island guardian that still stands at the entrance to New York Harbor. General Stone, with no charges ever brought against him, was released on August 16. He served for more than a year in the army after that, but finally resigned in September, 1864, feeling that his usefulness as an officer was over. After the war, by an odd quirk of fate, he was privately employed as an engineer in charge of constructing the foundations of the Statue of Liberty, in sight of Fort Lafayette where he had been so unjustly imprisoned.]

The Founder of the Pinkertons
Shadows a Beautiful Rebel Spy

by ALLAN PINKERTON
from *The Spy of the Rebellion,* 1883

[Here two of the best-known secret service agents of the Civil War are joined together in the uneasy relationship of the hunter and the hunted. Yet this naïvely told account, written by a man whose name was later to become synonymous with the word "detective," has a quality that is almost unknown in the literature of espionage, for he succeeds in being funny when he tells about his first amateurish efforts in playing at being a spy. Anyone less certain of his reputation would probably have suppressed or toned down the delightful details of this frantic chase in the rain.

Allan Pinkerton, who had come from Scotland to the United States, became Chicago's first professional detective in 1850. Much of his work was done for the railroads, and it was in connection with this that he first met George B. McClellan who had been president of the eastern division of the Ohio and Mississippi Railroad. Pinkerton helped to smuggle President-elect Lincoln through Baltimore to Washington in February, 1861.

Pinkerton assumed the name Major E. J. Allen and became McClellan's personal spy. He was sent into Virginia to estimate the strength of the Confederate Army there; because of his inexperience as a military observer he grossly exaggerated the number of Confederate troops in the field and so made the naturally cautious

McClellan even more cautious about attacking what was misrepresented as a much larger force than really existed.

Pinkerton went after Mrs. Rose O'Neal Greenhow because the Government had good reason to suspect that this redoubtable widow, who made no secret of her Confederate sympathies, had given Beauregard advance notice of the strength and intended movements of McDowell's forces at Bull Run in July and so was largely responsible for the rout of the Union Army there.

Of all the women agents in the Civil War, Mrs. Greenhow was certainly the best qualified for her work. She was at home in the highest circles of Washington society; she was widely traveled in various parts of North America; and, through her marriage to Dr. Robert Greenhow (who had died in California in 1854), she had received a liberal education in medicine, law, diplomacy, and history. In 1861 she was in her early forties, the mother of four daughters, and although she was at the peak of her intellectual powers, her beauty was beginning to fade. But she had always had a way with men which she was now to turn to the advantage of the Southern cause in which she so passionately believed. She said very candidly: "I employed every capacity with which God has endowed me, and the result was far more successful than my hopes could have flattered me to expect."

Her fine house in Washington became a center for Confederate espionage. She moved openly and arrogantly through the mazes of governmental Washington, but her greatest strength was also her greatest weakness. She thought she could afford to be daring because she felt sure that her high connections would protect her. But the Washington she had known was rapidly changing, and the little Scotsman from Chicago closed in.]

MY DEPARTMENT was in its infancy when . . . I secured a house in Washington and gathered around me a number of resolute, trustworthy men and discreet women. . . . I had not been many days in the city when one afternoon I was called upon by the Hon. Thomas A. Scott, of Pennsylvania, who was then acting as the Assistant-Secretary of War, who desired my services in watching a lady whose movements had excited suspicion. . . .

The residence of Mrs. Greenhow was situated at the corner of Thirteenth and I streets—quite a fashionable quarter of the city, and within a short distance of the White House. . . . It was a two-story-and-basement brick building, the parlors of which were elevated several feet above the ground; entrance was obtained by ascending a flight of steps in the center of the edifice. This lady was a widow, her husband having died some years before, and being possessed of considerable means, and mingling with the highest circles of Washington society, her home was the resort of most of the prominent people of the city.

The instructions of the Secretary of War were that a strict watch should be kept upon this house, and that every person entering or leaving the same should come under the close surveillance of my men, who should endeavor to ascertain who they were, and if they attempted in any manner to communicate with any suspicious persons. I was to report to him daily, and to continue my espionage until I received definite and official orders for its discontinuance. . . .

I took with me two of my men, and proceeded to the vicinity of the residence of Mrs. Greenhow. I was then quite a stranger in Washington, and localities were not as familiar to me as they afterward became, and I therefore preferred to reconnoiter by daylight, to depending upon a survey after nightfall.

The entire day had been dark, gloomy and threatening; clouds had been gathering in the heavens, and everything indicated the imminence of a severe storm. As I left my headquarters, a slight shower of rain was falling, which I knew was but the precursor of a storm more violent. On arriving at the designated locality I found everything to be as they had already been described to me.

The inside shutters to the windows were closed, and no sign was apparent that the house was occupied, and after carefully noting the situation and the exposed condition of the premises, I left the two men within a convenient distance of the place, and returned for the additional aid which I thought might be needed. Selecting three of my most discreet men, I again repaired to the scene of operations. We had not proceeded far, when the storm burst upon us in all its fury. The wind blew strong and chill, and the rain fell in deluging torrents. Umbrellas were a useless commodity, and, unprotected, we were compelled to breast the elements, which now were warring with terrible violence.

Arriving at Mrs. Greenhow's, under cover of the darkness I posted my men in such positions as I thought would be most advantageous for our purpose, and then calling in the two whom I had left there during the afternoon, I approached to within a short distance of the house. The darkness and storm, while decidedly uncomfortable, were of some benefit to us, as but few people were abroad, and these paid no attention to passing events, seeming to be only too anxious to reach their destination and to escape the pitiless rain.

The blinds at the windows were still closed, but a light was observed in two rooms upon the parlor floor, and I knew that the house was occupied. Of course I could see nothing within, as my view was entirely obstructed by the closed blinds, and, at length, becoming impatient at this unprofitable and unsatisfactory waiting, I determined to obtain a glimpse, at least, of the interior, and to ascertain, if possible, some knowledge of its occupants.

The parlor windows, through which the lights were gleaming, were too high from the ground to permit me to see within, and summoning the two men who were awaiting instructions I made use of their strong, broad shoulders. . . .

Ranging the two men side by side under the broad windows in front of the house, I removed my boots and was soon standing upon their shoulders and elevated sufficiently high to enable me to accomplish the object I had in view. I was now on a level with the windows, and noiselessly raising the sash and turning the slats of the blinds I obtained a full view of the interior of the room, but to my disappointment, it was unoccupied.

I was about to give expression to my chagrin at this discovery when a warning "Sh!" from one of my sturdy supporters induced me to be silent. Some one was approaching the house, and hastily clambering down from my perch, we hid ourselves under the stoop which led up to the front door. Scarcely had we ensconced ourselves in this convenient shelter when we heard the footsteps of the newcomer, and to our satisfaction, he stopped in front of the house, and ascending the steps rang the bell and in a short time was admitted.

By this time we were drenched to the skin—the rain had fallen in copious showers and during all the time we had been exposed to its dampening influences—but paying but little heed to this, we again took our position in front of the window, and I was soon remounted upon the shoulders of my operatives, prepared to take notes of what transpired.

As the visitor entered the parlor and seated himself— awaiting the appearance of the lady of the house—I immediately recognized him as an officer of the regular army, whom I had met that day for the first time. He was a captain of infantry and was in command of one of the stations of the Provost-Marshal. . . . I will call him Captain Ellison.

He was a tall, handsome man of a commanding figure and about forty years of age. He had removed his cloak, and as he sat there in his blue uniform, and in the full glare of the gaslight, he looked a veritable ideal soldier. As I watched him closely, however, I noticed that there was a troubled, restless look upon his face; he appeared ill at ease and shifted nervously upon his chair, as though impatient for the entrance of his hostess. In a few moments Mrs.

Greenhow entered and cordially greeted her visitor, who acknowledged her salutations with a courtly bow, while his face lighted up with pleasure as he gazed upon her.

Just at this moment I again received a warning from my supporters, and hastily jumping to the ground, we hid ourselves until the pedestrians had passed out of sight and hearing. When I resumed my station the Captain and Mrs. Greenhow were seated at a table in the rear part of the room, and their conversation was carried on in such low tones that, in consequence of the storm that was still raging, I could not catch but fragmentary sentences. At last, however, accustoming myself to the noise, I heard enough to convince me that this trusted officer was then and there engaged in betraying his country, and furnishing to his treasonably-inclined companion such information regarding the disposition of our troops as he possessed.

Presently, he took from an inner pocket of his coat a map which, as he held it up before the light, I imagined that I could identify as a plan of the fortifications in and around Washington, and which also designated a contemplated plan of attack.

After watching their movements for some time, during which they would frequently refer to the map before them, as though pointing out particular points or positions, I was again compellled to hide myself under the shelter of the convenient stoop, and when I resumed my position the room was empty. The delectable couple had disappeared. I waited impatiently for more than an hour, taking occasional glimpses into the room and watching for their re-appearance. At the end of that time they re-entered the parlor arm in arm, and again took their seats.

Again came the warning voice, and again I hastily descended, and as the retreating figures disappeared in the distance, I could hear the front door open and the step of the traitor Captain above me.

With a whispered good-night, and something that sounded

very much like a kiss, he descended the steps, and then, without paying any attention to the fact that I was without shoes, I started in pursuit of him, and through the blinding mist and pelting storms kept him in view as he rapidly walked away. It was then about half-past twelve o'clock, and the storm evinced no sign of a discontinuance.

I was not sufficiently acquainted with the city at that time to tell in what direction he was going, but I determined to ascertain his destination before I left him. I was compelled to keep pretty close to him, owing to the darkness of the night, and several times I was afraid that he would hear the footsteps of the man who accompanied me—mine I was confident would not be detected as, in my drenched stockings, I crept along as stealthily as a cat. Twice, I imagined that he turned around as though suspecting he was followed, but as he did not stop I reassured myself and plodded on. I could not, however, disabuse my mind of the fear that I had been seen, I could not relax my vigilance, and I resolved to take my chances of discovery. I knew who my man was, at all events, and now I must ascertain where he was going. He passed a guard on duty, and quickly passed into a building immediately in advance of me.

This movement was so unexpected that I had no time to turn back, and I was so close to him that it would have been very unwise to have done so, but I was more surprised when, as I reached the building into which the Captain had disappeared, I was suddenly confronted by four armed soldiers, who rushed suddenly out upon me, with fixed bayonets pointed at my breast. . . .

Realizing that an attempt at resistance or escape would be both foolish and useless, I attempted to make an explanation. All to no purpose, however. I informed them that I had been out late and had lost my way, but they refused to listen, and ordered my companion and myself to march at once into the guardhouse.

[The captain whom Pinkerton discreetly called Ellison was probably John Elwood of the Fifth Infantry. He had Pinkerton brought before him for an examination, during which he got very little information from his prisoner. Angered by Pinkerton's stubbornness, the captain sent the detective to a cell in which there were several drunks, common criminals, and two outspoken secessionists with whom Pinkerton's associate struck up a conversation. During the night the ever-resourceful detective persuaded one of the guards to deliver a message for him to Assistant Secretary of War Thomas A. Scott. Early in the morning, orders came to release Pinkerton and send him to Scott's home. Once he had told his story there, Scott summoned the suspected captain for questioning. It was soon established that the man was lying about his association with disloyal persons. He was placed under arrest. This ended his career in the Army, and the captain died in disgrace about a year later. In fact, it was said that he committed suicide. Immediately after his release, Pinkerton returned to Mrs. Greenhow's residence to keep watch over her.]

About eight days after this, orders were given for the arrest of Mrs. Greenhow herself. She was confined in her own house, and all her papers were seized and handed over to the custody of the Department of War. The intention of the government was to treat her as humanely and considerately as possible, but disdaining all offers of kindness or courtesy, the lady was discovered on several occasions attempting to send messages to her rebel friends, and finally her removal to the Old Capitol Prison was ordered, and she was conveyed there, where she was imprisoned for several months. After this she was conveyed across the lines, and reached in safety the rebel capital where she was greeted by the more congenial spirits of rebeldom.

Mrs. Greenhow afterwards went to Europe, in some trustworthy capacity for the Confederacy, and while there was noted for her bitter animosity to the Union and her vituperation of Northern men and measures.

[*Mrs. Greenhow's being sent to the Old Capitol Prison was one of the many strange coincidences of the war, for she had spent part of her girlhood in the big brick building which was then being run by her aunt as a boardinghouse. In the room assigned to her as a cell, she had watched John C. Calhoun, the leading apostle of nullification and states' rights, slowly sicken and die in 1850.*

Rose Greenhow remained in this prison from January to June, 1862, when she was released and sent through the lines to Richmond. There she was received with acclaim and was paid a fee of $2,500 out of Confederate secret service funds. She left Wilmington, North Carolina, on a blockade runner on August 5, 1863, carrying with her the manuscript of a book she had written about her experiences. This was published in London under the title My Imprisonment and the First Year of Abolition Rule at Washington. *It was a popular and financial success. Its wide circulation did much to help the Confederacy as a propaganda piece.*

Her book made Mrs. Greenhow a public figure in Europe. She worked with Confederate secret agents there and then returned to the South at the end of August, 1864, on a blockade runner named the Condor.

On the night before this ship entered the Cape Fear River to run up to Wilmington, another blockade runner, the Night Hawk, *had gone aground within a few hundred yards of the guns of Confederate Fort Fisher. A boarding party of Union sailors had then attacked the stranded ship and set it on fire. The local pilot who was bringing in the* Condor *through a heavy storm came upon the burned-out wreck of the* Night Hawk *in the darkness, and in trying to avoid this unexpected obstacle ran his ship aground.*

In the Secret Service files in the National Archives is an undated newspaper clipping from the London Daily Mail *which was* probably sent to Richmond by a Confederate agent stationed in England. It reads: "At 3 in the morning of the 1st [OF SEPTEMBER] . . . the Condor . . . had the misfortune, thanks to her blundering pilot, to run aground in the breakers. . . . The Condor was a new three-funnelled steamer, superbly adapted for her trade, with great carrying capacity, drawing only seven feet of water, and swift as a sea swallow. She was approaching Wilmington upon her first inward trip . . . from Greenock [SCOTLAND] whence she sailed in August last. . . . After the Condor took the ground, a Yankee vessel was seen approaching through the gloom, with a view to shelling or boarding the stranger. Mrs. Greenhow, remembering her long former imprisonment in Washington, and apprehensive of its repetition, insisted, against the advice of the captain, upon having a boat lowered, upon trusting herself to the tender mercies of the waves rather than to those of the Yankees. Into this boat she carried with her the mail bags [CONTAINING SECRET DISPATCHES FOR RICHMOND ENTRUSTED TO HER], and also Professor [JAMES B.] Holcombe, whom the Condor had picked up at Halifax, and whose name was last summer brought before the public in connexion with Mr. Greeley's abortive negotiations with a view to peace, which were entered into at Niagara Falls. To the pilot, who had just run the Condor aground, was committed the delicate task of steering Mrs. Greenhow's boat, which was lowered into a raging surf. Directly the boat left the leeside of the vessel she was caught, broadside on, by a huge breaker, and overturned. All the male passengers succeeded in clambering up and clutching the keel of the capsized boat, but in the darkness and amid the deafening thunder of the breakers, nothing was seen or heard of poor Mrs. Greenhow. Her body was subsequently washed ashore near Fort Fisher, and close beside it a heavy leather reticule, containing $2,000 in gold, which was believed to have been slung round her neck when the boat was upset. It is a strange proof of the strength of that boisterous sea that such a weighty article as this reticule should not have sunk, but should have been tossed up on the beach like a bit of seaweed. Upon the afternoon of the 2d Mrs. Greenhow's body was committed to the grave at Wilmington, according to the rites of the Roman Catholic Church."

The London paper does not tell the peculiar circumstances under which Mrs. Greenhow's body was found. A Confederate soldier had come across it early in the morning. He appropriated the gold and then pushed the body back into the breakers to cover the robbery. It floated ashore again later in the day and was found and identified by one of the owners of the Night Hawk. When it became known that the drowned woman was the celebrated Mrs. Greenhow, the conscience-stricken soldier who had taken the gold voluntarily turned in his plunder.]

The Future Head
of U.S. Secret Service Activities
Goes on His First Mission

by LAFAYETTE C. BAKER
from *History of the United States Secret Service,* 1867

[Lafayette C. Baker *grew up in Michigan, but he spent several years in San Francisco during the California gold rush. There he learned the rough-and-ready law enforcement methods used by the vigilantes who met violence with violence and hanged criminals publicly as a warning to others to behave or be executed in the same way. As a reward for his services early in the war, Baker was made a colonel and a special provost marshal in 1862. Not until 1865 did he attain the rank of general, but almost from the very beginning he arrogated to himself much more power than his rank warranted. When McClellan was removed from command in November, 1862, Pinkerton, who had served him well, followed him by retiring from the Eastern theater of war to investigate cotton frauds in the New Orleans area. Baker then rose rapidly to power.*

Baker is best known for his work in apprehending the Lincoln conspirators. His book, History of the United States Secret Service, *is filled with much valuable material but is marred by the sensationalism, charlatanism, and shameless mendacity that characterized the man himself.*

Here, at the beginning of his career in secret service work,

Baker *tells a simple and forthright story about his first exploit as a spy. It is more likely to be true than some of the later incidents in his book.*

Elmer Ellsworth, who is mentioned in Baker's account, was a young soldier friend of Lincoln. He was shot on May 24, 1861, by the proprietor of the Marshall House in Alexandria when he tore down the Confederate flag flying there.

It should be kept in mind that Baker's expedition into Virginia was made at a time when the armies were preparing for their first major encounter at Bull Run.]

In April, 1861, I went to Washington, to learn, if possible, in what capacity I could serve the loyal cause. At Willard's Hotel, I met . . . General Hiram Walbridge, of New York, and the Hon. William D. Kelley, of Philadelphia. We conversed freely upon the condition of the country, and the necessity of more reliable information respecting the strength and movements of the enemy.

General Walbridge then said to me, "Baker, you are the man of all others to go into this secret service; you have the ability and courage." General W., with the Hon. Mr. Kelley, strongly urged an interview with General Scott, who was in command of the Army of the United States; accompanied by him and the Hon. George W. Wright, of California, I went to his rooms. . . .

After a little general conversation, the venerable commander requested those present to leave the room, when he talked freely of my experiences as a detective, and the services required to ascertain the strength and plans of the enemy, requesting an interview the following day.

At the hour appointed, with a deliberate purpose to accept any service for the country he might desire, I was again closeted with the Lieut.-General. After stating that he had thus far found it impossible to obtain definite information respecting the rebel forces at Manassas, that of the five men who had been sent to

Richmond two were known to be killed, and the other three were probably taken prisoners, with patriarchal and patriotic interest, he said to me: "Young man, if you have judgment and discretion, you can be of great service to the country."

I then told him that I could not immediately engage in the service, but must at once return to New York, to arrange unsettled affairs. . . . The latter part of June, I was again in Washington, and had repeated interviews with the General. The result was, a definite arrangement for a journey toward Richmond, if not into the rebel capital. Directions in detail were given me respecting the difficult service I was expected to perform.

Taking from his vest pocket ten double eagles [twenty-dollar gold pieces] . . . General Scott handed them to me, expressing the warmest hopes of my success in the excursion to "Dixie."

July 11, 1861, I started for Richmond. Along the route of my travel toward the Confederate Capital, and while there, I was to learn, if possible, the locality and strength of the hostile troops, especially of the dreaded Black-horse cavalry, and also of their fortifications; leaving no opportunity to gather items of information concerning the movements and plans of the enemy which might be of any service to the Government.

To one unacquainted with the nature of the service, it may seem strange that our troops should not know my character and design. But such concealment is not only always practiced in the secret service, but was pre-eminently needful for us at that time, when we knew not whom to trust, because traitors were in the Government and in the army. To let the Union troops into the secret, would be to send it to Richmond before I had reached Manassas. Guarding the frontier of the Confederacy, the rebel army lay before Washington, stretching from a point three miles below Alexandria, toward the Potomac, eight miles above the capital. At Alexandria, then recently stained with the martyr blood of [Elmer] Ellsworth, Gen. Heintzelman was Provost-marshal. No passes were recognized by either the Union or rebel army, and I must necessarily run the risk equally, in the attempt to pass their lines, of being arrested as a spy. The surreptitious movements would begin, therefore, with the first step from Washington toward the "sacred soil of Virginia."

I went to a daguerrean establishment, and purchased for four dollars an old box which had once contained photographic apparatus, slung it across my back, after the fashion of an itinerant artist, and started for Alexandria. Four miles out of the city I came to the Second Maine Regiment, and proceeded at once to the headquarters of the colonel. He received me politely, and wished me to take a view of the camp, including his tent and the principal officers standing in the foreground. War scenes were new to the people, and the desire was natural enough, to gratify friends at home with pictures of the martial field. After a good dinner, I took my box, and told the colonel I would go to a neighboring hill and take views of the encampment, then return to photograph the headquarters. I was soon in the woods with my hollow box, eluding guards, and pushing forward through the tangled undergrowth, toward the heart of rebeldom. When across the Federal lines as I supposed, I was startled with the shout, "Who goes there?" I looked up, to see a sentinel, with lifted gun, standing upon a knoll just before me.

I had no alternative but to surrender, and march with him to the colonel's quarters. This officer was sure he had caught a spy, and, escorted by ten men, I was sent back along the railroad, the same way I came, to General Heintzelman's headquarters. The lieutenant in charge presented me to the commanding officer, with the following flattering and promising introduction: "Here is a spy, general, that we found lurking about our camp, trying to get through the lines."

"Oh! you villain you, you," said Heintzelman, with his usual nasal twang and an oath, "trying to get through my lines, are you?

I've a good notion to cut your head off! But I'll fix you, you rascal; I'll send you to General Scott." Another guard, with a message from the brave general, who was evidently gratified with the successful vigilance of his men, was ordered for me, and I was hurried away to Washington. The escort was dismissed by General Scott, and my story told. With an expression that indicated both amusement at the ruse, and its failure, and confidence in me, the old veteran said: "Well, try again!"

The uprising North was now sending her legions to the field of civil conflict, and in an almost unbroken line they were marching over Long Bridge into Virginia. That night, I took a position at the end of the bridge, and, when a regiment came down broken into considerable disorder, I stepped into the ranks, hoping to be borne along with the troops. Unfortunately, a lieutenant saw the movement, and, taking me by the collar, put me under guard, and sent me back to the rear. Another night was spent in Washington, but not wholly in sleep. My mind was busy with new plans for a successful visit to the Confederate capital.

With the dawn of the next morning I renewed my journey afoot through the lower counties of Maryland, toward Port Tobacco, traveling thirty-five miles that day, and reaching that town at night. Exhaustion prepared me for sound and refreshing sleep. In the morning I gave a Negro a twenty-dollar gold piece to row me across the river, when I was safely in the Confederacy, below Dumfries. The country was wooded, and an unfrequented road, whose general direction was toward Richmond, suggested the line of my advance into the Old Dominion. I pursued my solitary journey through the desolate country. . . .

Four miles . . . lay between me and the banks of the Potomac, when two Confederate soldiers made their appearance, too near me to make an escape possible. I was taken prisoner under an order to arrest as a spy any stranger passing that way, and marched off toward camp, eight miles distant. A beer shop by the roadside tempted the guard, and we all entered it. I was invited to drink. I saw my opportunity, and, although I never indulge in stimulants, accepted the offer of a glass of ale, and in return treated my captors. The generous indulgence was repeated, until my escort were stupidly under the influence of the potations, and fell asleep on the stoop of the beer-house, leaving me to go unmolested on my way.

I went up the road toward Manassas Junction, congratulating myself on my easy escape, when four rebel cavalrymen suddenly came out of the brush and ordered me to halt; then drawing their sabers, commanded me to surrender. I replied to them: "I am a peaceful citizen, unarmed, and on my way to Richmond." One dismounted, proceeded to search me, and succeeded in finding a number of letters introducing me to prominent rebels in Richmond. Among them were two written by the Rev. Mr. Shuck, . . . chaplain of a rebel regiment near Richmond. After obtaining possession of all my letters, the boastful chivalry could not read them. They requested me to be seated, while they heard from me the contents of the epistles.

Taking advantage of their ignorance, I read such portions as I chose. They at once directed me to proceed under guard to Brentsville, distant about ten miles—they riding, and keeping me on foot between them, and constantly conversing in a low tone of voice respecting the importance of the arrest. . . .

We arrived at Manassas Junction about daylight, and went to General Beauregard's headquarters—the Weire House. Completely exhausted by the walk, and the excitement attending the arrest, I laid down in front of the house and went to sleep. At nine . . . A.M., I was awakened by the warm, bright rays of the sun, shining in my face, and found myself in charge of the guard attached to the headquarters. I called for food, and was informed that General Beauregard desired to see me. I was taken into his presence, with whom were two or three staff officers. Pointing to an open letter . . . he said: "From this letter I see you have been found within our lines. What explanation have you to make?"

I replied, "I am from Washington, and going to Richmond, on private business. I have not intended to violate any law, regulation, or military rule, of the Confederate army. . . ."

"What is your name?"

"Samuel Munson."

"Yes, I see from your letters that that is your name; but what was your name before you turned spy?"

"I am no spy."

"I believe you are; and, if I was satisfied of it, I would hang you on that tree," pointing through an open window to an oak-tree in full view. "Orderly," he added, "take this man out and put him in the guard-house. . . ."

I was taken by the guard to a stockade or pen, inside of which was a log-house. Following the officer in command, I said: "Sir, I am very hungry—can you give me something to eat?"— taking from my pocket a gold eagle. At sight of the coin, he said —"What will you have?"

"Send out and get me the . . . best breakfast you can get."

He soon returned with a good warm breakfast and a bottle of sour wine. The wine I gave to the guard, and ate the breakfast.

Having put myself on good terms with the officer in command of the guard-house, he asked me what I was there for.

I replied I did not know—but, if not in violation of his orders, would like to go outside in charge of a guard. . . . The sight of a twenty-dollar gold piece relieved his mind of any doubt on the subject. . . . He called a soldier and said: "Take this man out, and walk him around awhile."

I went to the hotel, treated my escort, and then went with him to take a general survey of all the troops in the immediate vicinity of Manassas Junction. One of my instructions from General Scott . . . was to ascertain the numbers of the famous, and by the Union army much dreaded, Black-horse cavalry. In conversation with my half-drunken guard, I referred to this cavalry, and inquired where they were.

He replied, "Down on the railroad."

I expressed a wish to see them.

He said, "Certainly—them's the boys to whip the Yankees!"

We went down the line of the railroad half a mile, and there found the cavalry in camp. I asked him how many men there were in that command.

He said, "Two hundred."

I made a thorough inspection of these troops. My accommodating guard then took me to all the camps, pointed out the different intrenchments in course of erection, the names of the several regiments and brigades, who commanded them, their strength, etc. When I had obtained this information, my guard met drunken friends, and left me to go where I pleased. Fearing I should be missed, I immediately returned to the guard-house. I was not locked up, but allowed to remain in the stockade, where I met two fellow-prisoners, as I then supposed, who at once began asking me questions. It did not take me long, however, to decide that they were decoys, placed there for the purpose of eliciting from me, if possible, my real character. They complained bitterly of their treatment, and one even requested me to take a letter to his wife in Washington.

I consented to take the letter. It was written in a way well calculated to mislead me. I . . . called the lieutenant on guard, and said: "You have a spy in the stockade"—handing him the letter. He said, "I will send it up to headquarters." A few minutes later I saw the same man in private confidential conversation with the lieutenant, at the same time pointing to me across the yard.

This satisfied me of the truth of my suspicions. Repeated efforts were afterward made, during my stay in the stockade, to ascertain who I was, and my intentions. To all inquiries, however,

I had but one answer, and that was: That they had made a great mistake in arresting me.

[Baker was sent to Richmond by train and was confined in an engine house when he arrived. Jefferson Davis interrogated him several times, trying to obtain information about the Union troops guarding Washington. During the last of these interviews, Baker was confronted with a man from Knoxville, the city he had claimed as his former residence. By boldly taking the initiative and pretending to know this stranger, Baker succeeded in getting himself set free. He remained for a while in Richmond to gather military information and then started for Washington. It was an adventurous return journey through territory that was hostile to strangers who spoke with a Northern accent. In order to cross the Potomac, Baker had to steal a boat and paddle across the wide river in the darkness. He landed on the Maryland shore at a point very near the place where John Wilkes Booth was to make his historic crossing four years later.

Lucius E. Chittenden, Register of the Treasury, had a poor opinion of Lafayette C. Baker. In 1891 he said of him: "He took into his service . . . men who claimed to have any aptitude for detective work, without recommendation, investigation, or any inquiry, beyond his own inspection, which he claimed immediately disclosed to him the character and abilities of the applicant. How large his regiment ultimately grew is uncertain, but at one time he asserted that it exceeded two thousand men.

"With this force at his command, protected against interference from the judicial authorities, Baker became a law unto himself. He instituted a veritable Reign of Terror. He dealt with every accused person in the same manner; with a reputable citizen as with a deserter or petty thief. He did not require the formality of a written charge; it was quite sufficient for any person to suggest to Baker that a citizen might be doing something that was against

73

law. He was immediately arrested, handcuffed, and brought to Baker's office, at that time in the basement of the Treasury. There he was subjected to a browbeating examination, in which Baker was said to rival in impudence some heads of the criminal bar. This examination was repeated as often as he chose. Men were kept in his rooms for weeks, without warrant, affidavit, or other semblance of authority. If the accused took any measures for his own protection, he was hurried into the Old Capitol Prison, where he was beyond the reach of the civil authorities. . . . He [BAKER] seemed to control the Old Capitol Prison, and one of his deputies [w. w. WOOD] was its keeper. He always lived at the first hotels, had an abundance of money, and I am sure did more to disgust good citizens and bring the government into disrepute than the strongest opponents of the [DETECTIVE] system had ever predicted."]

How the Confederates Got Arms
and Ammunition in Europe

by CALEB HUSE
from *Supplies for the Confederate Army,* 1904

[At the beginning of the war the Confederates had practically no way of manufacturing arms or ammunition. Percussion caps, the small copper-encased explosive devices which had replaced flints as a means for igniting a charge of gunpowder, were badly needed. Since a large quantity of them could be packed into little space, they were tempting items to bring through the lines. When Captain Louis Zimmer went to New York in March, 1861, to try to obtain a million percussion caps, he had no trouble buying them openly at a store on Liberty Street. The big problem was to get them into the South. But he managed to do this with some difficulty and finally arrived with 800,000 of them in time to supply the Confederate Army before it went into battle at First Manassas.

Early in the war, Major Caleb Huse was authorized to go to Europe to buy arms for the Confederacy. He was given carte blanche because it was not known what arms he would find available or what they would cost in a market that was sure to become increasingly competitive.

Many of the guns which Huse obtained were run through the Federal blockade by James D. Bulloch when he took the Fingal to Savannah.]

75

ON ARRIVING in London I went to what was then a favorite hotel for Americans—Morley's in Trafalgar Square. . . . My orders were to purchase 12,000 rifles and a battery of field artillery, and to procure one or two guns of large caliber as models. A short time before the beginning of the war, the London Armory Company had purchased a plant of gun-stocking machinery from the Ames Manufacturing Company of Chicopee, Massachusetts. Knowing this, I went to the office of the Armory Company the day after my arrival in London, with the intention of securing, if possible, their entire output.

On entering the Superintendent's office, I found there the American engineer who superintended the erection of the plant. I had known him in Chicopee. Suspecting he might be an agent for the purchase of arms for the United States Government, I asked him, bluntly, if he was, and added, "I am buying for the Confederate Government." Such a disclosure of my business may seem to have been indiscreet, but at that time I thought it my best plan, and the result proved that I was right. He made no reply to my inquiry, but I was satisfied my suspicion was correct and resolved on the spot to flank his movement if possible.

As he had entered the office first, it was in order for me to outstay him, which I did. On his leaving, I asked for a price for all the small arms the company could manufacture.

The Superintendent said he could not answer me, but would refer me to the company President, . . . and would accompany me to his office. There I repeated my inquiry for a price for all the arms the company could make for a year, with the privilege of renewing the order. The President was not prepared to give me a price, but would do so the next day. On calling at his office the following day, he told me that the company was under contract for all the arms it could turn out, and considering all the circumstances, the directors felt they ought to give their present customer the preference over all others.

Confirmed in my belief that my competitor was no other than the man whom I had encountered the day before, I was now more determined than ever to secure the London Armory as a Confederate States arms factory. The Atlantic cable was not then laid, and correspondence by mail required nearly a month—an unreasonable time for a commercial company to hold in abeyance a desirable opportunity for profit. Within a few days I succeeded in closing a contract under which I was to have all the arms the company could manufacture, after filling a comparatively small order for the United States agent. This company, during the remainder of the war, turned all its output of arms over to me for the Confederate Army. . . .

Any Army officer . . . buying arms . . . at the outbreak of a war, would have acted, if necessary, without instructions, and secured everything he could find. . . . There were [smoothbore] muskets enough to be had for almost any reasonable offer, but of modern . . . rifles . . . there were only a few thousand in England, and none elsewhere except in Austria . . . owned by the Government. . . . Such an officer would have secured everything worth having—in other words, all the best—and only inferior arms of antiquated model would have been left for the Confederacy. The effect would have been not only to give the United States good arms in profusion, but utterly to discourage their opponents by the inferiority of their weapons. . . .

The civilized powers had but recently been equipped with modern arms. The United States had the Springfield; England had the Enfield, which was practically the same as the Springfield; Austria had a rifle bearing a close resemblance to both, and of about the same calibre; Prussia had a breech-loader which no Government would now think of issuing to troops; France had an inferior muzzle loader, and was experimenting with an imitation of the Prussian needle-gun, which finally proved ruinous to the Empire. There were few arms for sale. . . . Austria, however, had a considerable quantity on hand, and these an intermediary proposed I should buy.

I knew something of the armament of Austria, having visited Vienna in 1859 with a letter from the United States War Department, which gave me some facilities for observation. At first I considered the getting of anything from an Imperial Austrian Arsenal as chimerical. But my would-be intermediary was so persistent that finally I accompanied him to Vienna and, within a few days, closed a contract for 100,000 rifles of the latest Austrian pattern, and ten batteries, of six pieces each, of field artillery, with harness complete, ready for service, and a quantity of ammunition, all to be delivered on ship at Hamburg. The United States Minister, Mr. Motley, protested in vain. He was told that the making of arms had been offered to the United States Government and declined, and that, as belligerents, the Confederate States were, by the usage of nations, lawful buyers. However unsatisfactory this answer may have been to Washington, the arms were delivered, and in due time were shipped to Bermuda from Hamburg. Mr. Motley offered to buy the whole consignment, but was too late. The Austrian Government declined to break faith with the purchasers.

I confess to a glow of pride when I saw those sixty pieces of rifled artillery with caissons, field-forges, and battery-wagons, complete—some two hundred carriages in all—drawn up in array in the arsenal yard. It was pardonable for a moment to imagine myself in command of a magnificent park of artillery. The explanation of Austria's willingness to dispose of these batteries is that the authorities had decided on the use of gun-cotton in the place of powder; and the change involved new guns, although those sold to me were of the latest design for gunpowder. I believe gun-cotton was given up not long after.

The First Confederate Cruiser
Puts Out to Sea

by RAPHAEL SEMMES

from *Official Records of the Union and Confederate Navies*
Series I, Vol. I, 1894

[Since Raphael Semmes was one of the first officers to quit the United States Navy (on February 15, 1861), he was able to visit the Northern states before hostilities began. While there he ordered supplies and munitions for the Confederacy, which he succeeded in getting into the South before the first gun was fired at Fort Sumter. He was given command of a steam packet named the Havana and arrived in New Orleans on April 22 to rename her the Sumter and rebuild her for war duty. In less than two months he changed her into a fighting ship armed with a massive 8-inch pivot gun and four 32-pounders. While he was getting the Sumter ready for sea, several Federal warships arrived to prevent any Confederate vessels from leaving the Mississippi River. Among them was the Brooklyn, then the fifth largest ship in the Union Navy.

Semmes tells the story of his escape in his daily Journal:]

SUNDAY, JUNE 30. *Dies memorabilis.* At about 2 A.M. the steamer *Empire Parish* came alongside and put on board of us about 100 barrels of coal. At 10:30 A.M. . . . . a boatman pulled under our stern and informed us that the *Brooklyn* was nowhere to be seen, and that the pass was all clear. We immediately got underway and steamed down the pass . . . I hoisted my jack for a pilot, and . . . as I ran by the pilot station a bold fellow jumped on board. . . . We continued on our course rapidly for the bar. In the meantime we had some time before discovered the *Brooklyn* some 7 or 8 miles to the southward of the bar under steam and hurrying up to prevent our escape. We dashed by the *Bremen* . . . which considerately . . . let us pass. . . .

The *Brooklyn* had by this time approached us within about four miles, and was making every effort to overhaul us . . . [She] had the reputation of being very fast both under sail and steam, and I was very doubtful whether my gallant little ship had the heels of her. . . . The *Brooklyn* having emerged from a squall in which she had been hid loomed up very large with her heavy battery and tall spars, her flag being plainly distinguishable at her peak. At length it began to be perceptible that we were dropping her by slow degrees, and my excited nervous system experienced a partial relaxation from the tension to which it had been strained for the last three hours. At 3:30 the *Brooklyn*, seeing that we had the heels of her, gave up the chase and bore up to the northward. Called on hands, sent them into the rigging and gave three cheers for the Confederate flag, after which, by invitation, I met the officers in the wardroom and drank a glass of wine with them in honor of the event. It was a positive luxury as the evening set in to breathe the pure air and look over the vast expanse of blue waters, with the feeling of a liberated prisoner.

[*Word that the Sumter was at large in the Caribbean spread rapidly, causing ships from the Northern states to avoid that area. Half a dozen Federal gunboats were sent in pursuit of her, keeping the Sumter constantly on the go. After two months, during which Semmes made only two captures, he had to put in at St. Pierre, Martinque, for coal and water.*

Five days later, a Union warship, the Iroquois, came in sight.

When its captain learned that the Sumter was coaling up he anchored his vessel outside and waited for the Confederate cruiser to leave. He also arranged with men on the American schooners in port to signal to him any movements the Sumter might make. Semmes learned of this plan and cleverly made use of it to escape. He headed out on a straight course until he was sure the Iroquois was following these signal lights, then he turned suddenly, ran close to the shore and was lucky enough to encounter a rainstorm. Under the cover of this he successfully got away.

After capturing and burning three prizes the Sumter entered the port of Cadiz, Spain, for repairs early in January, 1862. Then the ship went on to Gibraltar, taking two more prizes on the way. At Gibraltar, the British authorities refused permission for the ship to obtain coal. Three Union warships then arrived to blockade the Sumter in port. Since she was in poor condition the Confederates condemned her and ordered her to be sold. She was afterwards refitted and became a blockade runner.

According to Semmes' own list, the Sumter captured only eighteen ships, of which seven were burned. But the Confederates' first cruiser did far more damage than the records show, for her presence on the high seas kept many Yankee ships in port, sent them on new and less profitable voyages, or caused them to transfer to foreign flags.]

The Confederacy's
First Government-Owned Blockade Runner
Begins Her Career

by JAMES D. BULLOCH
from *The Secret Service of the Confederate States*
in Europe, 1884

[*When it became evident that the Confederacy had to have a
navy of its own, James D. Bulloch was sent to London in June,
1861, to buy or build ships in Europe. When construction started
on the two cruisers that were to be named the Florida and the
Alabama, there were many privately owned blockade runners in
operation, most of which were earning fabulous sums for their
owners. Bulloch suggested to his fellow-commissioners that they
purchase a fast new ship with Confederate government funds, load
her with arms and ammunition, and take her on a hurried trip to
report progress to Richmond. This was agreed to, and Bulloch
looked for a suitable vessel. He was well-trained for his job, for
he had been an officer in the United States Navy and had also
worked in private shipping. His half-sister, incidentally, was the
mother of President Theodore Roosevelt.*

*He bought the almost new, propeller-driven steamer Fingal.
On a test run she made thirteen knots under steam, so she seemed
fast enough. He took possession of the ship in Greenock, Scotland.*]

IT WAS NECESSARY to act with caution and secrecy, because the
impression had already got abroad that the Confederate Govern-

ment was trying to fit out ships in England to cruise against American commerce, and . . . all vessels were closely watched. . . .

The shipment per *Fingal* was: *On account of the Navy Department*—1,000 short rifles, with cutlass bayonets, and 1,000 rounds of ammunition per rifle; 500 revolvers, with suitable ammunition; two 4½-inch muzzle-loading rifled guns, with traversing carriages, all necessary gear, and 200 made-up cartridges, shot and shell, per gun; two breech-loading 2½-inch steel-rifled guns for boats or field service, with 200 rounds of ammunition per gun; 400 barrels of coarse cannon-powder, and a large quantity of made-up clothing for seamen.

For the State of Georgia—3,000 Enfield rifles.

For the State of Louisiana—1,000 Enfield rifles.

No single ship ever took into the Confederacy a cargo so entirely composed of military and naval supplies, and the pressing need of them made it necessary to get the *Fingal* off with quick dispatch, and to use every possible effort to get her into a port having railway communication through to Virginia, because the Confederate army, then covering Richmond, was very poorly armed, and was distressingly deficient in all field necessaries. . . .

The *Fingal* was kept under the British flag for obvious reasons, and it was therefore necessary to employ a captain holding a Board of Trade certificate to clear her outward, and to ship the crew in accordance with the Merchant Shipping Act. Some pains were taken to engage good engineers and a few leading men, but no hint was given that the ship would go farther than Bermuda and Nassau. . . .

On the 11th [of October] we . . . learned by telegram that the *Fingal* was off from Greenock. During the night it came on to blow a hard gale, which continued for two or three days, with thick weather and much rain. We [in Holyhead] could get no tidings of the ship, and although I felt reasonably satisfied that she had put into some harbor or shelter, yet the uncertainty and delay were perplexing. During the 14th the gale broke. Towards evening the weather was fine, and we had hopes of seeing or hearing from the missing ship on the next day. At about 4 A.M. on the 15th, I was aroused by a loud knock at my bedroom door, and a house-porter came in with a dark lantern, followed by Mr. Low [the second officer]. It had been raining, and Low had on a 'souwester' and a long painted canvas coat, which were dripping with wet. I was only half awake. In the dim light of the lantern the figure before me loomed up like a huge octopus, or some other marine monster, and I was startled by a sepulchral voice which seemed to be mumbling under the breast of the peajacket, like the last tremulous quivering of a thunderclap. But my ear caught the sound of a few articulate words, among which *"Fingal,"* "brig," "collision," "sunk," were fearfully jumbled together. It is astounding with what electric velocity the mind acts in the few seconds of awaking when one is suddenly aroused from sleep. Before I could leap out of bed a painful scene of wreck and disaster passed vividly through my brain, and I fancied the *Fingal* at the bottom of Holyhead Harbor.

. . . Low was, however, steady, cool, and unimpassioned, and put the facts into my mind without waste of words, and they may be briefly summarized thus: The *Fingal* was creeping cautiously round the breakwater when she suddenly came upon a brig at anchor, with no light up. The steamer had barely steerage way, and the engines were quickly reversed, but her sharp stem took the brig's starboard quarter. There was just a slight sound, like the quick snap of a gun-hammer upon the uncapped nipple, then a shout from the deck of the unhappy craft, and before a boat could be lowered she went down all standing. This is what usually happens when an iron steamer comes in contact with a wooden ship. . . .

Day was just breaking when we got alongside of the *Fingal,* and in the dim twilight we could see the upper spars of the brig standing straight up out of the water, with the bunt of the main top-gallant sail just awash. The vessel proved to be the Austrian brig *Siccardi*. She was loaded with coal, which accounts for her going down so quickly and standing upright afterwards.

It was manifestly out of the question to remain where we were. Custom officers would soon be on board, the *Fingal* would be detained to settle, or give security for a satisfactory settlement, with the consignees of the *Siccardi*. . . . There would surely be inquiry, further detention, and perhaps a final break-up of the voyage. I thought of the rifles and sabers in the hold, and the ill-armed pickets on the Potomac, waiting and longing for them, and told the captain to weigh anchor at once.

There was no wish to defraud the owners of the *Siccardi* of any compensation they were entitled to. I wrote a hasty letter to Messrs. Fraser, Trenholm and Co., briefly reporting the circumstances and asking them to find out the consignees of the brig and make the best possible arrangement with them. (Messrs. Fraser, Trenholm and Co. communicated with the consignees very promptly. A friendly arbitration was agreed to, and the affair was satisfactorily settled.) The letter was dispatched on shore by a boat we had engaged to bring our luggage off, and the *Fingal* was round the point of the breakwater, and steaming down Channel, before the accident at the mouth of the harbor was known to anyone who would have had authority to stop her.

For several days after leaving Holyhead we had fine weather, and were well satisfied in most respects with the ship. She was staunch, comfortable, and well-fitted in all particulars, but in the anxiety to get as much in her as possible, she had been loaded too deep, and I found that we could not get a higher speed than nine knots, which was rather disappointing, in view of a possible chase between Bermuda and the coast. . . .

The *Fingal* . . . arrived at Bermuda on the 2nd of November. Here we had the pleasure to find the Confederate States ship *Nashville*. Captain R. B. Pegram, from whom we learned much about the state of affairs in the beleaguered Confederacy. . . .

handed me a dispatch from Hon. S. R. Mallory, Secretary of the Navy, acknowledging my reports sent per steamship *Bermuda* in August. He approved my contracts for the *Florida* and *Alabama*, and for naval ordnance stores, and also the proposition I had suggested of buying a steamer and returning in her to the Confederate States with supplies and for consultation. He furthermore informed me that he had sent out by the *Nashville* several pilots, and that Captain Pegram would let me have any one or more of them I might require. Mr. John Makin, a pilot for Savannah and the inlets to the southward, was transferred to the *Fingal*.

We were detained several days at Bermuda. The United States Consul suspected the ultimate object of the *Fingal's* voyage, and he did his best to put obstacles in the way of our getting coal and other supplies, and employed men to tamper with the crew and alarm them, and persuade them to leave the ship. However, the local merchants and the people generally were very friendly and we got at last all that was wanted, and sailed for the coast on the afternoon of the 7th of November.

Up to the time of our departure from Bermuda, not a word had been said to a member of the crew, nor even to the captain, about the purpose to run the blockade, and the ship was cleared out from St. George's for Nassau. . . .

The day after leaving Bermuda it was necessary to put the ship's head in the direction of the actual port of destination, and . . . all on board, would soon perceive that we were not steering the course for Nassau. It would not have been fair to conceal the object of the voyage from the men until a critical moment, and it would also have been imprudent to go on to the coast without knowing their minds, because they had not agreed to undertake any such risk.

I determined, therefore, to settle the matter there and then, and sent for all hands to come aft to the bridge. I told them very briefly that they had shipped in a British port, to make a voyage in a British ship to one or more British islands and back again to England; that I had no right to take them anywhere else without their consent, and I did not mean to use either force or undue pressure to make them do anything not set out in the shipping articles, but I thought they must have suspected that there was some other purpose in the voyage than a cruise to Bermuda and the Bahamas, and the time had arrived when it was both safe and proper for me to tell them the real port of destination, which was Savannah, and of course this meant a breach of blockade, with the risk of capture and some rough treatment as prisoners-of-war. I added, "If you are not willing to go on, say so now, and I will take the ship to Nassau and get other men who will go; but if you are ready and willing to risk the venture, remember that it is a fresh engagement and a final one, from which there must be no backing out."

I had thought over what to say, and was prepared with a few exhilarating and persuasive phrases; but . . . it flashed across my mind at once that no further talk was necessary, and I put the question plainly, "Will you go?" to which there was a prompt and unanimous consent. I thanked them, but said there was still something to explain, which I did to the following effect:

"The United States have been compelled to buy up steamers from the merchant service for blockaders. Many of them are neither so strong nor so efficient in any way as this ship, and they are not heavily armed. If we should fall in with any blockaders off Savannah at all, they are likely to be of that class, and [we] who represent the Confederate Government . . . do not feel disposed to give up this valuable and important cargo to a ship not strong enough to render resistance useless, or to open boats that may attempt to board us. So long as the *Fingal* is under British flag, we have no right to fire a shot, but I have a bill of sale in my pocket, and can take delivery from the captain on behalf of the Confederate Navy Department at any moment. This I propose to do, if there should appear to be any likelihood of a collision with a blockader, and I want to know if you are willing under such circumstances to help in defending the ship?"

They answered "Yes" to a man. These preliminaries being satisfactorily settled, all hands were set briskly to work to arm the ship. We mounted the two 4½-inch rifled guns in the forward gangway ports, and the two steel boat-guns on the quarterdeck. We got up a sufficient number of rifles and revolvers, with a good supply of ammunition, and converted the "ladies' saloon" into an armoury, shell-room, and magazine.

The cases containing the made-up cartridges for the guns were stowed out of easy reach, so we hoisted out of the hold a few barrels of powder and a bale of flannel, and made ten or fifteen cartridges for each gun. . . . The *Fingal* was on the next day ready to beat off a boat attack, or even to exchange shots with an impromptu blockader on a dark night, and thus perhaps prevent her closing. . . . Two or three . . . of the crew were old naval men, and took the leading positions at the guns. We had two or three drills, and found that we could handle the "battery" satisfactorily.

I had a talk with McNair [the chief engineer] after settling everything with the men. Although he did not say so, I felt sure from his manner that he had been expecting the information, because he received it quite as a matter of course, and told me that he had been putting aside a few tons of the nicest and cleanest coal, and if I could give him time just before getting on the coast to haul fires in one boiler at a time, and run the scrapers through the flues, he thought he might drive the ship, deep as she was, at the rate of eleven knots for a spurt of a few hours. These preparations seemed to put all hands in good spirits; indeed, the men were quite jolly over the prospect.

On the 11th McNair got the chance to clean his flues. It was my purpose to make the land at the entrance to Warsaw Sound, through which Makin said he could take the ship by inland creeks into the Savannah River, and the course was shaped so that at noon on the 11th we should be on the parallel of Warsaw. From that position we steered in on a due-west course, and timed the speed to make land . . . before daylight.

The moon set early, but the night was clear, and there was an unusually good horizon line. Several suitable stars passed the meridian between dark and 1 A.M., and Polaris was . . . available, so we were able to get the latitude every half hour, and thus to check the course. At about 1 A.M. on the 12th we got alongshore soundings inside the Gulf Stream. Up to this time it had been uncomfortably clear, with a light south-east breeze, but it now fell calm, and we could see a dark line to the westward. Makin said it was the mist over the marshes, and the land-breeze would soon bring it off to us. In half an hour or so we felt a cool damp air in our faces, then a few big drops of moisture, and we ran straight into as nice a fog as any reasonable blockade-runner could have wanted. There was not a light anywhere about the ship except in the binnacle, and that was carefully covered, so that the man at the wheel could barely look at the compass with one eye, and the engine-room hatches were well-hooded. Not a word was spoken, and there was not a sound but the throb of the engines and the slight "shir-r-r-" made by the friction of the ship through the water, and these seemed muffled by the dank vaporous air.

When we got into six fathoms the engines were eased to dead slow, and we ran cautiously in by the lead, straight for the land, the object being to get in-shore of any blockaders that might be off the inlet. We supposed the ship to be drawing fifteen or sixteen feet, and we stood on into three and a quarter fathoms, when we turned her head off to the light easterly swell, and stopped the engines. The fog was as thick as, and about the colour of, mulligatawny soup, and the water alongside looked darkish brown. From the bridge it was just possible to make out the men standing

89

on the forecastle and poop. We could not have been in a better position for a dash at daylight.

While we were thus lying-to and waiting, every faculty alert to catch the slightest sound, and every eye searching the fog for the first glimpse of land, or of an approaching ship, there burst upon our ears a shrill prolonged quavering shriek. The suddenness of the sound, coming upon our eagerly expectant senses, and probably much heightened in volume and force by contrast with the stillness, was startling. . . . None of us could conceive what it was, but all thought that it was loud and as piercing as a steam whistle, and that it must have been heard by any blockader within five miles of us. In a moment the sound was repeated, but we were prepared, and it was this time accompanied by a flapping and rustling noise from a hencoop in the gangway. "It is the cock that came on board at Bermuda," said someone. Several men ran to the spot . . . drew out an unhappy fowl, and wrung off its head with a vicious swing. But it was the wrong one, and chanticleer crowed again defiantly. "Try again," came up in an audible whisper from under the bridge; but [the man's] second effort was more disastrous than the first. He not only failed to seize the obnoxious screamer, but he set the whole hennery in commotion, and the "Mujan" cock, from a safe corner, crowed and croaked, and fairly chuckled over the fuss of feathers, the cackling, and the distracting strife he had aroused. At last the offending bird was caught. He died game, and made a fierce struggle for life . . . the body fell with a heavy thud upon the deck, and we were again favoured with a profound stillness.

By this time daylight began to break. Makin said the fog would settle and gather over the low marshes towards sunrise, and gradually roll off seaward before the light land-wind. I went aloft to look out for the first sight of the "inlet." Makin was right. In less than half an hour I could see the bushy tops of the tall pine-trees, then their straight slender trunks, then the brushwood, and finally the pale yellow streak of sand which formed the foreshore. I reported this to Makin, who could not see it all from the deck, and he asked me to come down and consult. I assured him we were right abreast of Warsaw Inlet, and of this he was satisfied, but he said the buoys would all be up, and the low-lying fog would probably cover the distant leading marks, and we might go wrong in the intricate channels. He thought it would be some time before the fog would clear off to seaward, but as it was settling over the land we would soon have a tolerably clear view inshore, he proposed making a dash for Savannah, about 18 miles to the north and east, where he felt sure we could get in, buoys or no buoys.

In a few moments the engines were doing their best, and the ship's head was laid for the outer bar of the Savannah River. McNair fulfilled his promise, for the *Fingal* was making a good eleven knots. Meanwhile the fog continued to settle and roll off the land, and the low sandy beach, with the tall pines in the background, and a gentle surf just creaming its outer edge, was soon in full view from the deck. We skirted the shore in the least water the ship's draft permitted, and were much favored. The land breeze dropped, and about half a mile off shore the fog hung heavily, a great gray mass, almost black at the water's edge. It served as a veil between us and any blockaders that might be enveloped in it.

We bowled along at a steady pace, and before long the beach and the line of pines trended abruptly away to the westward; we caught sight of the high brick walls of Fort Pulaski, and were off the estuary of the Savannah.

In another quarter of an hour . . . the *Fingal* was over the bar and plowing up channel. . . . We fired a gun and hoisted the Confederate flag at the fore, which was answered from the fort. The parapet of the main works and the *glacis* of the outer were lined with men, and as we drew near we saw the caps waving, although we could not hear their cheers.

[Bulloch returned to England to continue his work. But the Fingal, which he had brought across the Atlantic with such ease, turned out to be an unlucky ship for the Confederacy. She was bottled up in the Savannah River for so long by the Federal blockading fleet that it was decided to transform her into an entirely different kind of vessel. She was stripped and covered with thick armor which shielded four large naval guns. Renamed the Atlanta, she steamed down river as a fighting ironclad late in May, 1863. But she drew so much water with her deep hull and heavy armament that she soon went aground on a mudbank. She was floated off and repaired; then at 3:30 A.M. on June 17, she started out again to attack a fleet of Federal monitors. She went aground three times as she neared the little but well-armed monitors. When Captain John Rodgers, commander of the Weehawken, saw that the clumsy Atlanta was unable to move, he ordered his solidly armored monitor to close in and blast away at the stranded ship with enormous 15- and 16-inch guns fired at close range. The Atlanta was quickly forced to surrender. She was taken as a prize of war and was assigned to the Federal fleet.]

1862

On January 13, vigorous, hot-tempered Edwin M. Stanton replaced Simon Cameron as Lincoln's Secretary of War. And in February came the first decisive Union victories when Forts Henry and Donelson in Tennessee were taken. This was followed early in March by a mixed-up encounter at Pea Ridge, Arkansas, which both sides claimed as a victory. On April 6 and 7 came the bloody major battle of Shiloh where the Confederate general, Albert Sidney Johnston, was killed early in the fighting and the hitherto unknown U. S. Grant began to attract national attention.

The North was victorious on the water that spring, when the Confederate ironclad the Merrimac, which had been terrorizing Union shipping near Hampton Roads, Virginia, was driven back to port by the famous little "cheesebox on a raft," the Monitor. That day, March 9, 1862, spelled doom for wooden fighting ships.

During the fall of 1861 and the spring of 1862 a series of

amphibious operations enabled the Union forces to establish permanent bases along the coasts of North Carolina, South Carolina, Georgia, and Florida. These bases strengthened the Federal blockading fleet, because coal, ammunition, supplies, and shelter from sudden storms could be found there. Then, on April 29, 1862, New Orleans surrendered to Farragut, closing that important Mississippi River port to Confederate traffic. Blockade running, which had been relatively easy in 1861, now became increasingly difficult as Southern ports were captured, one by one. Meanwhile the Federal blockading fleet kept growing in size and firepower.

Late in March, General George B. McClellan landed his newly trained troops at Fortress Monroe and began the long Peninsular Campaign to take Richmond. Bitter fighting went on all spring, but the Union Army was driven back after it was almost in sight of the Confederate capital. On the last day of May, Lee was given command of the Army of Northern Virginia; during the summer "Stonewall" Jackson's Confederates fought a brilliant campaign in the Shenandoah Valley. At the end of August, Pope, who had temporarily replaced McClellan in favor at Washington, was beaten at Bull Run (Second Manassas) on the same ground where the first major battle of the war had taken place. Lee, taking advantage of this victory, pressed on to invade Maryland and the North. McClellan was hastily restored to the Union command; he rapidly reorganized the units that had been badly mauled at Bull Run and started out to meet Lee. The two great armies clashed head-on near a country village named Sharpsburg and fought along the shores of Antietam Creek. There, on September 17, 1862, occurred what has been called the bloodiest day of the war. Lee's invading army was stopped, and the Confederates had to return to Virginia. But McClellan did not follow up his victory; because of his inaction Lincoln removed him from command on November 5 and appointed Burnside in his place.

Burnside lasted from November 5, 1862, to January 25, 1863, just long enough to be in command during the dreadful battle of Fredericksburg on December 13, when the Union dead were piled up like logs of wood to shield the living.

The year, so far as fighting on land was concerned, was an indecisive one; but the loss of valuable seaports and the gradual strengthening of the Federal blockade was slowly cutting off the Confederacy's sources of manufactured goods and raw material which had to be imported. And since there was no way of shipping enough cotton out, the rebellious states were beginning to be smothered in the white fiber they had counted on to win English and French support.

Privateering had dwindled at the end of 1861 to almost nothing because shipowners had no ports into which they could bring their captured prizes. The Confederacy was badly in need of fighting ships that could destroy Yankee commerce on the high seas and be strongly enough armed to defend themselves if attacked. These roaming cruisers could be commanded by officers who had received their training in the United States Navy, but they would have to be manned by untrained Confederate crews or by seamen obtained from the ships of other nations. The few pro-Southern sailors on ships in the Federal Navy were watched carefully and given no chance to desert in ports from which they could reach the Confederate states.

The first Confederate cruiser to be built in Europe, the Florida, reached Nassau in May, 1862, where Captain John Newland Maffitt, one of the Confederacy's ablest seamen, took command of her.

Belle Boyd Starts Her Work
as a Spy

from *Belle Boyd in Camp and Prison,*
written by herself, 1867

[Most Civil War espionage was pretty amateurish, but to Belle Boyd spying was an exciting child's game for she was only seventeen when the war began. She had lived for most of her life in Martinsburg in the northern part of the Shenandoah Valley near Harpers Ferry. When some Union soldiers got drunk on July 4, 1861, and came to the Boyds' home to take down rebel flags allegedly displayed on the walls there, Belle shot and killed one of the invaders. She was acquitted and went free.

She then kept herself busy sending the Confederates written information about the Federal troops whose strength and movements she could easily observe. She was trapped by her own amateurishness, for she made no attempt to use a code or cipher or even to disguise her handwriting. When one of her messages was intercepted, she was again arrested and tried; again, as a young girl, she was allowed to go free. She promptly became even more active and carried messages through the lines to areas farther from home.

She was at Front Royal when "Stonewall" Jackson began moving his army north. Staying in the same cottage was G. W. Clarke, British-born correspondent of the New York Herald. According to Belle, this reporter for a Yankee newspaper had made improper advances to her. She was soon to play the leading role in a Victorian melodrama by helping the Confederates and at the same time get even with Clarke.]

ON THE EVENING of the 23rd May [1862] I was sitting at the window of our room, reading to my grandmother and cousin, when one of the servants rushed in, and shouted, or rather shrieked—

"Oh, Miss Belle, I t'inks de rebels am a-comin', for de Yankees are a-makin' orful fuss in de street."

I immediately sprang from my seat and went to the door, and I then found that the servant's report was true. The streets were thronged with Yankee soldiers, hurrying about in every direction in the greatest confusion.

I asked a Federal officer . . . what was the matter. He answered that the Confederates were approaching the town in force, under Generals Jackson and Ewell, that they had surprised and captured the outside pickets, and had actually advanced within a mile of the town without the attack being even suspected.

"Now," he added, "we are endeavoring to get the ordnance and the quartermaster's stores out of their reach."

"But what will you do," I asked, "with the stores in the large depot?"

"Burn them, of course!"

"But suppose the rebels come upon you too quickly?"

"Then we will fight as long as we can by any possibility show a front, and in the event of defeat make good our retreat upon Winchester, burning the bridges as soon as we cross them, and finally effect a junction with General Banks's force."

I parted with the Federal officer, and returning to the house, I began to walk quietly up-stairs, when suddenly I heard the report of a rifle, and almost at the same moment I encountered Mr. Clark [sic] who, in his rapid descent from his room, very nearly knocked me down.

"Great heavens! What is the matter?" he ejaculated, as soon

as he had regained his breath, which the concussion and fright had deprived him of.

"Nothing to speak of," said I; "only the rebels are coming, and you had best prepare yourself for a visit to Libby Prison."

He answered not a word, but rushed back to his room and commenced compressing into as small a compass as possible all the manuscripts upon which he so much plumed himself, and upon which he relied for fame and credit with the illustrious journal to which he was contributor. It was his intention to collect and secure these inestimable treasures, and then to skedaddle.

I immediately went for my opera-glasses, and, on my way to the balcony in front of the house, from which position I intended to reconnoitre, I was obliged to pass Mr. Clark's door. It was open, but the key was on the outside. The temptation of making a Yankee prisoner was too strong to be resisted, and, yielding to the impulse, I quietly locked in the "Special Correspondent" of the *New York Herald*.

After this feat I hurried to the balcony, and, by the aid of my glasses, described the advance-guard of the Confederates at the distance of about three-quarters of a mile, marching rapidly upon the town.

To add to my anxiety, my father, who was at that time upon General Garnett's staff, was with them. My heart beat alternately with hope and fear. I was not ignorant of the trap the Yankees had set for my friends. I was in possession of much important information, which, if I could only contrive to convey to General Jackson, I knew our victory would be secure. Without it I had every reason to anticipate defeat and disaster.

The intelligence I was in possession of instructed me that General Banks was at Strasbourg with four thousand men, that the small force at Winchester could be readily re-inforced by General White, who was at Harpers Ferry, and that Generals Shields and Geary were a short distance below Front Royal, while Fremont was beyond the Valley; further. and this was the vital point, that it had been decided all these separate divisions should co-operate against General Jackson.

I again went down to the door, and this time I observed, standing about in groups, several men who had always professed attachment to the cause of the South. I demanded if there was one among them who would venture to carry to General Jackson the information I possessed. They all with one accord said, "No, no. You go."

I did not stop to reflect. My heart, though beating fast, was not appalled. I put on a white sun-bonnet, and started at a run down the street, which was thronged with Federal officers and men. I soon cleared the town and gained the open fields, which I traversed with unabated speed, hoping to escape observation until such time as I could make good my way to the Confederate line, which was still rapidly advancing.

I had on a dark-blue dress, with a little fancy white apron over it; and this contrast of colors, being visible at a great distance, made me far more conspicuous than was just then agreeable. The skirmishing between the outposts was sharp. The main forces of the opposing armies were disposed as follows:—

The Federals had placed their artillery on a lofty eminence, which commanded the road by which the Confederates were advancing. The Confederates were in line, directly in front of the hospital, into which their artillery-men were throwing shells with deadly precision; for the Yankees had taken this as a shelter, and were firing upon the Confederate troops from the window.

At this moment, the Federal pickets, who were rapidly falling back, perceived me still running as fast as I was able, and immediately fired upon me.

My escape was most providential; for, although I was not hit, the rifle-balls flew thick and fast about me, and more than one struck the ground so near my feet as to throw the dust in my eyes. Nor was this all: the Federals in the hospital, seeing in what direction the shots of their pickets were aimed, followed the example and also opened fire upon me.

Upon this occasion my life was spared by what seemed to me then, and seems still, little short of a miracle; for, besides the numerous bullets that whistled by my ears, several actually pierced different parts of my clothing, but not one reached my body. Besides all this, I was exposed to a cross-fire from the Federal and Confederate artillery, whose shot and shell flew whistling and hissing over my head.

At length a Federal shell struck the ground within twenty yards of my feet; and the explosion, of course, sent the fragments flying in every direction around me. I had, however, just time to throw myself flat upon the ground before the deadly engine burst; and again Providence spared my life.

Springing up when the danger was passed, I pursued my career, still under a heavy fire. I shall never run again as I ran on that, to me, memorable day. Hope, fear, the love of life, and the determination to serve my country to the last, conspired to fill my heart with more than feminine courage, and to lend preternatural strength and swiftness to my limbs. I often marvel, and even shudder, when I reflect how I cleared the fields, and bounded over the fences with the agility of a deer.

As I neared our lines I waved my bonnet to our soldiers, to intimate that they should press forward, upon which one regiment, the First Maryland "rebel" Infantry, and Hay's Louisiana Brigade, gave me a loud cheer, and, without waiting for further orders, dashed upon the town at a rapid pace.

They did not then know who I was, and they were naturally surprised to see a woman on the battle-field, and on a spot, too, where the fire was so hot. Their shouts of approbation and triumph rang in my ears for many a day afterwards, and I still hear them not unfrequently in my dreams.

100

At this juncture the main body of the Confederates was hidden from my view by a slight elevation which intervened between me and them. My heart almost ceased to beat within me; for the dreadful thought arose in my mind, that our force must be too weak to be any match for the Federals, and that the gallant men who had just been applauding me were rushing upon a certain and fruitless death. I accused myself of having urged them to their fate; and now, quite overcome by fatigue, and by the feelings which tormented me, I sank upon my knees and offered a short but earnest prayer to God.

Then I felt as if my supplication was answered, and that I was inspired with fresh spirits and a new life. Not only despair, but fear also forsook me; and I had again no thought but how to fulfil the mission I had already pursued so far.

I arose from my kneeling posture, and had proceeded but a short distance, when, to my unspeakable, indescribable joy, I caught sight of the main body fast approaching; and soon an old friend and connection of mine, Major Harry Douglas, rode up, and, recognizing me, cried out, while he seized my hand—

"Good God, Belle, you here! What is it?"

"Oh, Harry," I gasped out, "give me time to recover my breath."

For some seconds I could say no more; but, as soon as I had sufficiently recovered myself, I . . . told him all, urging him to hurry on the cavalry, with orders to them to seize the bridges before the retreating Federals should have time to destroy them.

He instantly galloped off to report to General Jackson, who immediately rode forward, and asked me if I would have an escort and a horse wherewith to return to the village. I thanked him, and said, "No; I would go as I came;" and then, acting upon the information I had been spared to convey, the Confederates gained a most complete victory.

Though the depot building had been fired, and was burning,

our cavalry reached the bridges barely in time to save them from destruction: the retreating Federals had just crossed, and were actually upon the point of lighting the slow match which, communicating with the bursting charge, would have riven the arches in pieces. So hasty was their retreat that they left all their killed and wounded in our hands. . . .

[After her widely publicized exploit at Front Royal, Belle Boyd became an object of suspicion to the Union War Department. She did not cease her activities, but continued to carry messages—some of them private letters for which she was paid— to Richmond. On July 29, 1862, a detective from the United States Secret Service in Washington came to Front Royal to arrest her. She was taken under guard by carriage and train to Washington where she was placed in the Old Capitol Prison.

This famous prison, which at various times also housed Rose Greenhow and almost every other person suspected of espionage, disloyalty, or conspiracy against the Federal Government, had been the temporary Capitol of the United States after the British burned Washington in 1814. When the historic Capitol building was rebuilt and restored to use, the temporary brick structure became a boardinghouse and then a prison. It was located where the white marble Supreme Court building now stands. To the east were two yards surrounded by a thirteen-foot fence; within one of these yards was the gallows. Still farther east (where the Library of Congress is now) was a row of private residences which had been converted into Carroll Prison.

Here is a contemporary Confederate description of the Old Capitol, written by D. A. Mahony who spent some time within its dreaded walls:

"On the principal floor of the building, [ARE] the Halls of the Senate and House of Representatives, which are now divided into five large rooms, numbered respectively from 14 to 18—room 16 being the center and largest. These rooms . . . [ARE] fitted with similar bunks filled with filth of every imaginable kind, and entirely destitute of any furniture or necessary accommodations indispensable in the humblest cabin. These rooms usually contained from eighteen to twenty-five prisoners in each; their average size is under thirty feet square."

The superintendent of the prison, William P. Wood, was one of the most remarkable men in Washington. He had been an expert patent-model-maker before the war and was said to have altered the model on which the rights to the McCormick reaper were based. By this trick, Secretary of War Stanton, who was then counsel for McCormick, won the case.

Although Wood ruled the Old Capitol with iron discipline, the prisoners often attested to his fairness and good humor in dealing with them. He was particularly lenient with young and attractive female prisoners.

The superintendent was a skeptic about religion; on Sundays he would go through the prison hallways to announce loudly: "All ye who want to hear the Lord God preached according to Jeff Davis, go down to the yard; and all ye who want to hear the Lord God preached according to Abe Lincoln, go to [ROOM] Number 16."

Here is Belle Boyd's own account of her introduction to the Old Capitol and its superintendent:]

. . . Upon my arrival at the prison, I was ushered into a small office. A clerk, who was writing at a desk, looked up for a moment, and informed me the superintendent would attend to my business immediately. The words were hardly uttered when Mr. Wood entered the room, and I was aware of the presence of a man of middle height, powerfully built, with brown hair, fair complexion, and keen, bluish-gray eyes.

Mr. Wood prides himself, I believe, upon his plebeian extraction; but I can safely aver that beneath his rough exterior there beats a warm and generous heart.

"And so this is the celebrated rebel spy," said he. "I am very glad to see you, and will endeavor to make you as comfortable as possible; so whatever you wish for, ask for it and you shall have it. I am glad I have so distinguished a personage for my guest. Come, let me show you to your room."

We traversed the hall, ascended a flight of stairs, and found ourselves in a short, narrow passage, up and down which a sentry paced, and into which several doors opened. One of these doors, No. 6, was thrown open, and behold my prison cell!

Mr. Wood, after repeating his injunction to me to ask for whatever I might wish, and with the promise that he would send me a servant, and that I should not be locked in as long as I "behaved myself," withdrew, and left me to my reflections.

At the moment I did not quite understand the meaning of the last indulgence, but within a few minutes I was given a copy of the rules and regulations of the prison, which set forth that if I held any communication whatever with the other prisoners, I should be punished by having my door locked.

There was nothing remarkable in the shape or size of my apartment, except that two very large windows took up nearly the whole of one side of the wall. Upon taking an inventory of my effects, I found them to be as follows: A washing-stand, a looking-glass, an iron bedstead, a table, and some chairs.

From the windows I had a view of part of Pennsylvania Avenue, and far away in the country the residence of General Floyd, ex-United States Secretary of War, where I had formerly passed many happy hours. At first I could not help indulging in reminiscences of my last visit to Washington, and contrasting it with my present forlorn condition; but rousing myself from my reverie, I bethought myself of the indulgence promised me, and asked for a rocking-chair and a fire; not that I required the latter, for the room was already very warm, but I fancied a bright blaze would make it look more cheerful.

My trunk, after being subjected to a thorough scrutiny, was sent up to me, and, having plenty of time at my disposal, I unpacked it leisurely.

Upon each floor of the prison were posted sentries within sight and call of each other. The sentry before my door was No. 6, and when I had occasion for my servant I had to request him to summon the corporal of the guard. My attendant was an "intelligent contraband," [escaped Negro slave] who was extremely useful to me during my enforced residence in the Old Capitol.

I had not unpacked my trunk, when dinner was served, and here I shall do plain justice by transcribing the bill of fare; and it will be allowed I claim no commiseration on the plea of bread-and-water diet, though such had been ordered for me by Mr. Stanton: "BILL OF FARE—Soup / Beef Steak / Chicken / Boiled Corn / Tomatoes / Irish Stew / Potatoes / Bread and Butter / Cantelopes / Peaches / Pears / Grapes." This, with but little variety, constituted my dinner every day until released.

At eight o'clock, Mr. Wood came to my room, accompanied by the chief of the detectives [Lafayette C. Baker], who desired an interview with me on the part of the Secretary-at-War.

I begged this worthy to be seated—a request he immediately complied with; and he then delivered the following graceful exhortation, which I transcribe verbatim:

"Ain't you pretty tired of your prison a'ready? I've come to get you to make a free confession now of what you've did agin our cause; and, as we've got plenty of proof agin you, you might as well acknowledge at once."

"Sir," I replied, "I do not understand you; and, furthermore, I have nothing to say. When you have informed me on what grounds I have been arrested, and given me a copy of the charges preferred against me, I will make my statement; but I shall not

105

now commit myself." Thereupon the oath of allegiance was prof-
fered, and I was harangued . . . upon the enormity of my offence,
and given to understand the cause of the South was hopeless.

"Say, now, won't you take the oath of allegiance? Remember,
Mr. Stanton will hear of all this. He sent me here."

To this peroration I replied: "Tell Mr. Stanton from me, I
hope that when I commence the oath of allegiance to the United
States Government, my tongue may cleave to the roof of my
mouth; and that if ever I sign one line that will show to the
world that I owe the United States Government the slightest
allegiance, I hope my arm may fall paralyzed by my side."

This speech of mine he immediately took down in his note-
book, and, growing very angry at my determination, he called out:
"Well, if this is your resolution, you'll have to lay here and die;
and serve you right."

"Sir," I retorted, "if it is a crime to love the South, its cause,
and its President, then I am a criminal. I am in your power, do
with me as you please. But I fear you not. I would rather lie down
in this prison and die, than leave it owing allegiance to such a
government as yours. Now leave the room; for so thoroughly am
I disgusted with your conduct towards me, that I cannot endure
your presence longer."

Scarcely had I finished my defiance, which I confess was
spoken in a loud tone of voice, when cheers and cries of "Bravo!"
reached my ears. Until that moment, I was not aware that the
rooms on the floor with my own were occupied; for, having kept
my door shut all day, I had no means of noticing what was passing
around me.

My door, however, had been left open during my interview
with the detective, consequently my neighbors, whom I afterwards
ascertained to be Confederate officers and Englishmen, had over-
heard our whole conversation, and hailed with applause the firm-
ness with which I had rejected Mr. Stanton's overtures of liberty,

conditional as they were upon my renunciation of the Confederacy, and on my allegiance to the Federal Government. And now Mr. Wood, taking pity upon me, withdrew the detective, saying: "Come, we had better go; the lady is tired."

Within a few minutes of their departure, I heard a low, significant cough, and, as I turned in the direction from whence it proceeded, something small and white fell at my feet. I picked it up, and found that it was a minute nut-shell basket, upon which were painted miniature Confederate flags. Round it was wrapped a small piece of paper, upon which were traced a few words expressive of sympathy with my misfortunes. I afterwards found out that the author of this short communication was an Englishman; and I can assure him that his kindness was like a ray of light from heaven breaking into the cell of a condemned prisoner. I wrote a hasty reply, and, watching my opportunity, threw it to him. I then lay down on my bed in a tranquil—I had almost said a happy—frame of mind; and I closed my first day in a dungeon by repeating to myself, more than once:

"Stone walls do not a prison make,
    Nor iron bars a cage:
A free and quiet mind can take
    These for a hermitage."

[Since no specific charge had been made against Belle, she was released on August 28 and sent to Richmond where she was given an enthusiastic reception. She continued to work as a spy and went to England in May, 1864. While there she wrote her memoirs. She also married a Union naval officer whom she converted to the Confederate cause. After the war she went on the stage, not to play spy roles but standard parts in the popular dramas of the day. She died in 1900 in Kilbourn, Wisconsin, where she had gone to address the members of a G.A.R. post.]

A Union Spy Tells
How He Operated

from *Spencer Kellogg Brown, His Life in Kansas*
and His Death as a Spy, 1842–1863,
as disclosed in his diary, 1903

[Here is a plain, straightforward account of how a Union spy went about his daily business. It is especially interesting because it was written less than a month after the author returned from his mission, so the incidents were still fresh in his mind.

Spencer Kellogg Brown was just twenty in 1862, yet he had had a taste of violence before the war began. He had been in Osawatomie, Kansas, during the summer of 1856, and as a fourteen-year-old boy had taken an active part in the bloody fighting between those who were trying to expand slavery into the new territory and those who wanted to keep it free. The young boy was not related to fierce old John Brown, but he knew him well and was an ardent Abolitionist.

At the sack of Osawatomie, Spencer Brown saw his family's home burned, while he himself was taken prisoner and was placed in the home of a pro-slavery doctor who volunteered to bring him up and try to change his attitude toward slavery. Young Brown ran away from the doctor's home and went to upstate New York to spend several years with relatives there.

Early in 1860 he returned to Kansas. At the time of the Lincoln election he was warned to leave the Territory and was bluntly told that the fact that his name was Brown was against him in Kansas. He went to St. Louis to enlist in the United States Army to fight in the early battles in Missouri. When his term expired he was given an honorable discharge.

In 1861, he enlisted in the Navy and was assigned to the Essex, a former Mississippi river snag-boat which had been converted into a primitive flat ironclad. In command of this crude vessel was William D. Porter, the older brother of Admiral David Dixon Porter. They were sons of David Porter, who had commanded the raider Essex during the War of 1812.

A fleet of hastily built or converted ironclads was being assembled on the river to assist land troops in western Kentucky in the effort to capture Confederate Fort Henry on the Tennessee River and Fort Donelson on the Cumberland River. Brown's mission to obtain military information was made in connection with this campaign and also with the great battle of Shiloh (or Pittsburgh Landing) in Tennessee on April 6–7, 1862.]

DURING the last of January (1862) . . . Columbus [Kentucky], then still held by the rebels, was the point upon which much anxiety centered from both North and South.

At the time . . . I belonged to the gun-boat Essex, Porter commander. . . . After deliberating on the matter, I spoke first to a comrade, whom I knew well, and on the evening of the 29th of January asked permission of the executive officer, Captain Riley, to have an interview with Captain Porter. . . . I volunteered my services for an exploration of the river batteries at Columbus. . . .

The time allotted for our absence was ten days. . . . The next day the tug attending upon the Essex took us up to Cairo. . . . At noon, having satisfactorily acquitted all our business, we had a good dinner of fried oysters, etc., and we spent the afternoon at billiards, getting back to the boat about dark. . . . I had taken a pair of irons [handcuffs] with me . . . to get them twisted apart, although the work was done most awkwardly.

109

In the afternoon Captain Porter had caused a small skiff that was lying near us to be . . . attached to the stern of the gunboat, with oars handy. . . . We . . . left word . . . to wake my comrade and myself at half past two.

We woke late, however, but got on an extra amount of clothing (for it was extremely cold), and, dropping into the skiff, succeeded in making good our escape—the bell noting three o'clock as we left the vessel in the distance.

After half an hour, spent with frequent interruptions of warming ourselves by some little exercise, we succeeded in getting the irons upon my wrists, soon to remove them, however, on account of the intense cold; nor were they replaced until we were within sight of Columbus.

We searched ourselves carefully for letters and papers, destroying, among others, our leave of absence and pass, only keeping one for effect. Meanwhile, we muffled the oars with handkerchiefs, which were soon rendered useless by the water freezing upon them as hard as rock. We also, at first, secreted, each, a fine saw and file, to cut steel, but afterwards threw them over as useless, and, if found, criminating.

On the passage down the cold told upon us with fearful effect, benumbing us in spite of our most severe exertions. My comrade, who had been injured in one arm, suffered very severely. A little before dawn we passed the *Grampus* (a notorious craft) at anchor in the river, unnoticed and without hailing. At last, as the dawn was beginning to make things show a little, we passed the town, and finally effected a landing on the steamer *Charm*, our repeated hails having failed to bring any answer.

Here, once fairly on board, we succeeded in raising somebody, and, telling him we were deserters from the North, got him to take us up to the floating battery. Here we reported to Captain Guthrie as deserters, got kind treatment, and I was released from my irons. But still the suspicion was very great, and Captain Guthrie refused to allow us to leave the ship (we did not ask him), while he went up to Major-General Polk, then commanding at Columbus, and consulted about us. He asked us many questions, which we answered in a way that seemed remarkably like prevarication to each other.

However, after he came back from General Polk's we were put aboard the "Floating Battery," where we spent three days of idleness and anxiety under a cheerful countenance. On the fourth of February we were sent aboard the Confederate gun-boat *General Polk*, and were immediately sent below and put under guard. The day before, Captain Guthrie said that as we wanted to join the army he would send us to Island Number Ten, to Captain Gray's company, and so we were finally on the way. The gun-boat got under way in about two hours, after which we were brought up from the hold and sent forward among the men. They were very kind, giving and offering everything but clothes, of which the deficiency was everywhere apparent. At noon they made us drink grog with them, and gave us a dinner which seemed excellent.

Meantime we walked about, improving the opportunity for seeing, among other things, the peculiar construction of the boat, her four rifled Parrott guns, mounted on a carriage and slide of Southern invention, and apparently, by a unanimous verdict of two, superior to anything we had seen in the North.

After a while we were had up to a very severe cross-examination separately; but we had previously compared notes, and came through all right. . . .

We arrived the same evening at Number Ten, but did not leave the boat. . . . The next day the gun-boat steamed down to Madrid, giving us a good opportunity to see the fort and town; but we did not try to go ashore.

We did not stop at Madrid over two hours, and on going back to Number Ten we still stayed aboard. They used every effort to induce us to ship on their gun-boat, but the excuse (if we should be taken by our boat we should certainly hang) seemed so plausible that they could not insist. After spending the second night on the gun-boat, on the sixth of February we were finally sent ashore, and hired ourselves very readily to Captain Gray, of the Engineer Corps, as men of all work. Gray immediately set us to work building a house, leaving us the first opportunity to speak in perfect security and leave when we wished. We worked hard that day with the carpenters, and the next also on the house. Afterwards we were put to work cleaning a sixty-eight-pound gun that had just been mounted, which we put in perfect order. Later, having charge of the magazine, we moved it a couple of miles on a boat, and guarded it until we were relieved by soldiers. Then we did sailors' work with needle and palm, and all sorts of job-work. . . .

I did not know how long this would last, and begged Trussel, my comrade, to return with me; but he insisted upon our staying a while longer, and we finally agreed to do so. About this time Trussel went with Captain Gray to Columbus, where Gray stayed about four days, and, getting drunk, returned without him. Trussel stayed nearly a week longer in Columbus, getting complete information in regard to fortifications, guns, and torpedoes, and finally returned with an assistant engineer, Mr. Pattison, who proved to be our future "boss." But a rumour had already begun to circulate that Columbus was to be evacuated, and he thought he saw evidence of this while there, and so refused to return North with his information. He was in much better repute with the officers than I was, and his facilities for getting information were large. He demurred to the idea of returning until the matter of evacuation was permanently settled; and he was right.

One bright day, while we were at work surveying, with Mr. Pattison, boat-load after boat-load began to come in sight, land, and encamp; while ammunition and commissary stores poured in in enormous quantities. Of course there was immense waste in both.

At this time (of the evacuation) there were only seven guns mounted at Island Number Ten. . . .

Our work now was with Pattison, surveying, sometimes on the opposite shore, sometimes on the Island, and mostly on the mainland. . . . I managed to get all the important distances by stealing a glimpse at a map. We were then waiting impatiently for Madrid to be taken, to make our escape by floating down the river to that place.

Meanwhile our course of life began to improve under Pattison, Trussell being flag-man, while I walked alongside two lusty Negroes who carried the chain, noting the distances. At first I was tempted to give them inaccurately, but upon reflection acted differently, and with success, as the ground was afterward rechained and my chaining found correct.

On the day of the capture of Madrid we were nearly eleven miles from the island, surveying at the foot of Reelfoot Lake, to see if there was any passage by which Yankee soldiers could enter. Found none, but on our return found that Madrid was evacuated and the troops at Tiptonville. . . .

On arriving at Number Ten, I found a number of gun-boats (five), transports, and a few mortar-vessels, which began to shell the place soon. I could easily have escaped that night, but Trussel not being there I dared not leave him. On Sunday he returned, but altered much, suffering fearfully with his complaint, [diarrhoea] and almost unable to move. So I did nothing else but take care of him and watch our shells as they exploded all around. I went out frequently upon the bank of the river for that purpose, and must say they were of but little account there.

During Sunday night I made every arrangement for escape and return, but was again obliged to defer the attempt, as I dared not leave my comrade, although he begged me to do so. On Monday morning, while about to prepare some tea for him, being outside the house, I was suddenly arrested by an Irish lieutenant of the

Sappers, and strictly kept from giving Trussel the least hint of what had happened, or sending for my clothes or even sending the medicine to my comrade.

Being taken before the commanding officer, General Mc____ (I forget his name), and informed upon—"This young man, General, was standing on the bank yesterday all day long, and we suspect him of being a spy, and about to give information to the enemy"—I was by him immediately put in charge of Colonel Scott, Twelfth Louisiana Volunteers, who moved soon afterwards to Tiptonville. Marching, one of the men being overloaded I helped him carry his "traps," gaining thereby much goodwill and a pair of blankets to sleep under for the rest of the time that I was under guard. At Tiptonville we camped in the mud, where I sat all day under guard upon two rails, and slept about half of the night upon four rails.

Although five miles distant the mortar-shells could be distinctly seen bursting in the air all through the day. About midnight the regiment moved, taking me with them aboard a boat that soon afterward started for Fort Pillow.

Here I stood all night under guard before the furnace door, trying to warm myself but freezing all the time. I was neglected in the morning, and did not get any breakfast until, meeting one of the officers, I gave him a good blowing up, and got him to send the Colonel (Scott) to me. I asked him if he had orders to starve me, and he, repenting, took me upstairs and gave me a good breakfast. Immediately after, feeling better, I began to use my eyes, taking a good and comprehensive view of the fort, breastworks, caliber of the guns, etc. I was taken up the hill and placed upon the side of a bank, upon which a little grass had begun to grow (March 18th), and, the sun being pleasantly warm, slept nearly all day. I got a bite of dinner from some of the men, the officers neglecting me altogether until night, when one of them gave me some supper after dark, and I went to sleep on a borrowed blanket. It commenced

raining soon, and with extreme difficulty I got the guard to take me
under the shelter of the porch of the commissary store-house near
by. Once there, I slept like a top. . . .

At Fort Pillow I remained under guard two weeks to a day,
receiving, in the main, most kind treatment, winning the confidence in my innocence of most of the officers and men, teaching the
officers sword practice and the men bayonet exercise, and playing
many a game of whist and ball. The weather was fine, and I enjoyed myself famously, without any apprehensions for the future.
Finally I induced an officer (he made me promise to join his company) to speak to General Villipique, then commanding at the
place, in my favour. He immediately sent for me, asking only a few
questions, what I was going to do, etc., and upon my statement
that I was going to Corinth to enlist, he released me, and before I
left, gave me a pass, transportation, and five days' provisions. I did
not leave for three days, during which time I assure you I saw all
there was to see about Fort Pillow.

Started for Corinth, via Memphis, landing at the latter place
next day in the morning. Got my pass visaed at the provost marshal's office, and, seeing Memphis industriously until five o'clock
P.M., started for Corinth. General Trudeau and his aide were in the
cars, and, securing a seat near them, I obtained much valuable information from their conversation. Spent the night at Grand Junction. The next day, when about to leave, found a man belonging to
the First Louisiana Cavalry Volunteers, who, much to his own satisfaction, picked me up as a recruit to his company. He was at all
the expense upon our arrival at Corinth, where I stayed that day
and night, leaving the next day for Iuka, twenty-five miles farther
on, where his regiment was expected that night. I arrived at Iuka,
and his regiment came in during the evening, upon which I domiciled myself with his company (being acceptable, as it was small),
but would not be sworn in until he gave me the bounty-money,
fifty dollars, which not being on hand, I commenced serving with-

out being sworn in at all. Managed to pass the night in a semi-freezing condition near a small fire, and in the morning sponged some breakfast off one of the messes.

The sound of the fight at Pittsburgh Landing [Shiloh] began to reach our ears early in the morning, and continued with but little interruption during the entire day. About eleven o'clock A.M. all the available men in the regiment were ordered to be reported for service, and after some trouble I managed to get my name among them, getting an old double-barrelled shotgun and ten rounds of cartridges for arms, and an ambitious but extremely emaciated horse to ride—one that was never out of perpetual jiggle. We left camp soon after for the Tennessee River, passing many pretty houses, from which came ladies of various degrees of comeliness, wearing innumerable white and bandana handkerchiefs. From Iuka the Tennessee is distant nearly eight miles, but it was over mountains for a good part of the way, and the weather was intensely warm. The sound of the battle in progress, raging with a continual roar, caused anxiety to us all; but to me of a peculiar kind. I expected every moment to be brought into a fight against my friends, and you may imagine it caused me trouble.

However, we rode quietly along on a jog-trot, sweltering in the heat of the sun and in clouds of dust, until the road came at last to run along the side of a beautiful valley, in the midst of which flowed a babbling rivulet, which we crossed repeatedly in our course onward. Few knew where they were destined, yet jokes were current, and merriment and good-humour pervaded all. When we were within about a mile of the river a halt was ordered (I wished fervently that it might be to camp), and the colonel and a detachment went forward to reconnoitre. From the result a retrograde movement was ordered, and we began to retrace our line of march, leaving pickets at favourable places, and at last, striking a crossroad, moved down the river towards the scene of action. It had got to be quite dark by this time, and the roar of the smaller cannon had ceased, but occasionally there came, wafted on the breeze, a sullen boom which I knew full well to be the guns of our boats. Still we travelled on by moonlight until hardier men than I, overcome by weariness, slept in their saddles; while I, whose every nerve seemed pounded to a jelly, and whose eyelids seemed glued fast, was only kept awake by the hope of escape.

Meanwhile, in the distance it began to storm dreadfully, and every moment the sky grew darker above us, while still we followed the downward course of the river, until at last, long after midnight, we camped in some cow-lot; when, getting a few ears of corn and a little water for my jaded but still ambitious horse, I lay down on my blanket, without any meal since morning, and fell quietly and quickly into a sound sleep. In the morning, by questioning some boys, the sons of the owner of the aforesaid cow-lot, I found that the Tennessee River was about one and a half miles distant, and I made up my mind to cross it and break for home.

So, going back to camp, I fed and watered my horse carefully, and inquiring, found that no camp guard had been posted. Leaving my coat hanging on the fence, I strolled off naturally into the brush, but, once out of sight of the camp, I quickened my step, and in about fifteen minutes made the Tennessee River.

'Twas the first time I had ever seen it, and I gazed a moment with a natural curiosity; but that did not last long; everything was now at stake, and, although in a streaming perspiration with my rapid walk, I went to the water's edge, and, tearing off my shoes, trousers, and over-shirt, plunged in. The intensity of the cold nearly took away my breath, but I soon found I could not succeed in that manner, and I returned to the shore. This time I stripped completely naked, with the exception of my cap (a "Secesh" cap, from Fort Pillow), and, after some trouble and much cold, made an island in the middle of the river. Here, after a long search, I found an old, split dug-out, which carried me, up to my hips in water, across, about a mile below. Once out, you ought to have seen me

117

travel! After about two miles I saw a man ploughing. He was terribly scared; thought I was a wild man, but managed, in a trembling voice, to give me some false information. Travelling about five miles farther, I met a man who gave me some wretched clothes and a piece of bread and bacon, the first mouthful since the breakfast of the morning before. During the walk of the next three miles, which was over a rocky road, my feet were terribly lacerated by flints, and I bled from many scratches on my legs. At last, however, I found a Union man, who put me upon his mule and took me thirteen miles farther on to Savannah, where, among Union soldiers, I was at last home. I sought General Grant's headquarters, and immediately reported myself—only to be immediately put under guard. The battle was still raging, and the result was plainly against us. Almost every house in town was filled with wounded men, while hundreds lay upon the ground, and others were arriving constantly.

I was taken, soon after, up the river to Pittsburgh Landing, and stood in the rain shivering about two hours; then, at last, was taken before General Grant.

[When Spencer Brown returned to the Essex he made the greatest mistake a spy can make—he put down in writing this account of his activities and sent it in a letter to his grandfather in Utica, New York. There is no reason to believe that anyone in his family betrayed him, but a spy who was rash enough to write and mail such a letter in wartime may also have betrayed himself to others.

Early in August, 1862, Brown again volunteered for extra-hazardous duty, this time to attack and destroy a ferryboat which was being used by the Confederates to carry supplies across the lower Mississippi to Port Hudson. With the help of a transport carrying forty men, Brown captured the ferry and sank her on August 15. This was his last military action. Apparently feeling that he was safe while the transport was close by, he went ashore in a small boat. When he landed with only four armed guards, two civilians, who represented themselves as Unionists, drew him aside to engage him in conversation. While they were talking, a band of Confederate guerrillas suddenly sprang out of hiding and captured the overconfident young leader and his men.

He was sent to Richmond, tried for espionage, and was condemned to be hanged on September 25, 1863. He was taken out of Castle Thunder at 11:00 A.M., placed in a carriage surrounded by one hundred cavalry and infantrymen. The hostile Richmond Whig tells how he met his death:

"The cavalcade reached the scene of execution about half past twelve o'clock, where, as usual, a vast crowd of people, of both sexes and all ages, was congregated. . . .

"A short but impressive prayer was offered; at the conclusion of which the condemned man, unaccompanied, mounted the scaffold. In a few moments Detective Capehart followed and commenced to adjust the rope over the neck, . . . in which he (Brown) assisted, all the while talking with the officer. Taking off his hat, to admit the noose over his head, he threw it to one side, and, falling off the scaffold, it struck a gentleman beneath, when the prisoner turned quickly, and, bowing, said, 'Excuse me, sir.' After getting the rope on his neck arranged . . . Detective Capehart commenced to pinion the arms of the condemned, to which he submitted composedly, simply remarking, 'Isn't this hard, captain?' His ankles were then tied together and his hat given to him. Capehart then shook hands and left him. A Negro came on the scaffold with a ladder and proceeded to fasten the rope to the upper beam, the prisoner meanwhile regarding him with the greatest composure. The rope being fastened, the Negro was in the act of coming down, when the prisoner looked up at the rope and remarked, 'This won't break my neck. 'Tisn't more than a foot fall. Doctor, I wish you would come up and arrange this thing. I don't want to have a

119

botched job of it.' The rope was then re-arranged to his satisfaction, and the cap placed over his head. The condemned man then bowed his head and engaged a few seconds in prayer, at the conclusion of which he raised himself, and, standing perfectly erect, pronounced in clear voice, 'All ready!' "

Elizabeth Van Lew, the pro-Union observer in Richmond who acted—or posed—as an elderly eccentric while she recorded what went on in that city, wrote that while Brown was on the way to the place of execution, followed by the crowd to see him die, he looked toward them and then asked one who accompanied him: "Did you ever pass through a tunnel under a mountain? My passage, my death is dark, but beyond all is light and bright."]

A Female Spy Changes Her Color

by S. EMMA E. EDMONDS
from *Unsexed; or the Female Soldier*, 1864

[Just as Rose Greenhow's book about her personal experiences in the war served as propaganda for the Confederate cause, so did Emma Edmond's autobiography, which was first published in 1864, aid the Union cause. The original edition was called Unsexed, or the Female Soldier, but this title was toned down in later printings to Nurse and Spy.

Emma Edmonds was a Canadian girl from the province of New Brunswick. She came to the United States in 1856 and spent some time in the Far West. When war was declared, she immediately went to Washington to volunteer her services as a field nurse. She saw the Union army get its baptism of blood at Bull Run, and when McClellan shipped his huge army down to Fortress Monroe to begin the Peninsular Campaign, Emma Edmonds went with the troops.

While both Union and Confederate soldiers dug new trenches across the old ones left from the Revolutionary battle at Yorktown, the young nurse would go out alone into the country to seek fresh food for her patients. Once she narrowly missed being killed by a revolver bullet fired at her by a Confederate woman who had lost her husband, father, and two brothers in the recent fighting.

When she returned from one of these foraging expeditions, Miss Edmonds found that a young man whom she had known in New Brunswick—and with whom she was obviously in love—had

121

been killed while riding along the picket line. She arrived in camp just in time to see the burial party march back from his newly made grave.

The experience was a great emotional shock to her. She was no longer content to be a nurse; now she wanted to strike back at the Confederates, so she volunteered to become a spy.

This is her own account of her first experience behind the Confederate lines. Her disguise, not only of sex but also of color, makes her story a remarkable one in the annals of Civil War espionage.]

THAT MORNING a detachment of the Thirty-seventh New York had been sent out as scouts, and had returned bringing in several prisoners, who stated that one of the Federal spies had been captured at Richmond and was to be executed. This information proved to be correct, and we lost a valuable soldier from the secret service of the United States. Now it was necessary for that vacancy to be supplied, and, as the Chaplain had said with reference to it, it was a situation of great danger and vast responsibility, and this was the one which Mr. B. could procure for me. . . .

My name was sent in to headquarters, and I was soon summoned to appear there myself. . . . I was questioned and cross-questioned with regard to my views of the rebellion and my motive in wishing to engage in so perilous an undertaking. My views were freely given, my object briefly stated, and I had passed trial number one.

Next I was examined with regard to my knowledge of the use of firearms, and in that department I sustained my character in a manner worthy of a veteran.

I had three days in which to prepare for my debut into rebeldom, and I commenced at once to remodel, transform, and metamorphose for the occasion. Early next morning I started for Fortress Monroe, where I procured a number of articles indispensably necessary to a complete disguise. In the first place I purchased a suit of contraband clothing, real plantation style, and then I went to a barber and had my hair sheared close to my head.

Next came the coloring process—head, face, neck, hands, and arms were colored black as any African, and then, to complete my contraband costume, I required a wig of real Negro wool. But how or where was it to be found? There was no such thing at the Fortress, and none short of Washington. Happily I found the mail-boat was about to start, and hastened on board, and finding a postmaster with whom I was acquainted, I stepped forward to speak to him, forgetting my contraband appearance, and was saluted with— "Well, Massa Cuff—what will you have?"

Said I: "Massa send me to you wid dis yere money for you to fotch him a darkie wig from Washington."

"What the _____ does he want of a darkie wig?" asked the postmaster.

"No matter, dat's my orders; guess it's for some 'noiterin' business."

"Oh, for reconnoitering you mean; all right old fellow, I will bring it, tell him."

I remained at Fortress Monroe until the postmaster returned with the article which was to complete my disguise, and then returned to camp near Yorktown.

I was ready to start on my first secret expedition toward the Confederate capital. . . . With a few hard crackers in my pocket, and my revolver loaded and capped, I started on foot, without even a blanket or anything which might create suspicion. At half-past nine o'clock I passed through the outer picket line of the Union army, at twelve o'clock I was within the rebel lines, and had not so much as been halted once by a sentinel. I had passed within less than ten rods of a rebel picket, and he had not seen me. I took this as a favorable omen, and thanked heaven for it.

As soon as I had gone a safe distance from the picket lines I lay down and rested until morning. The night was chilly and the ground cold and damp, and I passed the weary hours in fear and trembling. The first object which met my view in the morning was a party of Negroes carrying out hot coffee and provisions to the rebel pickets. This was another fortunate circumstance, for I immediately made their acquaintance, and was rewarded for my promptness by receiving a cup of coffee and a piece of corn bread, which helped very much to chase away the lingering chills of the preceding night. I remained there until the darkies returned, and then marched into Yorktown with them without eliciting the least suspicion.

The Negroes went to work immediately on the fortifications after reporting to their overseers, and I was left standing alone, not having quite made up my mind what part to act next. I was saved all further trouble in that direction, for my idleness had attracted the notice of an officer, who stepped forward and began to interrogate me after the following manner:

"Who do you belong to, and why are you not at work?"

I answered in my best Negro dialect: "I dusn't belong to nobody, Massa, I'se free and allers was; I'se gwyne to Richmond to work."

But that availed me nothing, for turning to a man who was dressed in citizen's clothes and who seemed to be in charge of the colored department, he said: "Take that black rascal and set him to work, and if he don't work well tie him up and give him twenty lashes, just to impress upon his mind that there's no free niggers here while there's a d_____d Yankee left in Virginia."

So saying he rode away, and I was conducted to a breast-work which was in course of erection, where about a hundred Negroes were at work. I was soon furnished with a pickaxe, shovel, and a monstrous wheelbarrow, and I commenced forthwith to imitate my companions in bondage. That portion of the parapet upon which I was sent to work was about eight feet high. The gravel was wheeled up in wheelbarrows on single planks, one end of which rested on the brow of the breast-work and the other on the ground. I need not say that this work was exceedingly hard for the strongest man; but few were able to take up their wheelbarrows alone, and I was often helped by some good-natured darkie when I was just on the verge of tumbling off the plank. All day long I worked in this manner, until my hands were blistered from my wrists to the finger ends.

The colored men's rations were different from those of the soldiers. They had neither meat nor coffee, while the white men had both. Whiskey was freely distributed to both black and white, but not in sufficient quantity to unfit them for duty. The soldiers seemed to be as much in earnest as the officers, and could curse the Yankees with quite as much vehemence. Notwithstanding the hardships of the day I had had my eyes and ears open, and had gained more than would counterbalance the day's work.

Night came, and I was released from toil. I was free to go where I pleased within the fortifications, and I made good use of my liberty. I made out a brief report of the mounted guns which I saw that night in my ramble round the fort, viz.: fifteen three-inch rifled cannon, eighteen four-and-half-inch rifled cannon, twenty-nine thirty-two pounders, twenty-one forty-two pounders, twenty-three eight-inch Columbiads, eleven nine-inch Dahlgrens, thirteen ten-inch Columbiads, fourteen ten-inch mortars, and seven eight-inch siege howitzers. This, together with a rough sketch of the outer works, I put under the inner sole of my contraband shoe and returned to the Negro quarters.

Finding my hands would not be in a condition to shovel much earth on the morrow, I began to look round among the Negroes to find some one who would exchange places with me whose duty was of a less arduous character. I succeeded in finding a lad of about my own size who was engaged in carrying water to the troops. He said he would take my place the next day, and he thought he could find a friend to do the same the day following, for which brotherly kindness I gave him five dollars in greenbacks; but he declared he could not take so much money. . . . So by that operation I escaped the scrutiny of the overseer, which would probably have resulted in the detection of my assumed African complexion.

The second day in the Confederate service was much pleasanter than the first. I had only to supply one brigade with water, which did not require much exertion, for the day was cool and the well was not far distant; consequently I had an opportunity of lounging a little among the soldiers, and of hearing important subjects discussed. In that way I learned the number of reinforcements which had arrived from different places, and also had the pleasure of seeing General Lee, who arrived while I was there. It was whispered among the men that he had been telegraphed to for the purpose of inspecting the Yankee fortifications, as he was the best engineer in the Confederacy, and that he had pronounced it impossible to hold Yorktown after McClellan opened his siege guns upon it. Then, too, General J. E. Johnston was hourly expected with a portion of his command. Including all, the rebels estimated their force at one hundred and fifty thousand at Yorktown and in that vicinity.

When Johnston arrived there was a council of war held, and things began to look gloomy. Then the report began to circulate that the town was to be evacuated.

Having a little spare time I visited my sable friends and carried some water for them. After taking a draught of the cool beverage, one young darkie looked up at me in a puzzled sort of manner, and turning round to one of his companions, said: "Jim, I'll be darned if that feller ain't turnin' white; if he ain't I'm no nigger." I felt greatly alarmed at the remark, but said, very carelessly, "Well, gem'in I'se allers 'spected to come white some time; my mudder's a white woman." This had the desired effect, for they all laughed at my simplicity, and made no further remarks. . . .

A FEMALE SPY CHANGES HER COLOR

As soon as I could conveniently get out of sight I took a look at my complexion by means of a small pocket looking-glass which I carried for that very purpose—and sure enough, as the Negro had said, I was really turning white. I was only a dark mulatto color now, whereas two days previous I was as black as Cloe. However, I had a small vial of nitrate of silver in weak solution, which I applied to prevent the remaining color from coming off.

Upon returning to my post with a fresh supply of water, I saw a group of soldiers gathered around some individual who was haranguing them in real Southern style. I went up quietly, put down my cans of water, and of course had to fill the men's canteens, which required considerable time, especially as I was not in any particular hurry just then. I thought the voice sounded familiar, and upon taking a sly look at the speaker I recognized him at once as a peddler who used to come to the Federal camp regularly once every week with newspapers and stationery, and especially at headquarters. He would hang round there, under some pretext or other, for half a day at a time.

There he was, giving the rebels a full description of our camp and forces, and also brought out a map of the entire works of McClellan's position. He wound up his discourse by saying: "They lost a splendid officer through my means since I have been gone this time. It was a pity though to kill such a man if he was a d___d Yankee." Then he went on to tell how he had been at headquarters, and heard "Lieutenant V." say that he was going to visit the picket line at such a time, and he had hastened away and informed the rebel sharpshooters that one of the headquarter officers would be there at a certain time, and if they would charge on that portion of the line they might capture him and obtain some valuable information. Instead of this, however, they watched for his approach and shot him as soon as he made his appearance.

I thanked God for that information. I would willingly have wrought with those Negroes on that parapet for two months, and

127

have worn the skin off my hands half a dozen times, to have gained that single item. He was a fated man from that moment; his life was not worth three cents in Confederate scrip. But fortunately he did not know the feelings that agitated the heart of that little black urchin who sat there so quietly filling those canteens, and it was well that he did not.

On the evening of the third day from the time I entered the camp of the enemy I was sent, in company with the colored men, to carry supper to the outer picket posts on the right wing. This was just what I wished for, and had been making preparations during the day, in view of the possibility of such an event, providing, among other things, a canteen full of whiskey. Some of the men on picket duty were black and some were white. I had a great partiality for those of my own color, so calling out several darkies I spread before them some corn cake, and gave them a little whiskey for dessert. While we were thus engaged the Yankee Minie balls were whistling round our heads, for the picket lines of the contending parties were not half a mile distant from each other. The rebel pickets do not remain together in groups of three or four as our men do, but are strung along, one in each place, from three to four rods apart. I proposed to remain a while with the pickets, and the darkies returned to camp without me.

Not long after night an officer came riding along the lines, and seeing me he inquired what I was doing there. One of the darkies replied that I had helped to carry out their supper, and was waiting until the Yankees stopped firing before I started to go back. Turning to me he said, "You come along with me." I did as I was ordered, and he turned and went back the same way he came until we had gone about fifty rods, then halting in front of a petty officer he said, "Put this fellow on the post where that man was shot until I return." I was conducted a few rods farther, and then a rifle was put into my hands, which I was told to use freely in case I should see anything or anybody approaching from the enemy.

Then followed the flattering remark, after taking me by the coat-collar and giving me a pretty hard shake, "Now, you black rascal, if you sleep on your post I'll shoot you like a dog."

"Oh no, Massa, I'se too feerd to sleep," was my only reply.

The night was very dark, and it was beginning to rain. I was all alone now, but how long before the officer might return with some one to fill my place I did not know, and I thought the best thing I could do was to make good use of the present moment. After ascertaining as well as possible the position of the picket on each side of me, each of whom I found to be enjoying the shelter of the nearest tree, I deliberately and noiselessly stepped into the darkness, and was soon gliding swiftly through the forest toward the "land of the free," with my splendid rifle grasped tightly lest I should lose the prize. I did not dare to approach very near the Federal lines, for I was in more danger of being shot by them than by the enemy; so I spent the remainder of the night within hailing distance of our lines, and with the first dawn of morning I hoisted the well-known signal and was welcomed once more to a sight of the dear old stars and stripes. . . .

I made out my report immediately and carried it to General McClellan's headquarters, together with my trophy. . . . I saw General G. B., but he did not recognize me, and ordered me to go and tell A. to appear before him in an hour from that time. I returned again to my tent, chalked my face, and dressed in the same style as on examination day, went at the hour appointed, and received the hearty congratulations of the General. The rifle was sent to Washington, and is now in the capitol as a memento of the war.

Carrying a Memorized Cipher Message Through the Lines

by ADAM R. JOHNSON
from *The Partisan Rangers:*
Memoirs of General Adam R. Johnson, 1904

[In the early part of the nineteenth century the United States spawned brave fighting men as readily as Elizabethan England bred poets and playwrights and Renaissance Florence fostered great artists. Here we first meet two of Morgan's men whose bold activities for the Confederacy were to run through the dark pattern of underground warfare for the next three years.

Adam Rankin Johnson was just twenty-eight years old in 1862. Eight years before, the Kentucky-born boy had gone to Texas to spend five years surveying the western part of that frontier state. While working on the Overland Mail Route he fought off Indians and earned the title of "the Young Colonel."

He returned to Kentucky and married a sixteen-year-old girl in January, 1861. His parents and his two brothers were pro-Union in divided Kentucky, and his brothers fought in the Federal Army. Adam Johnson entered his family's home town (Henderson), which was then occupied by Union troops. He went to the local Army post, where he was known to be a Confederate. He asked to see his brothers, and was granted permission to spend some time with them. Everyone was very friendly, he said.

He had already volunteered to serve as a scout for the Confederate cavalry raider, Nathan Bedford Forrest, who had risen from private to the grade of lieutenant colonel. Johnson served with Robert Martin, Forrest's chief scout and one of the most daring men in an outfit noted for its daredevils.

Just before Union gunboats and land troops compelled Fort Donelson to surrender on February 16, Forrest led all his mounted men out of the doomed fort and got away to Nashville.

Forrest then sent Johnson and Martin on a long journey to Texas to carry secret dispatches to Governor Lubbock. During their travels they heard that the battle of Shiloh had been fought, and they were on their way to New Orleans when that city surrendered. They returned to Corinth, Mississippi, to meet Forrest. On May 10, 1862, they were sent for by their fellow Kentuckian, General John C. Breckinridge, who, of course, outranked Forrest, and so could ask for their services.

Most Civil War cipher messages were transmitted in writing. To be able to commit long series of meaningless and apparently unassociated numbers to memory is truly remarkable.]

WHEN we reached General Breckinridge's headquarters he . . . began questioning us as to our . . . experience as scouts and spies. He next informed us that he had need of two trusty, efficient men in our line to do special duty—two Kentuckians, and he believed that we were just the men he wanted, if reports he had heard of us were true. "In the meanwhile," he said, "you can go and enroll in my body-guard, where you can draw rations for yourselves and horses. . . ."

That evening the general called me alone to his room and asked me if I had a brother Ben. (Yes, I had a brother Ben.)

"He was one of the best friends I ever had and possessed one of the most remarkable memories I ever knew; if you are as much like him in that respect as you are in face, I think you will suit me exactly," Breckinridge replied as he earnestly scanned my face.

131

Evidently satisfied with his rigid examination he continued: "I have some dispatches in cipher which I wish to send to two different men. They are too important to trust upon paper and risk capture. The first one reads thus: 'Number 7 to 11; number 21 back to 11 except 13; the second like this: 'From 21 to 77 except 33, 41 and 56. Also figure 3 to 177 except 140, 50 and 60.' Now repeat these to me if you can," he finished, shooting a half-smiling incredulous glance at me. The incredulous smile broke into one of astonishment as I repeated both dispatches word for word. "The time has not yet come for you to go on this mission, and any change in these figures would be fatal, so I wish you to repeat them to me until I am perfectly sure you have them thoroughly planted in your memory," the general said, much pleased at finding one to carry information for him and to do scouting in the enemy's lines. Every day I went to the commander's headquarters to repeat my lesson to him while Martin was sent through the lines on various missions. . . .

Taking me aside, he asked me to repeat the cipher message, and on its being done correctly, said: "I shall now tell you the name of the man to whom this is to be delivered. It is our mutual friend David R. Burbank, of Henderson, Kentucky. The lives of many men depend upon your careful management of this affair and it will bring either good or evil to the Southern Confederacy." Calling Martin up, he said: "Now boys, I want you to flank this Federal army and bring out all the Kentuckians you can to serve as Southern soldiers. I wish you both to remember that you are commissioned officers on my staff, and if you bring out enough men you shall have the command of them. We are now the rear guard of the Confederate army, and I believe if there are any two men living that can and will carry out my orders you are the two."

This encouraging talk from our leader gave us a new inspiration, and we resolved to deserve all the trust he had placed in us. The personal influence of General Breckinridge was wonderful. In fact, he possessed more magnetism than any one I ever knew. . . . Shaking hands with this splendid commander, so eminent both as statesman and soldier, his two new aids turned their faces toward Henderson. . . .

Just before dark we came upon a farm house, and ascertaining that feed would be furnished for our animals and supper for ourselves, we took the corn and led our horses into a field. Leaving Martin in charge, I went back for his supper. The master of the house had just returned from the hospital, where he had been nursed on account of the loss of an arm in the battle of Shiloh. He was suffering greatly from poison-oak on his face, and as I entered his wife was applying a poultice. I was helping in this soothing ministration when I was startled by hearing the tramp of horses' feet as the house was surrounded by Federals. I was much alarmed at being caught there in a trap, but a happy thought struck me, and I ran at once to the door and asked one of the soldiers where the commander was. The aid was already giving orders in the kitchen for the cooking of all the provisions there. As soon as I could find the major in command I asked in an alarmed voice if they had a surgeon.

"What in the world do you want with a surgeon?"

"Why, we have a sick Confederate soldier in the house and we are afraid that he has smallpox," I answered glibly.

"The thunder you say!" exclaimed the Yankee officer in a surprised tone. "Here, Doctor, you had better go in and look at the man," he said, turning to a middle-aged man near him. Calling the captain, he gave orders to have the place well guarded and see that not one of the men was allowed to enter the house. As the captain started to obey the orders of his commander, I ran back to the invalid and tearing the poultice from his face, told him to let it remain exposed to the medical man's examination and to stick his wounded arm out and moan and groan and say that his bones were breaking with fever.

133

The Confederate soldier played this role to perfection, and when the doctor came in I held the candle to let him see what a terrible face he had. The poor fellow's face was swollen so that his eyes were entirely closed, his lips twice their ordinary size, while small portions of the poultice were smeared all over his distorted visage. No worse-looking countenance with confluent smallpox was ever presented to a visiting physician than the one now disclosed to the wondering eyes of this learned son of Esculapius, who solemnly pronounced it an undoubted case of smallpox in its worst form.

I followed the doctor out of the room and into the presence of the major, who was ordering all of his men to mount, and now asked . . . where he could get drinking-water. He was told that he could find it either up or down the creek, as there were farm houses all along the way. Commanding one of his staff to go back and inform those that were following, and ordering a yellow flag placed upon the gate, this Federal officer rode off ignorant of the ruse that had been played upon him and his duped command. As he rode off I heard him say: "I would take that fellow along to show us the way if he had not been so exposed to that case of smallpox."

To reassure Martin, I ran to the back door and threw it open, standing in the light so that my comrade could see that I was still there and not in the custody of the Yankees, whom he had of course heard surrounding the house. It was well that I gave this signal to my friend, for as the last tramping of the enemy's horses was heard, Martin stepped out from behind a tree, a revolver grasped in each hand. He had intended, in his bold, impetuous way, to attack the whole force if he found that I was a captive, trusting to the friendly dark and the confusion of the melee to give him an opportunity to escape. As Martin came up he asked, wonderingly: "Ad, what kind of a trick did you play on those foxy Yankees?" I told him what I had done, then took him in the room and showed him the terrifying face of our brother-in-arms. Martin broke into his usual great laugh when he was told of this effective hoax, and the others joined in the merriment.

Getting our cooked provisions and a new supply of forage for our horses, we again took a by-road and pushed on toward the Tennessee River. Nothing of consequence occurred upon our way and we crossed over and put at the ferry-house for the night. The host informed us that there was a Federal picket at the cross-roads about a mile distant. We secured a buggy and placing our saddles under the seat, covering our guns with a shawl and using a blanket for a lap robe, we fancied we resembled peaceable citizens rather than soldiers. Learning from a girl that the picket was in the habit of stopping every man to examine him, and that there were several Federals at the picket house, a little log cabin at the crossroads, we decided to pass them as early as possible in the morning. We placed our arms so that we could handle them readily and went forward. If only two of the men came to examine us I was to hand the one next to me a paper and shoot him as he took it, while, simultaneously, Martin was to shoot the other, then whip the horses into a run.

We reached the pickets just as the Federals were sitting down to breakfast, and one of them rose from the table and came to the door and scanned us closely for a moment, but as we were driving with apparent carelessness, slowly along, he seemed to think that we were two innocent country lads and did not halt us. I confess that I felt much relieved at their negligence, but Bob seemed actually sorry that we did not have a scrap with those Yankees. . . .

Upon reaching the farm of Mr. Charles Taylor near Highland creek, I met the very man to whom I was to deliver the ciphers, Mr. David R. Burbank, who was there on a visit to his father-in-law. Burbank was very glad to see me, and was carried away with excitement when the dispatches were repeated to him. . . .

135

By daylight the next morning I was out of doors, breathing in with delight the fresh morning air of old Kentucky. I was soon joined in my early walk by my old friend, Mr. Burbank, who took me to a quiet spot, and pulling out of his pocket a small memorandum book, handed it to me, saying: "Look at these figures, my boy, and see if they are correct." Examining them, I read these figures and words, as cabalistic as those I had verbally delivered to Mr. Burbank, viz: "7 to 11—Fine leaf," etc. They were written in his tobacco book . . . and each number was followed by a description of some kind of tobacco. The exceptions were all marked, "trash," a term used by tobacconists to signify a very inferior quality.

"If the Federals get hold of this they'll never get anything out of it," remarked Mr. Burbank with a very confident smile. "Now, Johnson, if you need any money you can get it," he said as he took a roll of bills out of his pocket, amounting to several hundred dollars. "Take this, and if you get a chance send it South to our old general, and if not, use it yourself, and when you want more let me know and you shall have it;" he smiled kindly into my face and gave me a friendly pat upon the shoulder. . . .

"Old Kentucky must go to the Confederacy. If they will only give us a half chance we'll put fifty thousand good soldiers in the field." The good man's face was alight with earnest feeling as he made this announcement, and after a few minutes he said, as he gave me a benign look: "I'll see that the messages you brought go straight. General Breckinridge will soon know that you've accomplished that part of your mission."

A Confederate Cruiser
Runs the Gantlet

by JOHN NEWLAND MAFFITT

from *Life and Services of John Newland Maffitt*, 1906
compiled by Emma Martin Maffit

[When James D. Bulloch returned to England in March, 1862, after having taken the Fingal to Savannah, work was far advanced on the two Confederate cruisers that were being built in British shipyards. But the United States State Department was well aware of what was going on, for Charles Francis Adams, American minister to the Court of St. James's, had notified Washington and alerted American consuls in all the chief blockading, stop-over ports such as Bermuda, Nassau, and Havana, to be on the watch for such vessels.

Bulloch wrote to Mallory, Secretary of the Confederate Navy, that Ship Number One, at first referred to as the Manassas (although she was built under the name Oreto, and was officially named the Florida when she went into service) was ready to put to sea late in March. She was planned to be a warship, but because of the neutrality laws, she had to sail without arms and under British registry. Her guns, gun carriages, gunnery equipment, and ammunition were sent out on another ship, the Bahama. The Oreto arrived in Nassau on April 28 where she was to be taken in command by Lieutenant John Newland Maffitt, one of the ablest officers in the Confederate Navy. But the moment the Bahama put into port, the British authorities prodded by the

137

American consul, seized the Oreto and held her until August 2, when the local court set her free. She was then given papers to clear for any Confederate port.

Maffitt evaded the Federal gunboats in the harbor and took his ship to Green Cay, nearly a hundred miles south of New Providence. With her went the Prince Albert, a small schooner carrying the arms brought across the ocean by the Bahama. Maffit's journal tells what happened during the next few days:

"Now commenced one of the most physically exhausting jobs ever undertaken by naval officers. All hands undressed to the buff, and with the few men we had commenced taking in . . . guns, powder, circles, shell and shot, etc. An August sun in the tropics is no small matter to work in. On the 15th C. Worrell, wardroom steward, died and we buried him on Green Cay. Several cases of fever appeared among the crew. At first I thought it but ordinary cases, originating from hard work and exposure to the sun, but in twenty hours the unpalatable fact was impressed upon me that yellow fever was added to our annoyances. Having no physician on board, that duty devolved upon me, and nearly my whole time, day and night, was devoted to the sick. . . . On the morning of the 17th got underway, hoisted and cheered the Confederate flag, and christened the Oreto by her new official cognomen of Florida, parted with the Prince Albert, and stood to the southward and westward. The yellow fever by this time had gained complete ascendency and in our absolute helpless condition were forced to enter a Cuban port. Moreover, we found that neither beds, quoins, sights or rammers, and sponges (for the guns) had been sent to us."

On August 19, they entered the port of Cardenas, Cuba. There Maffitt himself came down with yellow fever. For a week he was delirious and out of his mind; he recovered to find that his stepson was dying of the disease. Four other men also died that same day. The dead were buried on land, then they put in briefly at Havana, where they found it impossible to recruit a crew. Maffitt decided to head for Mobile, where only one blockading vessel was supposed to be guarding the port. He was still so weak that he had to be carried up on deck.]

It had become evident that the *Florida* would have to enter a Confederate port to be officered and properly equipped. This conviction determined me to sail for Mobile. . . .

On the 1st of September, 1862, we steamed out of Havana and made a direct course for Mobile Bay, avoiding the enemy's fleet gathered off the Moro, by running some distance close in shore. The voyage proved propitious, and at 3 P.M. on the 4th we sighted Fort Morgan, and two steamers, evidently blockaders, hastening to contest our entrance. Though still quite feeble, with assistance I was enabled to repair on deck and reconnoiter the situation. There was not a cloud in the sky, or a zephyr breath on the sea. . . . Lieutenant Stribling suggested that under the circumstances of our crippled condition, and inability to offer resistance, it would be advisable to stand off again and defer the attempt to enter the harbor until darkness should mantle our movements. This proposition I rejected, as the draught of the *Florida* did not permit of dalliance with the shoals, nor was there any surety of finding the channel without the aid of the lighthouse, which had been dismantled.

"But, sir," said Lieutenant Stribling, "in this attempt we cannot avoid passing close to the blockade-squadron, the result of which will be our certain destruction."

"The hazard is certainly very great, but it cannot be avoided. We will hoist the English colors as a 'ruse de guerre,' and boldly stand for the commanding officer's ship; the remembrance of the delicate *Trent* affair may perhaps cause some deliberation and care before the batteries are let loose upon us; four minutes of hesitation on their part may save us."

Moreover, having decided regardless of hazards to run the blockade, there was no time for hesitation, but dash ahead, trusting to fortune and a clean pair of heels. The English colors were set, and under a full head of steam we boldly stood for the flag-ship.

The *Oneida*, Captain Preble, of ten guns, made an effort to cut us off, but I sheered toward him, and feeling that he would be run down he backed—giving me a momentary advantage. When about some eighty yards distant from her she fired a warning gun, and ordered us to heave to, evidently deceived by our general appearance and bold approach into the belief that we were English. We paid no attention to the signal or command, but continued to press vigorously on. A second shot passed over our bow, when immediately their whole broadside was poured into us, the effect of which was to carry away some of our hammock nettings and much of our standing and running rigging. Had their guns been depressed, the career of the *Florida* would have ended then and there. The example of the flag-ship, the *Oneida*, was instantly followed by the other two ships of the squadron, and their fierce fusillade was hurled with the resolute determination of destroying the Confederate. In truth, so terrible became the bombardment, every hope of escape fled from my mind. One gunboat opened on my port bow, the other on our port quarter, and the cannonading became rapid and precise. Having passed the *Oneida* I gave a starboard helm to bring the gunboats in line and escape by this range the fire of one of them, for this grouping around me bid fair to send the little *Florida* to the bottom. One 11-inch shell from the *Oneida* passed through the coal-bunkers on the port side, struck the port forward boiler, and entering among the men on the berth deck wounded nine men and took off the head of James Duncan. Duncan was captain of the main top and one of our best men. If it had exploded, which it failed to do, I no doubt would have lost every man on the vessel except the two men at the helm, as I had ordered all the crew below, they being exposed to no purpose on deck. The officers of course remained at their stations, and though subjected to constant storms of destructive missiles, they miraculously escaped. Immediately after this a shot from the *Winona* entered the cabin and passed through the pantry, and an 11-inch shell from the *Oneida* exploded close to the port gangway and seriously injured the vessel. The fire from this vessel increased in warmth and destruction.

Finding that we did not distance the Federals, rapidly I sent the men aloft to loosen topsails and topgallantsails, and our sailors responded to the order with alacrity. As soon as they were seen on the yards all the gunboats commenced firing twenty-four pound shrapnel; the standing rigging was shot away, and we only succeeded so far as letting fall the topsails. Several men were wounded in the rigging; and one had the whole bottom of his foot taken off by a shrapnel shot, and afterward died from tetanus. The sheets and ties were shot away, so that I was not able to set the sails properly.

At this moment I hauled down the English flag under which we were sailing, and gave the order to one of the helmsmen to hoist the Confederate flag. At the time he was endeavoring to haul up the foot brail of the spanker, and lost his forefinger with a shrapnel shot, so that my order in regard to the flag could not then be complied with. The halyards were shot away, but soon re-rove and the Dixie flag floated in their faces. During all this time shell and shrapnel were bursting over and around us, the shrapnel striking the hull and the spars at almost every discharge.

We made no effort at resistance, for though armed we were not at all equipped, having neither rammers, sponges, sights, quoins, nor elevating screws. Properly manned and equipped, the excitement of battle would have relieved the terrible strain upon our fortitude, which nevertheless sustained us through the withering assaults of a foe who were determined upon capture or destruction.

141

The loud explosions, roar of shot and shell, crashing spars and rigging, mingled with the moans of our sick and wounded, instead of intimidating, only increased our determination to enter the destined harbor. Simultaneously two heavy shells entered our hull with a thud that caused a vibration from stem to stern. The 11-inch shell from the *Oneida* which came in and passed along the berth deck entered three inches above the waterline, and if there had been any sea on, our bilge-pumps could not have saved the vessel from sinking. Everything depended upon our engineers, and in that department the duty was performed with efficiency and zeal. . . .

Thus far we had borne the fierce assaults with the calmness that oft befriends the victims of desperation, and as nothing vital had been injured our gradual withdrawal from the close proximity of the guns of the enemy excited pleasurable hope. Finally we cleared the grouping circle and the prospects of escape began to brighten. This the enemy observed, as more fiercely their efforts increased, more furiously roared their artillery, and denser became the black clouds from their smokestacks, as they fed their fires with rosin and other combustible material to increase their head of steam.

Vain were these excessive exertions; fate had carved out for the *Florida* a more extended career, and this baptism of fire christened the gallant craft as a Confederate torch-bearer on the ocean of public events. The shot and shell gradually fall short, and a gentle northeast wind lifts the cloudy curtain and exhibits the indignant Federals hauling off from the bar, while in the channel-way, battered and torn, war-worn and weary, with her own banner floating in the breeze, the *Florida* . . . is welcomed to her anchorage by hearty cheers from the defenders of Fort Morgan.

We were soon visited by the officers of the fort. Colonel Powell says the scene was brilliant, and he considers it one of the most dashing feats of the war.

[For permitting the Florida to run past the Federal blockading fleet and enter Mobile Bay, Captain Preble was dismissed from the Union Navy on September 20. Maffitt's battle-damaged cruiser remained in port until January, 1863, by which time she had been repaired, painted a dull lead color, and was in fighting condition even though she still lacked a full crew. The unfortunate Preble was lucky that he was no longer in command of the blockading fleet on January 16, when the ever-daring Maffitt made a run for it to get out of Mobile Bay. Maffitt describes his escape in his Journal:

"January 16 (1863)—Blowing with avidity from the westward; rain at night; had up steam, but the pilot said it was too dark to see Lighthouse Island; in fact, nothing could be distinguished 20 yards. At 2 [A.M.] I was called; the stars were out, but a light mist covered the surface of the water. Got underway; the wind puffy from the W.N.W. At 2:40 passed a gunboat anchored just inside the bar, then a second one, but when abreast of the third a flame from the coal dust caused our discovery, and the ocean was lit up by the lights from the nine blockading vessels. Made sail and put on steam, and then commenced a most animated chase.

"Our passing unseen by the first Federal gunboats is hard to account for. My idea is that during the severity of the storm, then expecting us, a very anxious lookout had been kept, and that when the weather moderated all were exhausted and at the same time, from the clearness of the stars, concluded that if we had not already escaped no attempt would be made that morning. Moreover, the N.W. wind was very chilly, and the lookouts, no doubt, in a feeling of security, were comfortable under the lee of the bulwarks. I believe that had it not been for our soft coal we would have passed clear without any knowledge on the part of the enemy."

On his birthday that year, President Lincoln, perhaps taking the ineffectiveness of the entire Federal blockading fleet during

Maffitt's dash out of Mobile Bay into account, renominated Preble as a commander. On May 6, 1863, Lieutenant Maffitt was promoted to the rank of commander.

During that spring and summer the Florida captured and burned several million dollars worth of Yankee shipping. In August the hard-driven vessel had to put into Brest, France, for repairs. A few weeks later, her forty-four-year-old commander suffered from what seems to have been a heart attack and had to apply for sick leave. The Florida left France in February, 1864, under a new commander. She roamed the Atlantic raiding Yankee commerce until October 5, when she entered the Brazilian port of Bahia.

There the U.S.S. Wachusett was waiting for her. Neutrality laws compelled the two belligerent vessels to remain at peace while in the harbor. The Florida obtained permission to stay in port for forty-eight hours, and the technicality of the law required the Wachusett to remain for twenty-four hours after she left.

But Commander Collins of the Wachusett (who apparently was determined to live up to his given name, Napoleon) had no intention of abiding by the rules. At three o'clock in the morning of October 7, the Wachusett got under way and tried to ram the Florida. But she missed and scraped along the starboard side, smashing bulwarks and tearing down masts and rigging. There was small-arm shooting from both ships; then the Wachusett fired two of her broadside guns. The Florida, temporarily under command of a junior officer, surrendered. Her crew was taken on board the Wachusett which then proceeded to tow her prize out to sea while a small Brazilian gunboat sent several token shots after the invader in protest.

Collins took the Florida from Bahia to Hampton Roads, Virginia, where he sent some of her British guns to the Washington Navy Yard. While at Hampton Roads, the prize of war which had been taken under circumstances which threatened to embarrass the United States Government, was hit by an army transport by "an unforseen accident" and conveniently went to the bottom.

J. R. Soley called the capture of the Florida in a neutral port "as gross and deliberate a violation of the rights of neutrals as was ever committed in any age or country."]

1863

U<small>NTIL</small> <small>THE</small> <small>MIDDLE</small> <small>OF</small> 1863 <small>THE</small> C<small>ONFEDERATES</small> <small>HAD</small> <small>MORE</small> <small>THAN</small> *held their own. In the East, a succession of incompetent, over-cautious, or blundering Union generals had paralyzed the North. In the West, Grant and Sherman were rising to prominence but had not yet gained control of the essential Mississippi River. The Federal blockade, however, was steadily strengthening its hold on the Southern seacoast, making it more and more difficult for the Confederacy to get supplies from abroad.*

On January 25, General Joseph Hooker superseded the luck-less Burnside as commander of the Army of the Potomac. Desertions had been numerous, for men and officers were under-standably discouraged by continual defeat. Hooker did his best to reorganize the demoralized forces, and late in April began moving against Lee. At Chancellorsville, just west of Fredericksburg, in an area which was to be heavily fought over again during the next year, the two armies met on May 2. Although Lee lost his

146

top commander when "Stonewall" Jackson died of wounds accidently inflicted by his own men, Hooker lost the battle and soon afterwards lost his command.

The victorious Confederates then planned to invade the North again and started moving up the Shenandoah Valley early in June, heading toward Maryland and Pennsylvania.

In the West, the siege against the seemingly impregnable heights on which the Mississippi River port of Vicksburg was located had been dragging on all spring. Many moves on land and water had been made by the Union attackers, but the city, although desperately short of food and supplies, still stood firm. Farther down the river, Port Hudson was also holding out.

On June 28 Hooker was replaced by General George Gordon Meade. The new commander had to find Lee's widely scattered army in order to try to head it off. On July 1, almost by accident, the advance patrols of both armies met in the little Pennsylvania town of Gettysburg. For the next three days, as more and more troops kept moving into the area, the most truly decisive battle of the Civil War was fought. When Lee retreated into Virginia, and when Vicksburg surrendered on July 4, to be followed by Port Hudson four days later, the fate of the Confederacy had already been determined.

Meade, like McClellan at Antietam less than a year before, did not follow up his victory hard enough and so let Lee get away again. The war that conceivably could have been ended that month was to continue for nearly two more years, during which the Confederacy fought on stubbornly against odds which became increasingly hopeless.

The nature of the conflict changed after that first fatal week in July. Until then the Confederacy had counted on winning her independence on the battlefield. Now her leaders, sensing, although not openly admitting, that the much greater might of the North must eventually prevail, began to revise their thinking and their methods of fighting. Secret missions, which previously had played a relatively small part in the Confederacy's war efforts, were now given high priority. The transition, however, was not sudden; such a shift always takes time. Nor did the Confederates ever cease relying on strength of arms.

Confederate cavalry had thus far been superior to the best mounted forces the Union had been able to put into the field. Southern cavalry raiders like Mosby, Forrest, and John Hunt Morgan now increased their attacks. They struck swiftly and got away fast, sometimes disbanding temporarily to blend into the civilian population until called upon to go into action again.

Morgan's great cavalry raid into Indiana and Kentucky in 1863 was co-ordinated with Lee's invasion of the North. Morgan planned to join forces with Lee in Pennsylvania if the invading army got a firm foothold there, and he was heading in that direction when Lee's repulse at Gettysburg left Morgan's raiding party stranded in eastern Ohio near the Pennsylvania border. He and hundreds of his men were captured and sent to prison.

The Confederates' failure to win the decisive battle of Gettysburg had other repercussions that reached as far north as New York, some of the upstate New York cities, and New England. It cannot be proved that the Confederates incited the bloody draft riots which broke out in those places a few days after Gettysburg, but their secret agents did all they could to keep such disorders stirred up.

The year 1863 was noted not only for its important military actions but also for its extraordinary political developments—particularly in the Middle West. After his disastrous failure at Fredericksburg in December, 1862, Burnside was given command of the Department of the Ohio. This appointment turned out to be an unfortunate one, for the general with the sideburns was an overzealous but tactless administrator. And the area placed under his jurisdiction was an especially difficult one because it comprised the states of Ohio, Indiana, Illinois, and Kentucky, where many of the people were of Southern origin and still had close ties to the South. It was here that Copperheadism was at its strongest.

The word "Copperhead" during the Civil War was applied to citizens of Northern states who were pro-Confederate in their sympathies. Most of them were so-called "Peace" Democrats who sought peace at any price and were bitterly opposed to the administration's war efforts. The term was derived from badges or pins worn openly by members of various secret societies; these marks of identification were made by cutting out the Liberty head from one of the big copper pennies last issued in 1857 and making it into a lapel ornament. The word also had connotations of hidden menace such as that threatened by the copperhead snake which lies quietly and waits to strike.

During the spring of 1863 this peace-at-any-price movement found a leader in Clement L. Vallandigham, an Ohio-born Congressman who wanted to organize the various kinds of Peace Democrats for his own benefit. At a public meeting early in May, he denounced an order issued by Burnside which declared anti-war speeches treasonable. As a result, Vallandigham was arrested, tried, and sentenced to be confined in prison. Since Burnside's ill-considered order and the trial of a civilian by military court were both of doubtful constitutionality, President Lincoln—after some hesitation—very sensibly intervened. Before Vallandigham could be shipped off to Fort Warren in Boston Harbor, Lincoln ordered him banished to the Confederacy. This fanatic Northerner was received in the South with mixed feelings. In less than a month he was on a ship bound for Bermuda; from there he went to Halifax and Quebec. He spent most of the summer on the Canadian side of Niagara Falls holding court and issuing statements. The Peace Democrats in Ohio nominated him for governor, but he was badly defeated in the November election—especially when the soldier vote was counted. Vallandigham has become an obscure and rather ridiculous figure, but in his day he stirred up a great deal of trouble for the Lincoln administration.

During the autumn of 1863 the western theater of war became much more important than the eastern, where there was relatively little activity until the next spring. On the sea, however, the Union Navy was more active than ever. It made several attempts to reduce Fort Sumter and capture Charleston. These attempts, some of which were combined land and sea operations, were all unsuccessful, and the flag of rebellion still flew over the city where secession had begun.

In the West, the area around Chattanooga, Tennessee, became the center of action on September 19–20 when the Confederates won the battle of Chickamauga in northern Georgia and then moved on to attack Lookout Mountain and Missionary Ridge near Chattanooga on November 23–25. In this effort, however, they were defeated.

By the end of 1863, the Confederate cause was worse off than its leaders would admit. The war in the West was lost; there was to be no major fighting in that area again. Meanwhile, the stalemate in the East continued.

A Dummy Ironclad
Goes on a Secret Mission
with No One on Board

by DAVID DIXON PORTER
from *Incidents and Anecdotes of the Civil War*, 1885

[The war on the Mississippi went grimly on, but one Union officer
was making the best of a bad situation. This was Admiral Porter,
who lived well on his flagship and served elaborate breakfasts each
morning for the captains in his fleet so he could give them the
orders for the day. On February 17, 1863, a Federal gunboat, the
Queen of the West, was captured by the Confederates after having
been run aground—on purpose, it was said—by a local pilot. A
week later the newest Union ironclad on the river, the Indianola,
was sunk in shallow water by enemy action. This ship, a floating
fortress 170 feet long and 60 feet wide, had two enormous 11-inch
Dahlgren rifled cannon and battery of 24-pounders. She was cum-
bersome, awkward, and ugly, and at the moment was resting on
the bottom with her decks awash in a part of the river held by the
Confederates. Her enormously valuable guns were anybody's for
the taking—and both sides wanted them badly.

Porter made a rough drawing of an "ironclad" which was to
be built without iron. Within twelve hours the mock vessel was
completed and was sent down the river on February 27 to frighten
away the Confederates who were trying to salvage the Indianola's
guns.]

151

It WAS NECESSARY to try and prevent the rebels from raising the *Indianola*, and, as I was not ready to go down the river myself, as it would interfere with an important military movement, I hit upon a cheap expedient, which worked very well.

I set the whole squadron at work and made a raft of logs, three hundred feet long, with sides to it, two huge wheel-houses and a formidable log casemate, from the port-holes of which appeared sundry wooden guns. Two old boats hung from davits fitted to the "ironclad," and two smokestacks made of hogsheads completed the illusion; and on her wheel-houses was painted the following: "Deluded Rebels, Cave In!" An American flag was hoisted aft, and a banner emblazoned with skull and crossbones ornamented the bow.

When this craft was completed, she resembled at a little distance the ram *Lafayette*, which had just arrived from St. Louis.

The mock ram was furnished with a big iron pot inside each smokestack, in which was [sic] tar and oakum to raise a black smoke, and at midnight she was towed down close to the water-batteries of Vicksburg and sent adrift.

It did not take the Vicksburg sentinels long to discover the formidable monster that was making its way down the river. The batteries opened on her with vigor, and continued the fire until she had passed beyond the range of their guns.

The Vicksburgers had greatly exulted over the capture of the *Queen of the West* and the *Indianola*; the local press teemed with accounts of the daring of the captors, and flattered themselves that, with the *Indianola* and *Queen of the West* in their possession, they would be able to drive the Union Navy out of the Mississippi. What was their astonishment to see this huge ironclad pass the batteries, apparently unharmed, and not even taking the trouble to fire a gun!

Some of our soldiers had gone down to the point below Vicksburg to see the fun, and just before reaching Warrenton the mock monitor caught the eddy and turned toward the bank where these men were gathered.

The soldiers spent several hours in trying to shove the dummy off into the stream, when daylight overtook them in the midst of their work, and the Queen of the West, with the Confederate flag flying, was seen coming up the river and stopping at Warrenton. As we afterward learned, she came up for pumps, etc., to raise the Indianola.

In the meanwhile the military authorities in Vicksburg had sent couriers . . . to inform the people on board the Webb that a monster ironclad had passed the batteries and would soon be upon them. The crew of the Webb were busy in trying to remove the guns from their prize, and, when they heard the news, determined to blow her up.

Just after the Queen of the West made the Warrenton landing the soldiers succeeded in towing the mock ironclad into the stream, and she drifted rapidly down upon the rebel prize, whose crew never stopped to deliberate, but cut their fasts and proceeded down the river. Their steam was low, and for a time the mock ironclad drifted almost as fast as the Queen of the West; but at length the latter left her formidable pursuer far behind.

The Queen of the West arrived at the point where the Indianola was sunk just as the people on board the Webb were preparing to blow her up, bringing the news that the "great ironclad" was close behind. So the Webb cast off and, with her consort, made all speed down the river.

[The good admiral did not describe just how the frantic Confederates blew up the Indianola. They overloaded the two gigantic 11-inch Dahlgrens, swinging them so they pointed muzzle to muzzle, and then fired them at each other. The mighty blast tore the guns apart and wrecked everything that had remained above water on the sunken ship.

Word about Porter's clever ruse quickly spread up and down the river. The Vicksburg Whig excoriated the naïve crew from the Webb who had let themselves be taken in by an obvious Yankee trick. The Richmond Examiner was even more scornful when it said: "Here was perhaps the finest ironclad in the Western waters, captured after a heroic struggle, and destined to join the Queen of the West in a series of victories. Next we hear that she was of necessity blown up. Laugh and hold your sides, lest you die of a surfeit of derision, O Yankeedom! Blown up because, forsooth, a flat-boat, or mud-scow, with a small house taken from the back-garden of a plantation, put on top of it, is floated down the river."]

Morgan and His Men Escape
from Prison

by THOMAS H. HINES
from *Century Magazine*, January, 1891

[John Hunt Morgan was born in Alabama, but he grew up near
Lexington, Kentucky, and that city will always be associated with
his name. He fought in the Mexican War, and then became a
noted and daring cavalry raider for the Confederacy. About a
month before the battle of Gettysburg, he was given authority
from Braxton Bragg to make a raid into Kentucky in order to keep
Burnside from joining Rosencrans. Morgan's own plans were far
more ambitious than this; he intended to ride through Indiana
and Ohio to join Lee in Pennsylvania.

On July 2, 1863, he left Burkeville, Kentucky, with 2,400 men
and headed toward Louisville. On the way one of his brothers
was killed and had to be buried along the road. Morgan rode
around Louisville and crossed the Ohio River on July 8. The next
day, while at Corydon, Indiana, he learned about Lee's defeat at
Gettysburg, but he decided to keep on going. His spies, who had
preceded him several weeks before, were able to tell him who his
friends and enemies were along the route. And ahead of him had
gone the author of this article, Thomas H. Hines, one of the most
important of all the Confederate secret agents.

Militia forces were hastily assembled to oppose Morgan, but
the amateur farmers and clerks melted away before the hard-riding,

professional fighting men. When Morgan got near Cincinnati, he sent two men who knew the city into the downtown area to investigate. They rode back to report that the entire populace was demoralized and was momentarily expecting him to invade their homes. He led his troops through the outskirts of Cincinnati at night and then headed south to reach the Ohio River and try to get back to Kentucky. Heavy rains had swollen the river, and gunboats were actively patrolling it. He kept following the shore until he came to a ford, but found it defended in force by Federal troops. In the fighting that took place there, seven hundred of Morgan's men were captured; among them were two of his brothers.

Twenty miles farther up the Ohio, Morgan encountered some more Union gunboats and lost another two hundred men. Federal troops were now in close pursuit, and the great raid was rapidly collapsing. It came to an end near East Liverpool, Ohio, on July 26, when the over-daring cavalryman had to surrender with the few hundred men he had left. They were taken to Cincinnati and then to the penitentiary at Columbus, Ohio.

An attempt has been made to show that Morgan's raid was purely military and had no connection with the Copperheads, but Hines' activities among them disproves this. It is true that the Northern secret societies did not give Morgan any substantial aid, but that was because many of their members quickly became disillusioned with the Confederate raiders when they saw them on their own soil, killing, plundering, looting, and stealing horses and livestock.]

ON THE 31ST OF JULY and the 1st of August, 1863, General John H. Morgan, General Basil W. Duke, and sixty-eight other officers of Morgan's command were, by order of General Burnside confined in the Ohio State Penitentiary at Columbus. Before entering the main prison we were searched and relieved of our pocket-knives, money, and all other articles of value, subjected to a bath, the shaving of our faces, and the cutting of our hair. We were placed each in a separate cell in the first and second tiers on the south side in the east wing of the prison. General Morgan and General Duke were on the second range, General Morgan being confined in the last cell at the east end, those who escaped with General Morgan having their cells in the first range.

From five o'clock in the evening until seven o'clock in the morning we were locked into our cells, with no possible means of communication with one another; but in the day, between these hours, we were permitted to mingle together in the narrow hall, twelve feet wide and one hundred and sixty long, which was cut off from the other portion of the building, occupied by the convicts, by a plank partition, in one end of which was a wooden door. At each end of the hall and within the partitions was an armed military sentinel, while the civil guards of the prison passed at irregular intervals among us, and very frequently the warden or his deputy came through in order to see that we were secure and not violating the prison rules. We were not permitted to talk with or in any way to communicate with the convicts, nor were we permitted to see any of our relatives or friends that might come from a distance to see us, except upon the written order of General Burnside, and then only in the presence of a guard. Our correspondence underwent the censorship of the warden, we receiving and he sending only such as met his approbation. We were not permitted to have newspapers, or to receive information of what was going on in the outside busy world.

Many plans for escape, ingenious and desperate, were suggested, discussed, and rejected because deemed impracticable. Among them was bribery of the guards. This was thought not feasible because of the double set of guards, military and civil, who were jealous and watchful of each other, so that it was never attempted, although we could have commanded, through our friends in Kentucky and elsewhere, an almost unlimited amount of money.

On a morning in the last days of October I was rudely treated, without cause, by the deputy warden. There was no means of redress, and it was not wise to seek relief by retort, since I knew, from the experience of my comrades, that it would result in my confinement in a dark dungeon, with bread and water for diet. I retired to my cell and closed the door with the determination that I would neither eat nor sleep until I had devised some means of escape. I ate nothing and drank nothing during the day, and by nine o'clock at night I had matured the plan that we carried into execution. It may be that I owe something to the fact that I had just completed the reading of Victor Hugo's Les Misérables, containing such vivid delineations of the wonderful escapes of Jean Valjean, and of the subterranean passages of the city of Paris. This may have led me to the line of thought that terminated in the plan of escape adopted. It was this: I had observed that the ground upon the outside of the building, which was low and flat, and also that the floor of the cell was perfectly dry and free from mold. It occurred to me that, as the rear of the cell was to a great extent excluded from the light of air, this dryness and freedom from mold could not exist unless there was underneath something in the nature of an air-chamber to prevent the dampness from rising up the walls and through the floor. If this chamber should be found to exist, and could be reached, a tunnel might be run through the foundations into the yard, from which we might escape by scaling the outer wall, the air-chamber furnishing a receptacle for the earth and stone to be taken out in running the tunnel. The next morning when our cells were unlocked, and we were permitted to assemble in the hall, I went to General Morgan's cell, he having been for several days quite unwell, and laid before him the plan as I have sketched it. Its feasibility appeared to him unquestioned, and to it he gave a hearty and unqualified approval. If, then, our supposition was correct as to the existence of the air-chamber beneath the lower range of cells, a limited number of those occupying that

158

range could escape, and only a limited number, because the greater the number the longer the time required to complete the work, and the greater the danger of discovery while prosecuting it, in making our way over the outer wall, and in escaping afterward.

With these considerations in view, General Morgan and myself agreed upon the following officers, whose cells were nearest the point at which the tunnel was to begin, to join us in the enterprise: Captain J. C. Bennett, Captain L. D. Hockersmith, Captain C. S. Magee, Captain Ralph Sheldon, and Captain Samuel B. Taylor. The plan was then laid before these gentlemen, and received their approval. It was agreed that work should begin in my cell, and continue from there until completed. In order, however, to do this without detection, it was necessary that some means should be found to prevent the daily inspection of that cell, it being the custom for the deputy warden, with the guards, to visit and have each cell swept every morning. This end was accomplished by my obtaining permission from the warden to furnish a broom and sweep my own cell. For a few mornings thereafter the deputy warden would pass, glance into my cell, compliment me on its neatness, and go on to the inspection of the other cells. After a few days my cell was allowed to go without any inspection whatever, and then we were ready to begin work, having obtained through some of our associates, who had been sent to the hospital, some table knives made of flat steel files. In my cell, as in the others, there was a narrow iron cot, which could be folded and propped up to the cell wall. I thought the work could be completed within a month.

On the 4th of November work was begun in the back part of my cell, under the rear end of my cot. We cut through six inches of cement, and took out six layers of brick put in and cemented with the ends up. Here we came to the air-chamber, as I had calculated, and found it six feet wide by four feet high, and running the entire length of the range of cells. The cement and brick taken out in effecting an entrance to the chamber were placed in my bed-tick, upon which I slept during the progress of this portion of the work, after which the material was removed to the chamber. We found the chamber heavily grated at the end, against which a large quantity of coal had been heaped, cutting off any chance of exit in that way. We then began a tunnel, running it at right angles from the side of the chamber, and almost directly beneath my cell. We cut through the foundation wall, five feet thick, of the cell block; through twelve feet of grouting, to the outer wall of the east wing of the prison; through this wall, six feet in thickness; and four feet up near the surface of the yard, in an unfrequented place between this wing and the female department of the prison.

During the progress of the work, in which we were greatly assisted by several of our comrades who were not to go out . . . I sat at the entrance to my cell studiously engaged on Gibbon's Rome and in trying to master French. By this device I was enabled to be constantly on guard without being suspected, as I had pursued the same course during the whole period of my imprisonment. Those who did the work were relieved every hour. This was accomplished and the danger of the guards overhearing the work as they passed obviated by adopting a system of signals, which consisted in giving taps on the floor over the chamber. One knock was to suspend work, two to proceed, and three to come out. On one occasion, by oversight, we came near being discovered. The prisoners were taken out to their meals by ranges, and on this day those confined in the first range were called for dinner while Captain Hockersmith was in the tunnel. The deputy warden, on calling the roll, missed Hockersmith, and came back to inquire for him. General Morgan engaged the attention of the warden by asking his opinion as to the propriety of a remonstrance that the general had prepared to be sent to General Burnside. Flattered by the deference shown to his opinion by General Morgan, the warden unwittingly gave Captain Hockersmith time to get out and fall into line for dinner. While the tunnel was being run, Colonel R. C. Morgan, a brother of General Morgan, made a rope, in links, of bed-ticking, thirty-five feet in length, and from the iron poker of the hall stove we made a hook, in the nature of a grappling-iron, to attach to the end of the rope.

The work was now complete with the exception of making an entrance from each of the cells of those who were to go out. This could be done with safety only by working from the chamber upward, as the cells were daily inspected. The difficulty presented in doing this was the fact that we did not know at what point to begin in order to open the holes in the cells at the proper place. To accomplish this a measurement was necessary, but we had nothing to measure with. Fortunately the deputy warden again ignorantly aided us. I got into a discussion with him as to the length of the hall, and to convince me of my error he sent for his measuring line, and after the hall had been measured and his statement verified General Morgan occupied his attention, while I took the line, measured the distance from center to center of the cells—all being of uniform size—and marked it upon the stick used in my cell for propping up my cot. With this stick, measuring from the middle of the hole in my cell, the proper distance was marked off in the chamber for the holes in the other cells. The chamber was quite dark, and light being necessary for the work we had obtained candles and matches through our sick comrades in the hospital. The hole in my cell during the progress of the work was kept covered with a large hand satchel containing my change of clothing. We cut from underneath upward until there was only a thin crust of the cement left in each of the cells. Money was necessary to pay expenses of transportation and for other contingencies as they might arise. General Morgan had some money that the search had not discovered, but it was not enough. Shortly after we began work I wrote to my sister in Kentucky a letter, which through a trusted convict I sent out and mailed, requesting her to go to my library and get certain books, and in the back of a designated one, which she was to open with a thin knife, place therein a certain amount of Federal money, repaste the back, write my name across the inside of the back where the money was concealed, and send the box by express.

In due course of time the books with the money came to hand. It only remained now to get information as to the time of the running of the trains and to await a cloudy night, as it was then full moon. Our trusty convict was again found useful. . . . His time having almost expired, he was permitted to go on errands for the officials to the city. I gave him ten dollars to bring us a daily paper and six ounces of French brandy. Neither he nor any one within the prison or on the outside had any intimation of our contemplated escape.

It was our first thought to make our way to the Confederacy by the way of Canada; but, on inspecting the time-table in the paper, it was seen that a knowledge of the escape would necessarily come to the prison officials before we could reach the Canadian border. There was nothing left, then, but to take the train south, which we found, if on time, would reach Cincinnati, Ohio, before the cells were opened in the morning, at which time we expected our absence to be discovered. One thing more remained to be done, and that was to ascertain the easiest and safest place at which to scale the outside wall of the prison. The windows opening outward were so high that we could not see the wall. In the hall was a ladder resting against the wall, fifty feet long, that had been used for sweeping down the wall. A view from the top of the ladder would give us a correct idea of the outside, but the difficulty was to get that view without exciting suspicion.

Fortunately the warden came in while we were discussing the great strength and activity of Captain Samuel B. Taylor, who was very small of stature, when it was suggested that Taylor could go hand over hand on the under side of the ladder to the top, and, with a moment's rest, return in the same way. To the warden this seemed impossible, and, to convince him, Taylor was permitted to make the trial, which he did successfully. At the top of the ladder he rested for a minute and took a mental photograph of the wall. When the warden had left, Taylor communicated the fact that directly south of and at almost right angles from the east end of the block in which we were confined there was a double gate to the outer wall, the inside one being of wooden uprights four inches apart, and the outside one as solid as the wall; the wooden gate being supported by the wing wall of the female department, which joined to the main outer wall.

On the evening of the 27th of November the cloudy weather so anxiously waited for came; and prior to being locked in our cells it was agreed to make the attempt at escape that night. Cell No. 21, next to my cell, No. 20, on the first range, was occupied by Colonel R. C. Morgan. . . . That cell had been prepared for General Morgan by opening a hole to the chamber, and when the hour for locking up came General Morgan stepped into Cell 21, and Colonel Morgan into General Morgan's cell in the second range. The guard did not discover the exchange, as General Morgan and Colonel Morgan were of about the same physical proportions, and each stood with his back to the cell door when it was being locked.

At intervals of two hours every night, beginning at eight, the guards came around to each cell and passed a light through the grating to see that all was well with the prisoners. The approach of the guard was often so stealthily made that a knowledge of his presence was first had by seeing him at the door of the cell. To avoid a surprise of this kind we sprinkled fine coal along in front of the cells, walking upon which would give us warning. By a singular coincidence that might have been a fatality, on the day we had determined upon for the escape General Morgan received a letter from Lexington, Kentucky, begging and warning him not to attempt to escape, and by the same mail I received a letter from a member of my family saying that it was rumored and generally believed at home that I had escaped. Fortunately these letters did not put the officials on their guard. We ascertained from the paper we had procured that a train left for Cincinnati at 1:15 A.M., and as the regular time for the guard, to make his round of the cells was twelve o'clock, we arranged to descend to the chamber immediately thereafter. Captain Taylor was to descend first, and, passing under each cell, notify the others. General Morgan had been permitted to keep his watch, and this he gave to Taylor that he might not mistake the time to go.

At the appointed hour Taylor gave the signal, each of us arranged his cot with the seat in his cell so as to represent a sleeping prisoner, and, easily breaking the thin layer of cement, descended to the chamber, passed through the tunnel, breaking through the thin stratum of earth at the end. We came out near the wall of the female prison—it was raining slightly—crawled by the side of the wall to the wooden gate, cast our grappling iron attached to the rope over the gate, made it fast, ascended the rope to the top of the gate, drew up the rope and made our way by the wing wall to the outside wall, where we entered a sentry-box and divested ourselves of our soiled outer garments. In the daytime sentinels were placed on this wall, but at night they were on the inside of the walls and at the main entrance to the prison. On the top of the wall we found a cord running along the outer edge and connecting with a bell in the office of the prison..This cord General Morgan cut with one of the knives we had used in tunneling. Before leaving my cell I wrote and left, addressed to N. Merion, the warden, the following:

"Castle Merion, Cell No. 20, November 27, 1863: Commencement, November 4, 1863; conclusion November 24, 1863; number of hours for labor per day, five; tools, two small knives. *La patience est amère, mais son fruit est doux.* By order of my six honorable Confederates. / s / THOMAS H. HINES, *Captain, C.S.A.*"

Having removed all trace of soil from our clothes and persons, we attached the iron hook to the railing on the outer edge of the wall, and descended to the ground within sixty yards of where the prison guards were sitting round a fire and conversing. Here we separated, General Morgan and myself going to the depot, about a quarter of a mile from the prison, where I purchased two tickets for Cincinnati, and entered the car that just then came in. General Morgan took a seat by the side of a Federal major in uniform, and I sat immediately in their rear. The general entered into conversation with the major, who was made the more talkative by a copious drink of my French brandy. As the train passed near the prison wall where we had descended the major remarked, "There is where the rebel General Morgan and his officers are put for safe keeping." The general replied, "I hope they will keep him as safe as he is now." Our train passed through Dayton, Ohio, and there, for some unknown reason, we were delayed an hour. This rendered it extra hazardous to go to the depot in the city of Cincinnati, since by that time the prison officials would, in all probability, know of our escape, and telegraph to intercept us. In fact, they did telegraph in every direction, and offered a reward for our recapture. Instead, then, of going to the depot in Cincinnati, we got off, while the train was moving slowly, in the outskirts of the city, near Ludlow Ferry, on the Ohio River. Going directly to the ferry we were crossed over in a skiff and landed immediately in front of the residence of Mrs. Ludlow. We rang the door-bell, a servant came, and General Morgan wrote upon a visiting-card, "General Morgan and Captain Hines, escaped." We were warmly received, took a cup of coffee with the family, were furnished a guide, and walked some three miles in the country, where we were furnished horses.

[Despite Hines' denial of it, bribery was undoubtedly used to obtain information from the guards as well as the many candles needed to supply light while digging the tunnel. Charges were later made that no tunnel was dug at all, and that Morgan and his officers simply bought their way out of prison. Examination of contemporary records, however, establishes the fact that a tunnel was built and used as a means of escape.

After Morgan's escape from prison his path went rapidly downhill. He had made an enemy of Bragg by disobeying orders and going on to invade Indiana and Ohio. Since Bragg was now in the War Department in Richmond, he could do the rash young officer a great deal of harm. By the middle of January, 1864, Morgan was back in command, but his troops were of much lower caliber than those he had led before. In May and June he made another raid into Kentucky. It did not come off well, and some of his unscrupulous new officers robbed several banks and ran off with the money.

Early in June, Morgan's ragtag army was defeated in Cynthiana, Kentucky. He spent the summer trying to recruit and train a more efficient cavalry force. By the end of August word reached him from Richmond that he was to be tried for his faithless officers' thefts. He was never brought to trial. While staying in a private home in Greenville, Tennessee, his relentless Federal pursuers caught up with him. He tried to escape and fled from the house to be shot down on a rainy Sunday morning, September 4, 1864.

Two years later his brother's wife gave birth to a child who was named Thomas Hunt Morgan. When he grew up, the Confederate raider's nephew became one of America's outstanding scientists; in 1933 his pioneering work in genetics won the Nobel Prize.

John Hunt Morgan's real importance in the underground activities of the Confederacy is not so much what he did himself—

although there is good reason to believe that he was much more than a hard-fighting cavalry leader who carried open warfare into the Northern states—but that his small command supplied most of the secret agents who did most of the really dangerous work in 1864 and 1865. Nearly a dozen prominent Confederate under-cover agents are known to have come from Morgan's staff. There may have been even more; the common practice of using aliases on secret operations makes it impossible to identify all the men with the missions on which they may have gone.]

The Draft Riots

by JOEL TYLER HEADLEY
from *Pen and Pencil Sketches of the Great Riots*, 1877

[When Lee invaded Pennsylvania, the states in the Northeast were stripped of soldiers because militia had to be rushed to the defense of Gettysburg. Only men from the Invalid Corps, which was made up of veterans recovering from their wounds, and a few regulars, who were guarding the forts and military prisons, were left to defend the cities in that part of the country. It was a perfect time to stir up trouble and impede the war efforts of the North. Trouble began in New York hardly more than a week after Gettysburg. There is some reason to believe that an uprising was scheduled to begin the day after the end of the battle on July 4, but news of Lee's defeat postponed any overt move then.

New York was a peculiar city during the war. For many years its merchants had had strong commercial ties to the South. It was a trade rival of Boston and Philadelphia, and it was the money capital of the nation. It was also a corrupt and cynical city, most of whose people didn't care who won the war so long as they profited by it. In January, 1861, when Fernando Wood was mayor, he had proposed that New York City and Long Island secede from the nation and become a free port to trade with both sides.

In 1863 Manhattan Island had a population of 813,669; of these more than 200,000 were Irish who had flocked to the city after the Potato Famine of 1848. As the most recent arrivals, these half-starved and desperate people had to contend with the Negroes for the bottom jobs. There were also about 120,000 Germans and some 50,000 other people born in other countries. But the mobs who swept through New York, burning, pillaging, and killing were by no means all of foreign origin. They were composed of very poor people who had nothing to lose. And, mixed in among them were probably some secret agents from the Confederacy. It is difficult to prove this, but the few specialists who have studied the Draft Riots agree that although these crippling disturbances may not have been deliberately incited by the Confederates, emissaries were surely sent to the city to keep the pot boiling. In Felix G. Stidger's book, Treason History of the Sons of Liberty, this Union counterspy says (on page 95) that he met a former law partner of William L. Yancey (he could not recall the man's name) who told him that he had led the rioters on the third day to "the Headquarters of the Commanding General of U.S. troops in New York" intending to threaten to kill the general unless he called off the troops. But this bold fire-eater was captured, and the riots had then come to an end.

This is not firm evidence, of course. Either Stidger or his informant—or both—could have been lying, although Stidger's book seems to be truthful enough. But there is very little firm evidence to be found about Confederate or Copperhead complicity in the Draft Riots. What can be established is largely circumstantial. On the second night of the riots, for instance, a rocket was sent up near Union Square; three minutes later another rocket went up to be followed in four minutes by a large fire balloon. This was replied to in a few seconds by a rocket fired from Williamsburg, across the East River in Brooklyn. No one knows what this aerial display meant. It may have been a series of signals; it also may have been a prank.

But the riots did not just happen; they were caused—by parties still unknown. The ostensible reason for them was the Draft Bill which Lincoln had signed on March 3, 1863. This badly conceived measure made it possible to evade the draft by providing a substitute or by paying $300 to procure one. Such a loophole made it easy for well-to-do men to evade military duty while poor men had to serve. Anti-Negro feeling in New York also had a great deal to do with fanning the Draft Riots into flame. There had been a brief outburst of violence on April 13, when Irish workingmen attacked the Negroes who were rivals for their jobs.

Several suspicious characters appeared when actual conscription began. The first of these possible conspirators is the young man whose death is described in the account of the attack on the "wire factory" (also known as the Union Steam Works). The body of this mysterious person, who was wearing fine clothing underneath his rough workman's garb, was spirited away by the mob and never identified.

Still more interesting is the case of John U. Andrews, whose name was often printed in the New York newspapers in July, 1863. According to the New York Tribune for July 17, Andrews was of Virginia birth but had been living in New York since 1859. The Tribune also indicated that he might be connected with the anti-administration New York World. A letter written by Andrews, which is now in the Baker-Turner papers, shows that he was a notary public in 1862. The Tribune described him as being thirty-five years old in 1863, with brown hair, blue eyes, and a full sandy beard. It also said that he had a Southern accent.

Andrews harangued the crowd during the first day's attack on the draft office at Forty-sixth Street and Third Avenue and also on several other occasions, urging further acts of violence. He denounced Lincoln, the Negroes, and the war effort, and acted very much like a Confederate undercover agent trying to incite the mob to sack New York. In this he succeeded. He was arrested at No. 10 Eleventh Street, where he was found in bed with a colored woman who had kept a house of prostitution. Andrews was sent to Fort Lafayette in New York Harbor, where he vanished from public view like so many other things associated with the Draft Riots.

Another letter in the Baker-Turner papers dated October 21, 1863, makes a strange statement about the illusive Mr. Andrews. It was written by Robert Murray, United States Marshal for the Southern District of New York, to Major L. C. Turner in Washington. Murray indicates that Andrews had been sent to Fort Warren in Boston Harbor and asks that he be returned to New York to be brought to trial in order to silence the rumors that Andrews "was sent here by the Gov't to get up a disturbance that would accrue to the benefit of the Gov't." This charge that Andrews was an agent provocateur was being circulated by Democratic newspapers hostile to the administration, but it is interesting to note that Andrews disappears from history at this point and that the books about the Draft Riots written during the immediate postwar years refrain from mentioning him at all.

The riots spread from New York to other places, first to Brooklyn, Jamaica, Staten Island, Jersey City, and Newark; then to Troy, Boston, and Portsmouth, New Hampshire. Only in New York, however, did violence reach epic proportions. There the mob terrorized the entire city, bringing traffic and business to a halt for several days.

Since the disorders were spread over so large an area of the city, no one person could possibly see and record all that went on. Fourteen years later, Joel T. Headley (not to be confused with John W. Headley, the Confederate secret agent) published an account of the riots which he assembled from interviews with the police and various municipal and military officers who had played major roles in suppressing New York's worst outbreak of violence.]

THE THREAT OF VIOLENCE (Saturday, July 11)

THE DRAFT COMMENCED . . . in the Eleventh and Ninth Districts, and passed off quietly; and it was thought the same order would be maintained throughout, and if any force were necessary to repress violence, it would be when the conscripts were required to take their place in the ranks.

Still Superintendent [John] Kennedy of the Police Department feared there might be some difficulty experienced by the officers in charge of the draft, even if no serious resistance could be offered. Some of the enrolling officers, a short time previous, while taking the names of those subject to draft, had been assailed with very abusive language, or their questions received in sullen silence or answered falsely; fictitious names often being given instead of the true ones. . . .

Provost Marshal Captain Joel T. Erhardt came near losing his life in the performance of this duty. At the corner of Liberty Street and Broadway a building was being torn down, preparatory to the erection of another, and the workmen engaged in it threatened the enrolling officer who came to take down their names, with violence, and drove him off.

Captain Erhardt . . . requested of Colonel Nugent a force of soldiers to protect the officer in the discharge of his duty. But this the latter declined to do, fearing it would . . . bring on a collision, and requested the captain to go himself. . . . Erhardt . . . said he would go, but only on one condition, that if he got in trouble and asked for help, he would send him troops. To this he [Nugent] agreed, and Captain Erhardt proceeded to . . . the corner of Broadway and Liberty Street, and . . . asked a man on a ladder for his name. The fellow refused to answer, when an altercation ensuing, he stepped down, and seizing an iron bar advanced on the provost marshal. The latter had nothing but a light Malacca cane in his hand, but as he saw the man meant murder he drew a pistol from his pocket, and levelled it full at his breast. This brought him to a halt; and after looking at Erhardt for a while he dropped his bar. Erhardt then put up his pistol, and went on with his enrolling. The man was dogged and angry, and waiting his opportunity, suddenly made a rush at the provost marshal. The latter had only time to deal him, as he sprang forward, one heavy blow with his cane, when they closed. In a moment both reeled from the plank and fell to the cellar beneath, the provost marshal on top. Covered with dirt, he arose and drew his pistol, and mounted to the sidewalk.

The foreman sympathized with the workmen, and Erhardt could do nothing. Determined to arrest them for resisting the draft, he despatched a messenger to Colonel Nugent for the promised force. None, however, was sent. He, in the meantime, stood with drawn pistol facing the men, who dared not advance on him. Aid not arriving, he sent again, and still later a third time. He stood thus facing the workmen with his pistol for three hours, and finally had to leave without making any arrests. This failure of Colonel Nugent to fulfill his promise and perform his duty came near costing Erhardt his life, and then and there starting the riot. The next day he had the foreman arrested, and completed his work of enrolling. . . .

THE FIRST DAY (Monday, July 13)

Meanwhile, events were assuming an alarming aspect in the western part of the city. Early in the morning men began to assemble here in separate groups, as if in accordance with a previous arrangement, and at last moved quietly north along the various avenues. Women, also, like camp followers, took the same direction in crowds. They were thus divided into separate gangs, apparently to take each avenue in their progress, and make a clean sweep. The factories and workshops were visited, and the men compelled to knock off work and join them, while the proprietors were threatened with the destruction of their property, if they made any opposition. The separate crowds were thus swelled at almost every step, and armed with sticks, and clubs, and every conceivable weapon they could lay hands on, they moved north towards some point which had evidently been selected as a place of rendezvous. This proved to be a vacant lot near Central Park, and soon the living streams began to flow into it, and a more wild, savage, and heterogeneous-looking mass could not be imagined. After a short consultation they again took up the line of march, and in two separate bodies, moved down Fifth and Sixth Avenues, until they reached Forty-sixth and Forty-seventh Streets, when they turned directly east.

The number composing this first mob has been so differently estimated, that it would be impossible from reports merely, to approximate the truth. A pretty accurate idea, however, can be gained of its immense size, from a statement made by Mr. King, son of President King, of Columbia College [then at 49th Street and Fifth Avenue]. Struck by its magnitude, he had the curiosity to get some estimate of it by timing its progress, and he found that although it filled the broad street from curbstone to curbstone, and was moving rapidly, it took between twenty and twenty-five minutes for it to pass a single point.

A ragged, coatless, heterogeneously weaponed army, it heaved tumultuously along toward Third Avenue. Tearing down the telegraph poles as it crossed the Harlem & New Haven Railroad track, it surged angrily up around the building where the drafting was going on [at Forty-sixth Street and Third Avenue.] The small squad of police stationed there to repress disorder looked on bewildered, feeling they were powerless in the presence of such a host. Soon a stone went crashing through a window, which was the signal for a general assault on the doors. These giving way before the immense pressure, the foremost rushed in, followed by shouts and yells from those behind, and began to break up the furniture. The drafting officers, in an adjoining room, alarmed, fled precipitately through the rear of the building. The mob seized the wheel in which were the names, and what books, papers, and lists were left, and tore them up, and scattered them in every direction. A safe stood on one side, which was supposed to contain important papers, and on this they fell with clubs and stones, but in vain. Enraged at being thwarted, they set fire to the building, and hurried out of it. As the smoke began to ascend, the onlooking multitude without sent up a loud cheer. Though the upper part of the building was occupied by families, the rioters, thinking that the officers were concealed there, rained stones and brick-bats against the windows, sending terror into the hearts of the inmates.

Deputy Provost Marshal Vanderpoel, who had mingled in the crowd, fearing for the lives of the women and children, boldly stepped to the front, and tried to appease the mob, telling them the papers were all destroyed, and begged them to fall back, and let others help the inmates of the building, or take hold themselves. The reply was a heavy blow in the face. Vanderpoel shoved the man who gave it aside, when he was assailed with a shower of blows and curses. Fearing for his life, he broke through the crowd, and hastened to the spot where the police were standing, wholly powerless in the midst of this vast, excited throng.

In the meantime, the flames, unarrested, made rapid way, and communicating to the adjoining building, set it on fire. The volumes of smoke, rolling heavenward, and the crackling and roaring of the flames, seemed for a moment to awe the mob, and it looked silently on the ravaging of a power more terrible and destructive than its own.

At this time Superintendent Kennedy was quietly making his way . . . toward the offices of the provost marshal, Jenkins. But noticing a fire as he approached, he left his wagon . . . and walked toward Third Avenue. The street was blocked with people, but they seemed quiet and orderly as any gathering in presence of a fire, and differed from it only in that the countenances of all seemed to wear a pleased gratified look. As he unsuspiciously edged his way forward toward the fire, he heard some one cry out,

"There's Kennedy!" "Which is him?" asked a second; and he was pointed out.

Kennedy was dressed in ordinary citizen's clothes, and carried only a slight bamboo cane. Thinking the allusion to him was prompted only by curiosity, he kept on, when suddenly he felt himself violently pushed against. Turning around, he encountered a man in a soldier's old uniform, and sternly demanded what he meant by that. The words had hardly escaped his lips, when a heavy blow was planted full in his face. Instantly the crowd closed around him, and rained blows in rapid succession on him, until he fell over and down the graded street, some six feet, into a vacant lot. The crowd, with yells, poured after him. Kennedy, springing to his feet, started on a run across the lot towards Forty-seventh Street, distancing his pursuers. But as he reached Forty-seventh Street, and attempted to ascend the embankment, another crowd, which had witnessed the pursuit, rushed upon him, and knocked him back again in front of his pursuers. He quickly sprang up, though bleeding and stunned, for he knew his only chance for life was in keeping his feet. But the crowd closing around on both sides gave him no chance to run. One huge fellow, armed with a heavy club, endeavored to break in his skull, but Kennedy dodged his blows. Careful only for his head, he let them beat his body, while he made desperate efforts to break through the mass, whose demoniacal yells and oaths showed that they intended to take his life. In the struggle the whole crowd, swaying to and fro, slowly advanced toward Lexington Avenue, coming, as they did so, upon a wide mud-hole. "Drown him! drown him!" arose at once on every side, and the next moment a heavy blow, planted under his ear, sent him headforemost into the water.

Falling with his face amid the stones, he was kicked and trampled on, and pounded, till he was a mass of gore. Still struggling desperately for life, he managed to get to his feet again, and made a dash for the middle of the pond. The water was deep, and his murderers . . . ran around to the other side to meet him. . . . But Kennedy was ahead of them, and springing up the bank into Lexington Avenue, saw a man whom he knew, and called out: "John Eagan, come here and save my life!" Mr. Eagan, who was a well-known and influential resident of that vicinity, immediately rushed forward to his assistance, and arrested his pursuers. But the superintendent was so terribly bruised and mangled, that Eagan did not recognize him. He, however, succeeded in keeping the mob back, who, seeing the horrible condition their victim was in, doubtless thought they had finished him. Other citizens now coming forward, a passing feed wagon was secured, into which Kennedy was lifted, and driven to police head-quarters. [Police Commissioner Thomas C.] Acton, who was in the street as the wagon approached, saw the mangled body within, but did not dream who it was. The driver inquired where he should take him. "Around to the station," carelessly replied Acton. The driver hesitated, and inquired again, "Where to?" Acton, supposing it was some drunkard, bruised in a brawl, replied rather petulantly, "Around to the station." The man then told him it was Kennedy. Acton, scanning the features more closely, saw that it indeed was the superintendent himself in this horrible condition. As the officers gathered around the bleeding, almost unconscious form, a murmur of wrath was heard, a sure premonition what work would be done when the hour of vengeance should come. . . .

Having stopped the draft in two districts, sacked and set on fire nearly a score of houses, and half killed as many men, [the mob] now, impelled by a strange logic, sought to destroy the Colored Orphan Asylum on Fifth Avenue, extending from Forty-third to Forty-fourth Street. There would have been no draft but for the war—there would have been no war but for slavery. But the slaves were black, ergo, all blacks are responsible for the war. This seemed to be the logic of the mob, and having reached the sage conclusion to which it conducted, they did not stop to consider

177

how poor helpless orphans could be held responsible, but proceeded at once to wreak their vengeance on them. The building was four stories high, and besides the matrons and officers, contained over two hundred children, from mere infants up to twelve years of age. Around this building the rioters gathered with loud cries and oaths, sending terror into the hearts of the inmates. Superintendent William E. Davis hurriedly fastened the doors; but knowing they would furnish but a momentary resistance to the armed multitude, he, with others, collected hastily the terrified children, and carrying some in their arms, and leading others, hurried them in a confused crowd out at the rear of the building, just as the ruffians effected an entrance in front. Then the work of pillage commenced, and everything carried off that could be, even to the dresses and trinkets of the children, while heavy furniture was smashed and chopped up in the blind desire of destruction. Not satisfied with this, they piled the fragments in the different rooms, and set fire to them.

The Second Day (Tuesday, July 14)

Inspector [Daniel] Carpenter [and his men], coming down Twenty-first Street, struck Second Avenue, and wheeling, moved in solid column through the crowd up to Thirty-second Street. The force was assailed with hoots and yells, and all kinds of opprobrious epithets, but no violence was shown, until it had crossed Thirty-second Street. The mob not only filled the street, but numbers, with piles of stones and brick-bats, had climbed to the roofs of the houses. These deeming themselves secure, suddenly, with one accord, rained their missiles on the rear of the column.

The men fell rapidly, and two were dangerously hurt. Carpenter immediately halted his command, and ordered fifty men to enter the houses, and mounting to the roof, clear them of the assailants. Barricaded doors were at once broken in, and every one that opposed their progress clubbed without mercy, as they made their way to the upper floors. Captain Mount of the Eleventh Precinct, led this storming party. Officers Watson and Cole distinguished themselves by being the first on the roof, fighting their way through a narrow scuttle. As the police, one by one, stepped on to the roof, they rushed on the desperadoes with their clubs, and felled them rapidly. Those who attempted to escape through the scuttles were met by the police in the rooms below; or if one chanced to reach the street, he was knocked down by those keeping guard there. Some dropped from second and third story windows, and met with a worse fate than those who stayed behind. One huge fellow received such a tremendous blow, that he was knocked off his feet and over the edge of the roof, and fell headlong down a height of four stories to the pavement beneath. Crushed to death by the force of the fall, he lay a mangled heap at the feet of his companions.

The fight was sharp and fierce, and kept up for nearly an hour, and bodies scattered around showed with what deadly force the club had been wielded. But with the clearing of the houses there came a lull in the conflict, and the immense crowd looked on in sullen silence, as the police reformed in the street, and recommenced their march. The military force that had accompanied the police, had formed in the avenue, about a block and a half above where the latter were stationed, while the detachment was clearing the houses. Two howitzers were placed in position commanding the avenue.

Colonel O'Brien, of the Eleventh New York Volunteers, who was raising a regiment for the war, had gathered together, apparently on his own responsibility, about fifty men, and appearing on the field . . . assumed command. For a short time the rioters remained quiet but as the police marched away, they suddenly awoke out of their apparent indifference. Maddened at the sight of the mangled bodies of their friends stretched on the pavement, and enraged at their defeat by the police, they now turned on the soldiers, and began to pelt them with stones and brick-bats. O'Brien rode up and down the centre of the street a few times, evidently thinking his fearless bearing would awe the mob. But they only jeered him, and finding the attack growing hotter and more determined, he finally gave the order to fire. The howitzers belched forth on the crowd, the soldiers levelled their pieces, and the whistling of minié-balls was heard on every side. Men and women reeled and fell on the sidewalk and in the street. One woman, with her child in her arms, fell, pierced with a bullet.

The utmost consternation followed. The crowd knew from sad experience that the police would use their clubs, but they seemed to think it hardly possible that the troops would fire point-blank into their midst. But the deadly effect of the fire convinced them of their error, and they began to jostle and crowd each other in the effort to get out of its range. In a few minutes the avenue was cleared of the living, when the wounded and dead were cared for by their friends. Order had been restored, and O'Brien, with some twenty or thirty men, marched down to police head-quarters, and offered his services to General [Harvey] Brown. Colonel Frothingham thanked him, but soon saw that the Colonel was not in a fit state to have command of troops, and so reported to General Brown. O'Brien appeared to comprehend the state of things, and asked to be excused on the plea of sickness. [He was intoxicated.] He was excused, and rode away.

Whether he disbanded his handful of men, or they disbanded themselves, was not stated, but he was soon back again at the scene of the riot. His residence was close by, but had been deserted that morning by the family, which had fled in alarm to Brooklyn. Scowling visages lowered on the colonel, as he rode slowly back among the crowd, and low muttered threats were heard. Although an Irishman, and well-known in that neighborhood, his sympathy with the Government had awakened more or less hostile feeling against him, which his conduct to-day kindled into deadly hate. Apparently unconscious or reckless of this, he dismounted, and entered a neighboring drug-store or saloon. . . . Drawing his sword, and taking a revolver in the other hand, he deliberately walked out into the street. He had taken but a few steps, when a powerful blow on the back of his head made him stagger forward. In an instant a rush was made for him, and blows were rained so fast and fierce upon him, that he was unable to defend himself. Knocked down and terribly mangled, he was dragged with savage brutality over the rough pavement, and swung from side to side like a billet of wood, till the large, powerful body was a mass of gore, and the face beaten to a pumice. The helpless but still animate form would then be left a while in the street, while the crowd, as it swayed to and fro, gazed on it with cool indifference or curses. At length a Catholic priest, who had either been sent for, or came along to offer his services wherever they might be needed, approached the dying man and read the service of the Catholic Church over him, the crowd in the meantime remaining silent. After he had finished, he told them to leave the poor man alone, as he was fast sinking. But as soon as he had disappeared, determined to make sure work with their victim, they again began to pound and trample on the body. In the intervals of the attack the still living man would feebly lift his head, or roll it from side to side on the stones, or heave a faint groan.

The whole afternoon was spent in this fiendish work, and no attempt was made to rescue him. Towards sundown the body was dragged into his own back-yard, his regimentals all torn from him, except his pantaloons, leaving the naked body, from the waist up, a mass of mangled flesh clotted with blood.

But the dying man could not be left alone in his own yard. A crowd followed him thither, among which were women, who committed the most atrocious violence on the body, until at last, with one convulsive movement of the head, and a deep groan, the strong man yielded up his life. . . .

181

A bloody conflict also took place between the police and mob in the same avenue [Second Avenue] where Colonel O'Brien fell, below Thirtieth Street. There was a wire factory [The Union Steam Works at Twenty-second Street] here, in which several thousand carbines were stored. Of this, some of the rioters were aware, and communicated the fact to others, and a plan was formed to capture them. Having discovered from the morning's experience that the military had been called in to aid the police, arms became imperatively necessary, if they hoped to make a successful resistance. All public depositories of arms they knew were guarded, but this factory was not, and hence they resolved to capture it without delay. Swarming around it, they forced the entrance, and began to throw out the carbines to their friends. The attack, however, had been telegraphed to head-quarters, and Inspector Dilks was despatched with two hundred men to save the building, and recover any arms that might be captured. He marched rapidly up to Twenty-first Street, and down it to the avenue. Here he came suddenly upon the mob, that blocked the entire street. As the head of the force appeared, the rioters, instead of being frightened, greeted it with jeers and curses.

It was two hundred against a thousand; but the inspector did not hesitate a moment on account of the inequality of numbers, but instantly formed his men and ordered a charge. The mob, instead of recoiling, closed desperately on the police, and a fierce hand-to-hand encounter took place. The clubs, however, mowed a clean swath along the street, and the compact little force pushed like a wedge into the throng, and cleared a bloody space for itself. The orders were to recapture all the arms; for this was of more vital importance than the capture of men. Wherever, therefore, a musket was seen, a man would dash for it, and, seizing it, fight his way back into line. On the pavement, the sidewalk, and in the gutters, men lay bleeding and dying, until at last, the more resolute having been knocked on the head, the vast crowd, like a herd of buffalo, broke and tore madly down the street.

One of the leaders was a man of desperate courage, and led on the mob with reckless fury, though bleeding freely from the terrible punishment he received. As his comrades turned to flee, leaving him alone, a fearful blow sent him reeling and staggering towards the sidewalk. As he reached it, he fell heavily over against the iron railing, and his chin striking one of the iron pickets, the sharp point entered it and penetrated through to the roof of his mouth. No one noticed him, or if they did, paid no attention to him in the headlong flight on the one hand, and swift pursuit on the other. Thus horridly impaled, his body hanging down along the sidewalk, the wretched man was left to die. At length Captain Hedden noticed him, and lifting up the corpse, laid it down on the sidewalk. It was found, to the surprise of all, to be that of a young man of delicate features and white, fair skin. "Although dressed as a laborer, in dirty overalls and filthy shirt, underneath these were fine cassimere pants, handsome, rich vest, and fine linen shirt." He was evidently a man in position far above the rough villains he led on, but had disguised himself so as not to be known. He never was known. The corpse, during the fight that followed, disappeared with the bodies of many others.

THE THIRD DAY (Wednesday, July 15)

Colonel Sherwood's battery of rifled cannon arrived in the afternoon, and was put in position in front of the arsenal [located at Seventh Avenue and Thirty-fifth Street], where the firing of pickets all day would indicate that an attack was momentarily expected. . . .

At about five o'clock, it was ordered by [General Charles W.] Sandford, with an infantry force of one hundred and fifty, to the corner of Twenty-seventh Street and Seventh Avenue, to quell a mob assembled in large numbers at that point, and which were gutting, and plundering, and firing houses. As they approached, they saw flames bursting from windows, while, to complete the terror of the scene, the body of a Negro hung suspended from a lamp-post, his last struggle just ended. At the same time that the military arrived, firemen, who had come to put out the fire, reached the spot in another direction. One portion of the mob immediately took shelter behind the latter, so that the troops dared not fire and clear the streets, while another ran up to the house-tops, armed with guns and pistols, for the purpose of firing into the ranks below. The colonel told his men to keep a sharp lookout, and at the first shot fire. Scores of guns were immediately pointed towards the roofs of the houses. In the meantime, from some cause not fully explained, the imposing force, after this demonstration, marched away, leaving the mob in full possession of the field. It had hardly reached the protection of the arsenal again, when the plundering and violence recommenced; and in a short time two more Negroes were amusing the spectators with their death throes, as they hung by the neck from lamp-posts. . . .

Towards evening word was brought to the Seventh Regiment Armory that the mob had gathered in great force in First Avenue, between Eighteenth and Nineteenth Streets.

Colonel Winston, in command, immediately ordered out a force . . . and with a battery of two howitzers . . . marched rapidly to the scene of disturbance. Passing down Nineteenth Street to the avenue, it halted, and unlimbering the pieces, trained them so as to command the avenue, while the infantry formed in line to support them. As soon as the rioters saw the guns bearing on them, they dodged into basements, and mounted to the windows and roofs of the tenement buildings that abounded in that vicinity. A number of them armed with muskets and pistols, and the rest with stones and brick-bats, began a fierce and determined attack on the troops. The howitzers, loaded with grape and canister, at once swept the street. After the first discharge, but few ventured to show themselves in the avenue, until after they heard the report, when they would dodge from behind corners and fire back. But from the tops of the houses an incessant fusillade was kept up. The soldiers endeavored to pick them off, but the rioters presented a small mark compared to that which the troops, massed in the open streets, furnished; and it was soon apparent that the fight was unequal. If they had only had a police force to enter the buildings, and hunt the men from the roofs, the fight would soon have been over. But the commander, thinking he could not spare a sufficient number to do this work, or that the soldiers, cumbered with their muskets, which, after the first discharge, would have to be clubbed, could make no headway in such a hand-to-hand fight, made no effort to dislodge the wretches, who loaded and fired with the most imperturbable coolness. One man was seen to step round the corner, after the discharge of the battery, and resting his gun on the shoulder of a fellow-rioter, take as deliberate aim at Colonel Jardine as he would at a squirrel on the limb of a tree, and fire. The ball struck the colonel in the thigh, and brought him to the pavement. Other officers shared his fate, while at every discharge, men would drop in the ranks.

The howitzers rattled their shot on the deserted pavements and walls of the houses, but did no damage to the only portion of the enemy they had to fear, while the fight between the infantry and the rioters was like that between soldiers in the open field and Indians in ambush. Colonel Winston soon saw that it was madness to keep his men there, to be picked off in detail, and ordered a retreat. At the first sign of a retrograde movement, a cry rang along the avenue; and from the side streets, and basements, and houses, the mob swarmed forth so furiously, that it assumed huge proportions at once, and chased the retiring soldiers with yells and taunts, and pressed them so hotly that they could not bring off all their killed and wounded. Among those left behind was Colonel Jardine. He took refuge in a basement, where the mob found him, and would have killed him on the spot, had not one of them recognized him as an old acquaintance, and for some reason or other protected him from further violence; he was eventually carried to the house of a surgeon near by.

The mob were left masters of the field, and soon began their depredations. The state of things was at length reported to police head-quarters, and General Brown sent off Captain Putnam, with Captain Shelby and a hundred and fifty regulars and two field-pieces, to disperse the mob and bring away the dead and wounded of Winston's force that might remain. They reached the spot between ten and eleven o'clock at night. The dimly lighted streets were black with men, while many, apprised of the approach of the military, mounted again to the roofs as before. Putnam immediately charged on the crowd in the street, scattering them like a whirlwind. He then turned his guns on the buildings, and opened such a deadly fire on them that they were soon cleared. Having restored order, he halted his command, and remained on the ground till half-past twelve.

At the same time a mob was pulling down the Negro houses in York Street, which they soon left a heap of ruins. Houses plundered or set on fire in various parts of the city, combined with the ringing of fire-bells, thunder of cannon, and marching of troops, made this night like its predecessor—one of horror. . . .

The illumination of the windows from the *Times* building this evening shed a brilliant glow over Printing-house Square, and flooded the Park to the City Hall with light, while an armed force within was ready to fire on any mob that should dare expose itself in the circle of its influence. . . .

The Seventh Regiment . . . was expected to reach the city that night by special train. Policemen were therefore kept on the watch, but the regiment did not arrive till after daylight. About half-past four in the morning, the steady ranks were seen marching along Canal Street towards Broadway, and soon drew up in front of St. Nicholas Hotel. . . .

THE FOURTH AND FIFTH DAYS (Thursday and Friday, July 16 and 17)

The arsenal had not been attacked. . . . Many colored people
. . . took refuge in it; and about noon on this day, a body of
police arrived before it, with the children of the Colored Orphan
Asylum that had been burned on Monday, in charge. They had
since that time been scattered round in station-houses, but were
now to be escorted to Blackwell's Island, for better security. It
was an impressive spectacle this army of children presented, as
they drew up in line in front of the arsenal to wait for those within
to join them. The block was filled with them. The frightened
little fugitives, fleeing from they scarce knew what, looked bewildered at their novel position. It seemed impossible that they
ever could have been the objects of any one's vengeance. With a
strong body of police in front and rear, and a detachment of soldiers on either side, they toddled slowly down to the foot of
Thirty-fifth Street, from whence they were taken by boats to the
Island.

The Sixty-fifth New York Regiment arrived from Harrisburg
in the afternoon, and just before midnight the One Hundred and
Fifty-second also reached the city, and marched up Broadway to
police headquarters. . . to get some rest.

A heavy storm that set in during the evening helped to
scatter the crowd that would otherwise have gathered on this warm
July night, but it at the same time gave a sombre aspect to the
city. The crescent moon was veiled in black, and thunderous
clouds that swept heavily over the city, deepened the gloom, and
seemed portentous of greater evil. The closing of all the stores
and shop-windows at nightfall, through fear, left the streets lighted
only by the scattering lamps. This unusual stretch of blank dead
walls, emitting no ray of light, rendered the darkness made by the
over-hanging storm still more impenetrable. Flashes of lightning
would reveal small groups of men bent on plunder, in sections

where the military and police were not stationed, but no open violence was attempted. In other directions, the bayonets of the soldiers would gleam out of the dense shadows, as they silently held the posts assigned them, ready to march at a moment's notice. This was the fourth night, and the cannon planted in the streets, and the military force, showed that peace was not fully restored.

This week of horrors—a week unparalleled in the history of New York—was drawing to a close. . . . Friday, the fifth day of this protracted struggle, dawned bright and tranquil. The storm of the night before had passed away, and the streets, thoroughly washed by the drenching rain, stretched clean and quiet between the long rows of buildings, emblematic of the tranquillity that had returned to the city.

The [horse-] cars were seen once more speeding down to the business centres, loaded with passengers. Broadway shook to the rumbling of the heavy omnibuses; shutters were taken down, and the windows again shone with their rich adornments. The anxious look had departed from the pedestrians, for the heavy cloud, so full of present woe and future forebodings, had lifted and passed away. . . .

The End of the Riots

There were, perhaps, in the city this morning [Saturday] not far from ten thousand troops—quite enough to preserve the peace, if the riot should break out afresh; and orders therefore were given to arrest the march of regiments hastening from various sections to the city under the requisition of the Governor. Still, the terror that had taken possession of men could not be delayed in an hour, and although the police had resumed their patrols, and dared to be seen alone in the streets, there was constant dread of personal violence among the citizens. Especially was this true of the Negro population. Although many sought their ruined homes, yet aware of the intense hatred entertained toward them by the mob, they felt unsafe, and began to organize in self-defence. But the day wore away without disturbance, and the Sabbath dawned peaceably, and order reigned from the Battery to Harlem. The military did not show themselves in the street, and thousands thronged without fear the avenues in which the fighting had taken place, to look at the ruins it had left behind. . . .

The Grand Jury indicted many of the prisoners; twenty were tried and nineteen convicted and sentenced to . . . imprisonment. Of course a large number on preliminary examinations got off, sometimes from want of sufficient evidence, and sometimes from the venality of the judges before whom they were brought. . . . The number of rioters killed, or died from the effects of their wounds, was put down by the Police Commissioners at about twelve hundred. Of course this estimate is not made up from any detailed reports. The dead and wounded were hurried away, even in the midst of the fight, and hidden in obscure streets, or taken out of the city for fear of future arrests or complications. Hence, there was no direct way of getting at the exact number of those who fell victims to the riot. The loss of life, therefore, could only be approximated by taking the regular report of the number of deaths in the city for a few weeks before the riots, and that for the same length of time after. As there was no epidemic, or any report of increased sickness from any disease, the inference naturally was, that the excess for the period after the riots was owing to the victims of them. Many of these were reported as sunstrokes, owing to men exposing themselves to the sun with pounded and battered heads. . . .

[Although the police commissioners believed that twelve hundred people died in the New York Draft Riots, no one really ever knew. There was plenty of vacant land in the city which could have been used for surreptitious burials, and the waters around Manhattan Island doubtless carried many corpses out to sea.

189

Confederate reaction to the disturbances in the North was so gleeful that there is little doubt that those who left written statements about it would have been delighted if Southern agents were responsible for stirring up the trouble. J. B. Jones, writing his *A Rebel War Clerk's Diary* in Richmond, commented on July 17: "But we have awful good news from New York: an INSURRECTION, the loss of many lives, extensive pillage and burning, with a suspension of the conscription!" (He was wrong, of course, about the draft being suspended.) And the Richmond Enquirer referred to the riots as "this good work," and then said, "We wish it good speed."

One of the many remarkable—and mysterious—things about the Draft Riots is the fact that although thousands of people went on the rampage, arrests and convictions were exceedingly few. This, however, points more to disaffection and corruption in New York's municipal government than it does to Confederate complicity, although one odd fact is that the daily record of activities and expenditures for Lafayette C. Baker's office in New York shows no evidence whatsoever that the detectives stationed there paid any attention to the great riots that were going on all around them. Detectives from New York's Metropolitan Police, however, disguised themselves in rough workingmen's clothes and mingled with the various mobs to get information for police headquarters about the rioters' plans.

But at least one of the men arrested in New York was certainly no ragamuffin from the slums. This was a dentist named Nelson Edwards, a thirty-five-year-old British subject who gave his address as 726 Broadway, which was then in the heart of the city's hotel district. Five witnesses charged him with exhorting the mob to violence on several occasions. What eventually happened to this obviously middle-class person is not known. He appeared briefly in the spotlight and then was swept away forever into the dustbin of history.

190

One thing ties that week of horror to our own time. On July 17, 1863, a Relief Fund was started by public subscription for the benefit of the families of the policemen who were killed or seriously injured in the effort to restrain the mob. The original fund was so well invested and administered over the years that it still yields an annual income of about $8,000 which is paid to the families of New York policemen who are killed or injured in performance of their duty.]

1864

January, 1864, was one of the most uneventful months of the war. The leaders of both armies were sparring for time while they planned their major strategy for the spring and summer campaigns. The number of blockade runners captured or destroyed, however, was stepped up then, so that it became increasingly difficult for the Confederates to maintain communications with the outside. Union cavalry too, was at last coming into its own. Late in February a daring raid was made by Kilpatrick which carried his troopers to within a few miles of Richmond; at the same time Custer's men devastated the country around Charlottesville.

During the Kilpatrick raid, young Colonel Ulrich Dahlgren was shot. The Confederates claimed to have found a paper on his body stating that he was going to try to release the Union prisoners on Belle Island and with their help attack and burn Richmond. They were then to kill Jefferson Davis and members of his Cabinet. Oddly enough, however, Dahlgren's supposed signature on this document was misspelled "Dalhgren," which led many to believe that the controversial paper was a forgery produced by the Confederates as a propaganda move.

Perhaps inspired by the escape of John Hunt Morgan and his men from jail a few months before, 109 Federal officers confined in Richmond's Libby Prison tunneled their way to freedom on February 9. Forty-eight of them were captured and sent back. During Kilpatrick's raid J. B. Jones noted in his A Rebel War Clerk's Diary that "when it was supposed probable that the prisoners of war at the Libby might attempt to break out, Gen. Winder ordered that a large amount of powder be placed under the building, with instructions to blow them up, if the attempt were made."

This was only the first of many desperate moves the Confederates were to make in 1864 when the war was going against them. Weapons such as naval and land mines were being used more and more. And the submarine, although still almost as crude as Robert Fulton's primitive Nautilus of half a century before, was being tried out. Crew after crew was drowned in these early attempts, but volunteers were always ready to man the plummeting coffins again.

The most important strategical move of the year—and perhaps of the whole war—took place early in March when Grant was given command of all the Union armies, thus ending the division of responsibility that had hampered the North's war effort from the beginning. The taciturn Western general decided to take the field with the Army of the Potomac, although he left Meade in actual command. Sherman was to have charge in the West, where he was about to launch his massive campaign against Atlanta and march from there to the sea.

On April 17 Grant issued orders that no more able-bodied Confederate prisoners were to be exchanged. The North, with its greater population could stand the loss of manpower involved in such a decision, but the South, with its fighting forces already

193

seriously depleted, could not. Grant was out to make a kill, and so was Sherman.

The days of the Confederacy seemed numbered in the early spring of 1864. The Army of the Potomac was almost twice as large as the Army of Northern Virginia and was much better equipped. One factor, however, had not been taken into full account; that was the brilliant generalship of Robert E. Lee and his skillful handling of his small but always effective Army of Northern Virginia. When Grant's 119,000 men moved against Lee's 64,000 poorly armed, poorly fed troops on May 3, it seemed as though the much larger Union force would quickly beat down all Confederate resistance and sweep on triumphantly to occupy Richmond, which was only about sixty miles away.

During that dreadful month of May, Grant hammered and bludgeoned. Men died by the thousands in the greening woods and fields of central Virginia. Obscure places like the Wilderness, Spotsylvania, and Cold Harbor were written in letters of blood on the pages of history, but a month later Grant had lost 55,000 men while Lee's army, although seriously reduced, was still unconquered, and the Confederate capital was intact.

Grant was repulsed but not beaten. He suddenly shifted his tactics and moved his men to the southeast of Richmond to attack Petersburg, which was then fortified but almost undefended. On June 15, when General William F. ("Baldy") Smith advanced against that city early in the morning, his men could have overrun the thinly held earthworks and kept on going until they reached Richmond. But by one of the strange delays that had all too often impeded the progress of the Army of the Potomac, Smith hesitated and was lost, for Confederates were rushed to the almost empty trenches in time to save the two cities.

As a result, Grant had to begin an elaborate siege operation that was to last until the end of the war. On July 30, a huge mine was exploded under the Confederate earthworks. Union troops

194

were supposed to dash into the breach and overpower the surprised Confederates. It was an ingenious plan, but again bad timing and delay spoiled the Union's chances, and what should have been an easy victory became a terrible defeat when the Confederates rallied their forces and caught the much-too-late invaders in the vast crater of mud which then became a death-trap. Afterwards the opposing armies settled down to a long stalemate of entrenched warfare very much like that which paralyzed the Germans and the Allies in the First World War.

On May 18, at a crucial moment during Grant's campaign in Virginia, gold speculators sent a fraudulent proclamation signed with the President's name to the New York newspapers, hoping to drive up the price of the precious metal for their own profit. This forged document ordered a new draft and recommended that May 26 be made "a day of fasting, humiliation and prayer" because of military reverses in various parts of the country. Fortunately, only two New York papers were incautious enough to print the forgery, which was immediately denounced. Secretary of War Stanton closed the offending newspapers down for two days and sent Joseph Howard, the actual perpetrator of the fraud, to Fort Lafayette, where he remained until August 23 and was then released because Henry Ward Beecher (Howard's former employer) interceded for him with President Lincoln. The brokers who had backed Howard were not punished, although they succeeded in driving the price of gold up 8 per cent on the day the bogus proclamation was printed.

On May 28, in far-off Vera Cruz, Mexico, something was taking place which was to have an important effect on American foreign policy for the next three years. Landing there in regal splendor was the Austrian archduke Maximilian, who was being made Emperor of Mexico by Napoleon III in order to re-establish France's lost foothold in the New World. The cause of this sorry

195

catspaw, whose career was to end before a firing squad in 1867, was favored by the Confederates, who planned to colonize northern Mexico with Southerners and set up a haven for slavery there in case the Confederacy was defeated. The tide of fortune turned quickly against this puppet emperor, but his presence on the North American continent was to be a disturbing factor during the rest of the war.

On June 7, while the nation was still reeling from the shock of Grant's heavy losses at Cold Harbor, the Republican Presidential Nominating Convention met at Baltimore. The party had temporarily changed its name to National Unionist; it nominated Lincoln and Andrew Johnson. The Democratic Party nominated General George B. McClellan on August 31. Two days later, Sherman's army entered Atlanta. This resounding Union victory, followed in October by Sheridan's conquest of the Shenandoah Valley, helped Lincoln win the election on November 8 by a far greater majority than anyone—including Lincoln himself—had expected. In the Electoral College, McClellan carried only Kentucky, Delaware, and New Jersey—all states with a large pro-Southern population.

Aggressive action against the Northern states by surprise raids and sudden forays from unexpected bases went on for months. Some were open warfare, like Early's lightning raid against Washington (July 6 to 14), when his troops came within sight of the Capitol dome and the President of the United States was under fire at Fort Stevens. Others were secret operations, some of them so carefully concealed that the full truth about them has never been fully revealed.

One especially interesting mission was the expedition to terrorize Yankee shipping along the coasts of New Jersey, Long Island, and New England, when the raider Tallahassee captured and burned vessels in that area. Only recently has it been shown that this apparently isolated raiding voyage was part of a much larger plot—a plot to stir up revolution in the Northern states and make their people call off the war.

To understand the complexities of this gigantic conspiracy one has to know who ran it. It was directed from Canada by three commissioners whom the Richmond government had appointed in April, 1864, to harrass the North by underground warfare.

These commissioners were an odd lot to direct a cloak-and-dagger operation of so vast dimensions. Their leader, Jacob Thompson, who had been a Congressman from Mississippi and Secretary of the Interior under Buchanan, was the ablest of them, yet he was not suited by training, nature, or physical constitution to head such a mission. His second in command, Clement C. Clay, who had been a Senator from Alabama until the outbreak of the war, was constantly in poor health and utterly lacking in forcefulness. He quarreled with Thompson as soon as they arrived in Canada; the two split up, with Thompson going to Toronto while Clay remained in Montreal with $93,614 in Confederate funds at his disposal, which enabled him to operate almost independently. The third member of the commission, James P. Holcombe, formerly a professor of law at the University of Virginia, was an erudite scholar, but he too was hardly the sort to be one of the heads of a secret mission.

On August 24, 1864, Holcombe left Halifax, presumably for Europe with dispatches for Mason and Slidell, the Confederate commissioners stationed there. Oddly enough, however, the ship he took was on its way to Wilmington, North Carolina. This was the Condor, the ill-fated blockade runner that was carrying Rose O'Neal Greenhow to her death in the breakers near Fort Fisher. Holcombe escaped drowning and went on to Richmond to advise Jefferson Davis that the underground effort against the North should be continued with undiminished vigor.

Helping the three Confederate commissioners in Canada were William C. Cleary, the secretary of the mission, George N. Sanders, and Beverley Tucker. Active on the military front were Thomas H. Hines, John B. Castleman, Robert Martin, John W. Headley, and others, many of whom had been with Morgan's raiders. The three heads of the mission seem to have floundered occasionally in their thinking and were sometimes hesitant in making decisions, but most of their subordinates were daring and ruthless. The group never lacked money. It spent hundreds of thousands—and perhaps millions—of dollars during its short existence. Much of the money came from the sale of contraband cotton; a good deal of it was taken by force from Northern banks, trains, express company safes, and Federal army-payroll funds.

One of the commissioners' first moves was to try to organize the Copperheads into an effective fighting force. The secret order of the Knights of the Golden Circle had become the Order of American Knights and was now masquerading under the name of the Sons of Liberty with the seriocomic Clement Vallandigham as its head. The Confederates in Canada made contact with all the dissident groups it could find and began an elaborate plot to promote revolution against the Federal Government in the Midwest. Efforts were also to be made to attack Maine, seize shipping on the Great Lakes, and burn the cities of the North.

The Confederates' most ambitious plan was the celebrated Northwestern Conspiracy, which was directed at Indiana, Illinois, Ohio, and the states bordering on them. On June 9, Hines met Vallandigham at Windsor, Ontario, where Thompson also came two days later. Vallandigham was cautious at first about committing himself and his followers, but he re-entered the United States breathing fire and using the threat of "a vast multitude" of determined men he could summon to his aid. He was soon glad to accept Confederate cash and outright support. The date of this first meeting between Vallandigham and Hines is significant. By the middle of June it was evident that Grant's fiercely launched spring campaign of 1864 had spent its force at Cold Harbor. Since there was much dissatisfaction with the war effort among the people of the North, the Confederates could not have chosen a better time to create dissension. This was also just after the Republican Convention on June 7, and the Confederates were eager to do everything possible to prevent the Lincoln administration from being reelected.

Plans were made to free thousands of Confederate prisoners who were being held in numerous camps throughout the Midwest. During the summer large quantities of weapons were purchased in Northern cities (despite the fact that there was a war on), and cases of them disguised as religious books were shipped west. Hines was given command of the Chicago area where Camp Douglas was a target, while John B. Castleman was sent to Rock Island, Illinois, which also had a large prison camp and a Government arsenal as well.

Two things—in addition to the Copperheads' own timidity— broke up the ambitiously planned Northwestern Conspiracy; one was the fact that informers in the Confederates' own ranks were selling out to the Federal authorities. The other was vigorous counterespionage on the part of the Northern government. In Indiana, where the strongly pro-Union governor, Oliver P. Morton, was willing to break with all precedent in order to stamp out Copperheadism in his state, a young man named Felix G. Stidger was acting as a spy, ferreting out the secrets of the underground organization by joining it and working his way to the top. It was the information he gathered that finally wrecked the Northwestern Conspiracy.

Again and again the Copperheads and their Confederate backers found themselves blocked just as they were about to go into action. When Morgan rode on his last raid—which was to be a signal for the Copperheads to rise—he was suddenly outnumbered and defeated by Federal cavalry. Stands of arms hidden by the Copperheads were then discovered and confiscated. Copperhead leaders were arrested, and even some of the secret Confederate agents from Canada were caught and sent to prison. The uprising planned for Chicago had to be postponed several times until it finally could not be put off any longer. August 29, the date set for the opening of the Democratic National Convention, was then chosen as the time for action. There would be thousands of "Peace" Democrats and Copperheads in the city then; a group of trained fighting men was to be sent in; and nearly six thousand Confederate prisoners in Camp Douglas were to be set free so they could all work together to terrorize northern Illinois. But informers in the Confederates' midst had tipped off Colonel Benjamin G. Sweet, the commandant of Camp Douglas, and several thousand Union soldiers were marched into Chicago before the convention was held. The plot collapsed without a blow being made anywhere. Hines said contemptuously that the Copperhead organizations were "as harmless as an association of children."

But if the Copperheads were scared children, the secret agents working with them were not. They were relatively few in number, but the most effective of them were soldiers with plenty of experience in guerrilla warfare. And even though their civilian leaders had no fighting experience, they were shrewd and cunning.

Inspired perhaps by the gold speculators' forged proclamation of May 18, Secretary of State Judah P. Benjamin in Richmond directed Jacob Thompson in Canada to undertake one of the cleverest moves of the war. Reporting to Benjamin later, Thompson told how he had plotted to upset the gold market in the United States by using adroit propaganda and a small amount of Confederate cash. He wrote that he had "urged the people in the North to convert their paper money into gold and withdraw it from the market. I am satisfied this policy was adopted and carried into effect to some extent, but how extensively I am unable to state. What effect it had on the gold market it is impossible to estimate, but certain it is that gold continued to appreciate until it went to 290. The high price may have tempted many to change their policy, because afterward gold fell in the market to 150. When it was about 180, and exportation of gold was so small that there appeared to be but little or no demand for it, Mr. John Porterfield, formerly a banker in Nashville, but now a resident of Montreal, was furnished with $100,000, and instructed to proceed to New York to carry out a financial policy of his own conception, which consisted in the purchase of gold and exporting the same, selling it for sterling bills of exchange, and then converting his exchange into gold. This process involved a certain loss, the cost of transshipment. He was instructed by Mr. Clay and myself to go on with his policy until he had expended $25,000, with which he supposed he would ship directly $5,000,000, and induce others to ship much more, and then, if the effect upon the gold market was not very perceptible, he was to desist and return to Canada and restore the money unexpended. By his last report he had caused the shipment of more than $2,-000,000 of gold at an expense of less than $10,000."

Confederate funds were also used to subvert certain Northern newspapers, notably the New York Daily News, whose editor, Phineas Wright, offered to influence public opinion in his journal for a cash payment of $25,000. A much larger sum was paid in Illinois in an unsuccessful effort to elect James C. Robinson, the Peace Democrats' candidate in 1864 for the governorship of Illinois. And John Bigelow, United States Consul General in France, reported from Paris on October 15 that a man carrying $15,000,000 in Federal greenbacks (probably counterfeit) was being sent to New York to bribe three hundred influential men—and ward heelers—to buy votes there. If he distributed the money it was wasted, for the 1864 electoral vote of New York State went to Lincoln.

The United States had a small warship, the U.S.S. Michigan, stationed on Lake Erie. Since she was the only armed vessel on the Great Lakes, officers in the Confederate Navy quickly saw her value, and as early as February 7, 1863, proposed a plan to capture her. This plan was accepted; then the Richmond government became wary about violating the neutrality laws and perhaps causing England "to stop the building of some ironclads which were on the stocks" there, so the plan was temporarily dropped. Later that year, when the prison camp on Johnson's Island near Sandusky, Ohio, was crowded with thousands of Confederate prisoners, Richmond was willing for a new attempt to be made to seize the Michigan and use her guns to force the commandant of the Johnson's Island camp to turn the prisoners loose. Twenty-two men, supplied with $110,000 in gold, were sent into Canada on October 7, 1863. They planned to embark on one of the many lake passenger steamers, overpower her officers, and use the captured ship to take the Michigan. But an informer told the Canadian government what they were doing. The Governor-General of Canada immediately notified Washington, and Stanton telegraphed to all the Lake cities to be on guard. This plot of 1863 to seize the Michigan had to be abandoned just as it was about to be put into effect.

In 1864 the Federal warship was still a tempting prize; on July 14, Jacob Thompson ordered Captain Charles H. Cole, of the Confederate Navy, to investigate the possibility of capturing her. Two months later the Confederates had their plans complete and were ready to act. While Cole dined and wined the Michigan's captain, whose acquaintance he had carefully cultivated, John Yates Beall, who had learned how to seize ships on Chesapeake Bay, was to capture the passenger steamer Philo Parsons and use it against the Michigan.

Beall and a trained crew disguised as civilians boarded the Philo Parsons, carrying an unusually heavy trunk loaded with firearms. They seized the ship on September 19 and then captured another passenger steamer, the Island Queen. They put the passengers of both ships ashore, sank the Island Queen, and proceeded toward Johnson's Island in the darkness. Signal rockets which were to be fired there did not appear, so it was evident that something had gone wrong. The crew grew uneasy, and begged Beall to abandon the attempt. The ship was turned around, taken to the Canadian side of the lake, and burned. Meanwhile, Cole, who had arranged to give an elaborate dinner on the Michigan that evening, was arrested at his hotel in Sandusky. Like so many of the other carefully conceived Confederate plots, the whole scheme came to nothing. Again an informer had revealed the details to Federal authorities. The parallel between this and the earlier plot of 1863 is amazingly close. The Confederates tried to use the same plan twice—and were twice betrayed by informers.

Election Day, November 8, was a crucial moment for the destiny of the United States. The future of the nation might have been decided on that day by means other than the ballot, for Confederate secret agents were making plans to create such havoc in Chicago and New York that voters would be kept away from the polls by a show of violence.

Disappointed in their effort to rouse the Copperheads into action on August 29, when the Democratic National Convention was held in Chicago, Hines and his men were going to make another try, this time without even seeking help from timorous Copperhead civilians. Again an effort was to be made to set free the Confederate prisoners in Camp Douglas, now numbering more than eight thousand, so they could collaborate with trained professional soldiers who were being sent into the city. And prisoners from nearby camps were also to be freed, armed, and banded together into military units to cut their way through miles of Union territory to rejoin the dwindling armies of the South.

But Federal detectives and Confederate informers again broke the conspiracy. On Sunday night, two days before the Presidential election was to be held, practically all the top Confederate agents working in Chicago—except the redoubtable Captain Hines—were arrested. Large stores of weapons and ammunition hidden by Confederate agents were seized and used to arm volunteers who patrolled the streets of Chicago to keep the peace on Election Day.

As soon as telegraphed word of this fiasco reached New York, the plans to terrorize that city on November 8 had to be postponed until later in the month. And the plans to take over the North's largest city, if they had been successful, would have attracted world-wide attention. According to James D. Horan: "In New York the United States Sub-Treasury on Wall Street was to be seized, City Hall turned into a fortress, Broadway to echo with the tramp of twenty thousand traitors. Policemen who were members of the Sons of Liberty would seize Police Headquarters on Worth Street. The Federal Courthouse and all government buildings were to be taken. Five cans of gunpowder buried under the main gate of Fort Lafayette in the Narrows off Brooklyn would be touched off to pierce the thick stone walls. General John A. Dix was to be held as a hostage in his own dungeon. All Confederate prisoners were to be released and armed. The Stars and Bars of the Confederacy would fly over City Hall in twilight's purple light. By nightfall, as one of them recalled, all New York City would be a sea of flames."

On July 24, 1864, there had appeared a mysterious notice in the Richmond Whig which may very well have been an appeal to adventurous-minded Southerners to join this scheme to bring violence to the civilian population of the North. It read:

THE DEVOTED BAND

It is believed that there are five or ten thousand men in the South ready and willing to share the fate of Curtius, and devote themselves to the salvation of their country. It is proposed that all who are willing to make this sacrifice shall arm themselves with a sword, two five-shooters, and a carbine each, and meet on horseback at some place to be designated, convenient for the great work in hand. Fire and sword must be carried into the houses of those who are visiting those blessings upon their neighbors. Philadelphia, and even New York, is not beyond the reach of a long and brave arm. The moral people of these cities cannot be better taught the virtues of invasion than by the blazing light of their own dwellings.

None need apply for admission to the "Devoted Band" but those who are prepared to take their lives in their hands, and would indulge not the least expectation of ever returning. They dedicate their lives to the destruction of their enemies.

A.S.B.D.B., Richmond

All Southern papers are requested to give this notice a few insertions.

Little attention was paid to this appeal when it first appeared, but after efforts were made to burn Northern cities, Union newspapers dug the neglected item out of their files and reprinted it widely.

The incendiary attempts began in Louisville in July, 1864, when several buildings at Main and Eighth streets, which were being used to store Federal military supplies, were set ablaze by the use of Greek Fire. The next move was made in Mattoon, Illinois, where army warehouses were set on fire by the ubiquitous Captain Hines. Then he and Castleman attacked Federal shipping along the St. Louis waterfront, again using Greek Fire, although they were becoming wary of its efficacy because it sometimes failed to burst into flame. Greek Fire was also employed by Bennett Young in his raid on St. Albans, Vermont, on October 19, but it received its main test in New York when the attack originally planned for

Election Day was finally put into effect on November 25 by Robert Martin, John W. Headley, and a few others. Fortunately, Headley left his own acount of this attempt, which was the last major overt act of Confederate underground warfare in the North. By this late date, many of the Confederacy's secret agents were in hiding, in prison, or dead. And the Confederacy itself was dying.

The Confederate Torpedo Service

by R. O. CROWLEY
from *Century Magazine*, June, 1898

[By 1864 the technology of warfare had advanced so far that both Confederate and Union naval forces were using steam-powered launches carrying a torpedo at the end of a long spar. Compare this account with the Union one by Lt. William B. Cushing of blowing up the ram *Albemarle* with a similar device, and it will be seen that the Confederate mechanism for exploding a spar torpedo by contact was much simpler than the elaborate Union method which called for exactly timed hand controls.

The Confederates, who were on the defensive, had more need for the protection of underwater explosive devices and mines than the Federals did. They had used a floating mine in the Potomac River even before Bull Run, for the U.S.S. Pawnee had discovered one there on July 10, 1861. And they planted small land mines at Yorktown in May, 1862, on the beaches around Charleston during the summer of 1863, and in the defenses before Richmond in the spring of 1865. Railroad torpedoes were also used on tracks to derail trains.

The men who developed the technology of torpedo warfare for the Confederates belonged to one of the most secret organizations in the South. Rains' Torpedo Bureau was headed by Gabriel James Rains, whose equally ingenious brother was in charge of manufacturing gunpowder. Rains met much opposition early in the war from other Confederate leaders who deplored the use of concealed lethal mechanisms against which there was then practically no protection; but, as is usual in an all-out war, Rains, as the exponent of ruthless methods won his point and persuaded Jefferson Davis to approve his new weapons.

The Confederates also used primitive submarines, which differed from torpedo launches only in that they were supposed to be submersible. These small cigar-shaped boats were exceedingly dangerous to operate, yet volunteers were always willing to try. One of these little "Davids"—as they were called—torpedoed the Federal sloop-of-war Housatonic near Charleston on February 17, 1864. The ship was seriously damaged; but the submarine and its crew were lost in the attempt.

Another method of destroying Union shipping was to use a bomb disguised as a large piece of coal. This was mixed with the regular coal put aboard the ship; when it was thrown into a hot furnace, the explosion would blow up the boiler and sometimes sink the ship. One of these coal-bombs wrecked General Butler's headquarters' ship while he and Admiral Porter were on board it. The unloaded shell of another was found on Jefferson Davis' desk when Union troops entered Richmond on April 3, 1865.

Oddly enough, the author of the following article does not mention Rains' contribution to the development of the torpedo although the organization for which Crowley worked as an electrician was called Rains' Torpedo Bureau.]

At the outbreak of the war, one of the most pressing needs of the Confederacy was some effective method of defending its water approaches, especially the James River, leading direct to Richmond, its capital city. The South had no ships of war, and the few old-fashioned brick-and-mortar forts . . . were mostly armed with smooth-bore iron cannon, relics of a past age, and rusty from neglect.

To look back now, it seems wonderful how very defenseless

we were at the start, and how apparently easy it would have been for a single second-class war vessel to have steamed up to Richmond in the early days of the conflict. For the defense of the rivers, men's minds turned toward torpedoes, which were then but little known in the military world. Scores of plans were submitted to the War and Navy departments, some advocating mechanical torpedoes—that is, those which exploded by contact or by timed mechanism—others strenuously urging electrical torpedoes. Those generally intended for use on land naturally fell into the hands of the War Department, while electrical torpedoes for use under water came within the province of the Navy Department.

The idea of using torpedoes on the Confederate side originated, I believe, with the Hon. S. R. Mallory, Secretary of the Navy; and he directed the distinguished Captain M. F. Maury to make experiments, with a view to their general employment, if practicable. His work began in the spring of 1862, and continued for a few months only with electrical torpedoes. He had arrived at no definite conclusion from his experiments when he was despatched on an important mission to Europe, where he continued to make experiments in electricity applicable to torpedo warfare, discovering an ingenious method of arranging and testing mines.

At that time the Federal government had no system of torpedoes; indeed, they did not consider it "honorable warfare." They had no necessity for submarine defenses, because early in the war we had no ships to attack them. Frequent reports reached us that they intended to hang or shoot any man they should capture who was engaged in the torpedo business. It was, therefore, a very risky business on our part, as we were constantly exposed to [the chance of] capture. . . .

The experiments made under the supervision of Captain Maury consisted of placing a series of hollow spherical shells of iron, containing about fifty pounds of powder, and extending across the bottom of the river, and connecting them electrically by insulated copper wires leading to galvanic batteries on shore. Inside these, shells' fuses were placed, which were to be ignited by the passage of an electric current through a fine platinum wire.

It was confidently expected that the simultaneous explosion of these shells under a passing vessel would instantaneously destroy the vessel and all on board. Experiments soon demonstrated, however, that fifty pounds of powder in from ten to fifteen feet of water would scarcely do any harm; and very soon the whole plant was entirely disarranged, the wires broken, and the shells lost, by a heavy freshet in the river.

Captain Maury was succeeded by Lieutenant Hunter Davidson, and it was at this time that the writer was appointed electrician of the Torpedo Division. Our headquarters were on board a small but swift steam-tug called the *Torpedo*, and two Parrott rifles were put aboard of her for emergencies. In the cabin of this little steamer we studied, planned, and experimented for months with various fuses, galvanic batteries, etc., and finally we determined on a system.

Our first object was to prepare a sensitive fuse of fulminate of mercury, to be exploded by . . . electricity. We succeeded in this, and our fuses were made by taking a piece of quill, half an inch long, and filling it with fulminate of mercury. Each end of the quill was sealed with beeswax, after fixing a fine platinum wire through the center of the quill and connecting . . . the protruding ends of the platinum wire with insulated copper wire. Enveloping the fuse was a red-flannel cartridge-bag stuffed with rifle-powder. The fuse, thus prepared, was ready to be placed in a torpedo-tank containing cannon-powder.

I have been thus particular in describing the fuse because on it depends entirely the certainty of explosion. Our torpedo-tanks were made of half-inch boiler iron. There was an opening to pour in the powder and to receive the fuse. The opening was then fitted with a screw-plug, in which there were two holes for the passage of the wires, and packed with greased cotton waste to prevent leakage of water to the inside. There was a heavy ring by which the tank was slung into position, and through this ring was passed a heavy iron chain attached to a mushroom anchor about twenty feet distant. . . .

We experimented a long time with tanks of various sizes, and at various depths of water, and finally decided that a tank containing two thousands pounds of cannon-powder was sure to destroy utterly a ship of any size at a depth of not more than thirty feet.

To give some idea of the many difficulties we encountered, I will mention, first, the scarcity of cannon-powder; secondly, we had only about four miles of insulated copper wire in the entire Confederacy; thirdly, we could obtain only about four or five feet of fine-gage platinum wire. Battery material was very scarce, and acids could be purchased only from the small quantity remaining in the hands of druggists when the war broke out.

In the autumn of 1862 we planted three of these copper torpedoes, each containing one hundred and fifty pounds of powder, in the Rappahannock River, below Port Royal, the intention being to destroy any Federal gunboat passing up. Our plans, however, were disclosed to the enemy by a Negro, and no attempt was made to steam over the torpedoes. In December of that year, when Burnside was about to attack at Fredericksburg, it was deemed prudent to abandon our station near Port Royal, to avoid being cut off if the Federal army should succeed in making Lee retreat.

To this end, I was instructed to proceed without delay to Port Royal, to save all the wire possible, and bring off our galvanic batteries and other material. This was a hazardous undertaking, as our station was outside the Confederate lines, and the enemy was in strong force on the opposite bank of the Rappahannock. In pursuance of orders, I arrived at the station about sunset one evening, and after making due preparations for the transportation of our men and material, the galvanic battery was charged and the circuit closed, and a tremendous explosion took place, throwing up large columns of water, and arousing the inhabitants for miles around. . . .

Having our system now perfected, we established a torpedo station, some five or six miles below Richmond, by submerging two iron tanks, containing one thousand pounds of powder each, in twelve feet of water, leading the wires ashore, and connecting them with a galvanic battery concealed in a small hut in a deep ravine. From the battery-house the wires were led to an elevated position near by, where the man in charge could keep a lookout for passing vessels. The position of the torpedoes in the water was indicated by two sticks, planted about ten feet apart on the bluff, and in a line with each other and the torpedoes; and the watchman's instructions were to explode them by contacting the wires as soon as an enemy's vessel should be on a line with the two pointers. All this being prepared, we awaited the approach of a Federal gunboat. As was usually the case, one came when least expected, on a beautiful clear day, when our entire force except the man stationed as lookout was absent in Richmond, preparing other war material.

We were apprised by telegraph of the rapid approach of the gunboat, and immediately hastened toward our first station; but we arrived too late. The man in charge had not seen the United States flag for a long period, and never having previously seen a gunboat so near, lost his presence of mind, and fired one of the 1,000-pound powder-tanks when the gunboat was at least twenty to thirty yards distant. A great explosion took place, throwing up a large column of water to a considerable height; and the gunboat by her momentum plunged into the great trough, and caught the downward rush of a wave on her forward deck. The guards were broken away, half a dozen men were thrown overboard, and other damage to the gunboat was caused. The steamer then turned about as quickly as she could, and prepared to retrace her route down the river, after picking up the men who had been washed overboard. There was a brilliant opportunity to accomplish her total destruction by firing the remaining torpedo as she passed back over it. But alas! the man had been so astounded at the first explosion that he had fled. . . .

The partial success of this attempt at exploding torpedoes by electricity immediately established the reputation of the Torpedo Division, and created great excitement all over the South, it being an undisputed fact that but for this explosion a Federal gunboat would have been moored at the wharf at Richmond that morning, and would have captured the city. . . .

Immediate steps were now taken to establish other torpedo stations at several points lower down the river, using in every instance 2,000 pound torpedoes. . . . The lowest torpedo station was at a place called Deep Bottom, about five miles above City Point by land, but more by water. As there were a good many free Negroes in the vicinity of Deep Bottom, we had to do our work with great secrecy, generally planting the torpedoes at night, in a position previously surveyed by day. At Deep Bottom we located the galvanic battery on the right bank of the river, in a pit about four or five feet deep, the top covered over with twigs and brush, and another pit, some distance off, a place was prepared for the lookout; this pit was also concealed by twigs and brush.

We were duly advised of the advance of General Butler's army from Bermuda Hundred toward Drewry's Bluff [in May, 1864], the entire Federal fleet also advancing up the river. . . . The Federals had been told by the Negroes that there were torpedoes at Deep Bottom, and used great caution in advancing. As soon as the fleet rounded the point below Presque Isle, the Federals began shelling our tower, and it was soon demolished; but no one was hurt, as our men took away the telegraph instruments, and rapidly retreated up the river road. A force of marines was landed on both sides of the river, in order to discover the whereabouts of our batteries. A squadron of boats, heavily armed, went into advance of the fleet, dragging the river for wires and torpedoes. Their grapnels, however, passed over our wires, without producing any damage; our lookout, from his concealed station in the pit, noting all the movements of the men in the boats, and hearing every word of command. After a while the Federal commander, apparently satisfied that there were no torpedoes there, ordered the *Commodore Jones,* a double-ender gunboat carrying eight guns and manned by a force of two hundred men, to move up to Deep Bottom, make a landing, and report. This was done, the gunboat passing over our torpedoes; but our man in the [lookout] pit kept cool, and did not explode them, because, as he afterward said, he wanted to destroy the ironclad *Atlanta,* recently captured by the Federals from us near Savannah, Georgia.

The *Commodore Jones* steamed up to the wharf at Deep Bottom, and found our quarters deserted. This looked suspicious, and the order was then given for her to fall back. Our man now concluded that the entire fleet would retire, and he determined to destroy the *Commodore Jones.* As she retreated she passed immediately over one of the two torpedoes planted there. All at once a terrific explosion shattered her into fragments, some of the pieces going a hundred feet in the air. Men were thrown overboard and drowned, about forty being instantly killed. The whole Federal fleet then retreated some distance below.

The Federal marines on shore continued their explorations, and our man in the battery-pit suddenly jumped out, and was as suddenly killed by a shot from the marines. The small boats again began dragging for our wires, and finally caught them, and by underrunning them to the shore at length discovered the man in the lookout pit, who was immediately taken prisoner and carried on board one of the vessels composing the fleet. He was subsequently imprisoned at Fort Warren, but about a year afterward was exchanged. Both he and his assistant, when taken aboard the fleet, were securely placed in a conspicuous position on the wheel-house of a double-ender gunboat—the foremost vessel—in order, as they were told, that if any further explosion took place they should share the consequences.

Thus was accomplished at one blow . . . the complete destruction of a war steamer by submarine torpedoes. So far as I know, it was the first instance of the kind in the annals of war. Its effect astonished the world, and its immediate result was the safety of Richmond from a second peril. . . .

So far we had been acting on the defensive, and the torpedoes described might be called defensive torpedoes. It was now determined to apply offensive torpedoes; if the enemy would not come to us to be blown up, we would go to them.

The first thing to be done was to prepare a fuse which was not dangerous to handle, and which would explode quickly on contact with any substance.

To this end we made some sheet-lead tubes, the rounded end being of much thinner lead than the other part.

These tubes were about three inches long and one inch in diameter. Into this tube was inserted a small glass tube, of similar shape, filled with sulphuric acid, and hermetically sealed. The vacant space about the glass tube was then tightly packed with a mixture of chlorate of potash and pulverized white sugar, and the mouth of the lead tube was closed by fastening a strip of muslin over it.

Now, if the rounded end of the leaden tube is brought into contact with any hard substance, the thin lead will be smashed, the interior glass tube broken, and the sulphuric acid becoming mixed with the preparation of chlorate of potash and sugar, an immediate explosion is the result. We then prepared a copper

215

cylinder capable of containing about fifty pounds of powder, and placed several of the leaden fuses in the head, so that no matter at what angle the butt struck the hull of a ship, one of the fuses would be smashed in, and flame from the potash and sugar ignite the powder. At the bottom of the copper cylinder there was a socket made to fit on the end of a spar.

We discussed the matter of exploding spar torpedoes by electricity, but the difficulty of arranging a contrivance to close the electric circuit when the torpedo came in contact with the hull of a ship, and want of conveniences for stowing a galvanic battery in the launch, induced us to adopt the fuses above mentioned instead.

This was a formidable weapon, and one extremely dangerous to handle. We first experimented with an empty cylinder fitted with leaden fuses. The copper cylinder was fastened to a spar attached to the bow of a small steam-launch. Thus prepared, we "rammed" an old bulkhead, or wharf, at Rocketts, in the lower part of Richmond, at first unsuccessfully. We then tried it loaded with twenty-five pounds of powder, and, lowering the spar torpedo about two feet under water, again rammed the bulkhead. The effect of the explosion shattered the old wharf and threw up a column of water, completely drenching the occupants of the launch.

Our steam-launch, or "torpedo launch," as it was called, was prepared for an expedition against the enemy's fleet snugly anchored off Newport News. Just at this time a new difficulty presented itself. The launch burned bituminous coal, the smoke from which could be discerned at a long distance, and the sparks from which at night would disclose its presence to an enemy. Some one suggested that we might obtain anthracite coal by dredging at the wharves and in the docks at Richmond. This was accordingly done, and we obtained a supply of the anthracite, for which an almost fabulous sum was paid.

Our launch was about twenty feet long, about five feet beam, and drew three feet of water. She was fitted with a small double [steam] engine amidships, and there was sufficient space in her bow for three men, and aft for an engineer, who also acted as fireman. An iron shield was then fixed on her, completely covering the men from plunging rifle-shots.

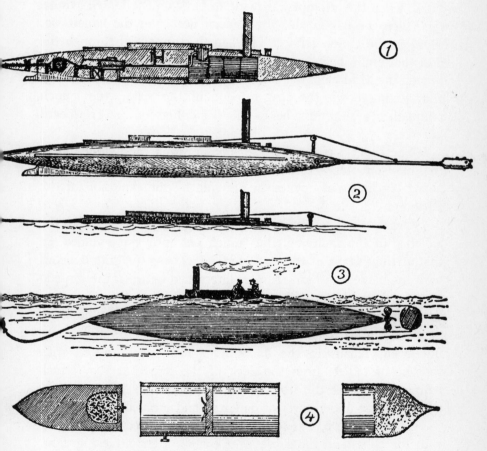

CONFEDERATE SUBMARINES AND TORPEDOES

1. A Confederate "David" shown equipped with a steam engine 2. A Confederate Torpedo Boat with a contact torpedo carried ahead on a long spar 3. A Confederate torpedo boat, as described by an observer 4. A Confederate spar torpedo

Thus equipped, and all being ready, we towed the launch down the James River on a dark night, to a point about ten or fifteen miles below City Point, and then let her go on her dangerous mission. . . .

She steamed down toward Newport News until the approach of daylight, and then hid in a swamp until the next night [April 9, 1864], when the attempt was made to blow up the U.S.S. *Minnesota*, then the flag-ship of the Federal fleet, and the largest war vessel in the Union service. The launch steamed all through the fleet that night, being frequently challenged by the deck lookouts. Finally the *Minnesota* was seen looming up grimly in the darkness, and, letting down the spar torpedo in the water, the launch rammed the ship just below the water-line on her starboard quarter.

The effect was terriffic, the shock causing the *Minnesota* to tremble from stem to stern. Several of her guns were dismounted and a big hole was opened in her side by the explosion of the 50-pound torpedo.

Owing to the strong tide prevailing at the time, and the violence of the ramming, the launch perceptibly rebounded, so that at the instant of the explosion, which was not simultaneous with the blow, a cushion of water intervened between the torpedo and the hull of the *Minnesota*, thus weakening the effect and probably saving the ship. She was so thoroughly disabled, however, as we afterward understood, that she had to be towed off, and underwent repairs in the docks. Our men were greeted with showers of bullets from the deck of the ship, but they struck harmlessly against the iron shield of the launch which quickly steamed away under cover of darkness, and escaped.

This, I believe, was the first instance of successful ramming with torpedoes and the subsequent escape of the attacking crew, most other cases happening subsequently resulting in the death or capture of the attacking party.

The Tallahassee Terrifies New York and New England

by JOHN TAYLOR WOOD

from *Century Magazine*, July, 1898

[The captain of a Confederate raider tells here how he attacked
Yankee ships along the coast from North Carolina to Canada during the summer of 1864. He planned to run into New York
Harbor, set fire to the shipping there, bombard the Brooklyn Navy
Yard, and dash up the East River to Long Island Sound. In 1898,
when this account was first printed, no more was known about the
real purpose of the Tallahassee's adventurous cruise than her captain admits to here.

When the Baker-Turner papers in the National Archives
were made public in September, 1953, James Horan discovered
the facts behind the Tallahassee's voyage. In his book, Confederate
Agent, he showed that the raider's northward cruise was part of a
conspiracy to invade the state of Maine. During the summer of
1864, a number of Confederate topographers had been sent to the
Maine coast to pose as artists while they mapped isolated bays
and harbors. Troops, officered by trained guerrilla leaders from
Morgan's, Wheeler's, and Stuart's commands, were to be brought
to Maine by blockade runners. There they were to be joined by
more troops sent from Canada. The Confederate raider Florida
was to work with the Tallahassee in this bold attempt to seize a
New England state. And the whole effort, which was closely tied

219

in with the Northwestern Conspiracy, was directed by the Confederate commissioners in Canada.

Before the complicated machine of this elaborate plot could be put into action, three of the men connected with the scheme tried to hold up a bank in the border town of Calais, Maine, on July 16, 1864. The local people had been tipped off that the three Confederates were on their way and had a sheriff's posse waiting for them when they arrived. After their arrest, one of them, Francis Jones, made a complete confession. Assistant Judge Advocate.L. C. Turner was sent from Washington to Maine to conduct a secret inquiry. He suppressed the testimony so successfully that no word of the plot to attack Maine appeared until 1954 when Horan's book was published.]

AMONG THE STEAMERS coming to Wilmington I had long been on the lookout for a cruiser, and finally selected the *Atlanta*, an iron twin-screw of seven-hundred tons gross, and two-hundred feet long. She had been built at Millwall, below London, ostensibly for the Chinese opium trade; and was a first-class, well-constructed vessel . . . making fourteen and a quarter knots on her trial trip. She had two engines, which could be worked together or separately. The necessary changes were soon made to receive the crew and armament. The latter consisted of one rifled 100-pounder amidships, one rifled, 60-hundredweight 32-pounder forward, and one long Parrott aft. The officers and crew were all volunteers from . . . Confederate gunboats. . . . She was formally put in commission on July 20, 1864, and rechristened the *Tallahassee*. . . .

Ten days sufficed to get things in working order, and the crew into shape, when we dropped down the river to wait a favorable time for running the gantlet, which was only when there was no moon and when the tide served. . . . Everything was secured for sea. The lights were all carefully housed, except the binnacle, which was shaded; fires were cleaned and freshened, lookouts were stationed, and the men were at their quarters. The range lights were placed; these, in the absence of all buoys and lights, were necessary in crossing the bar, and were shown only when vessels were going in and out. . . .

Steaming down to Fort Caswell, we waited in darkness. . . . As the moon went down on the night of August 6, at ten, we approached the bar. . . . and as the leadsman called out the water in a low tone, our hearts rose in our throats as it shoaled: "By the mark three, —and a quarter less three, —and a half two, —and a quarter two." She touched, but did not bring up. Then came the joyful words: "And a half two."

We had just grazed the "Lump," a bad shoal in mid-channel, and were over the bar. Chief Engineer Tynan was by my side on the bridge. I turned to him and said: "Open her out, sir, but let her go for all she is worth." With a bound he was in the engine-room, and in a few moments I knew from the tremor of the vessel that the order was obeyed, and with a full head of steam we leaped on. "A sharp lookout ahead!" was the order passed forward. We were hardly clear of the bar when back came the words: "A steamer on the starboard bow! A steamer ahead!" The two made us out at the same time, and signaled. I hailed the forecastle, and asked how the steamer under our bows was heading. "To the southward," was the reply. The helm was accordingly ported, and we passed between them, so close under the stern of the one that was ahead that a biscuit could have been tossed on board. As we dashed by we heard the sharp, quick words of command of the officer in charge of the after pivot: "Run out!—Starboard tackle handsomely!—Elevate!—Steady!—Stand clear!" Then the flash from the muzzle, like a gleam of lightning, illumined the water for a moment, and a heavy shell flew singing over our heads, leaving a trail like a comet. It was an excellent line shot. That order, "Elevate" had saved us. The steamer on the starboard side opened and our opponents, now on our quarter, joined in; but their practice was wild, and in a few moments they were out of sight. I did not return their fire, for it would only have shown our position, and I did not wish our true character to be known, preferring that they should suppose us an ordinary blockade-runner.

During the night we ran to the southward until clear of Frying-Pan Shoals, and then hauled up to the eastward. More to be feared than the inshore squadron were the vessels cruising offshore from forty to fifty miles, in a position to sight at daylight the vessels that might come out during the night, and these were the fastest and most efficient blockaders. I was not surprised when at daylight the next morning, a cruiser was reported in sight astern, hull up. As we were outlined against the eastern sky, she had seen us first, and from the dense smoke issuing from her funnel I knew she was in sharp chase. At eight another steamer was made out ahead. I changed our course eight points, bringing one on each beam, and the chase became interesting. One we made out to be a large side-wheeler, and she held her own, if she did not gain. Mr. Tynan made frequent visits to the engineroom, trying to coax out a few more revolutions; and he succeeded, for we brought them gradually on our quarter, and by noon had lowered their hulls two or three strakes. It was at times like this that the ship and engines proved themselves reliable; for had a screw loosened or a journal heated we should have been lost.

The ship was very deep with an extra supply of coal, and probably out of trim, so we were prepared, if hard pressed, to sacrifice some of it. Fortunately it was calm, and they could not use their canvas to help them. . . . By 4 P.M. our pursuers were astern, hull down, and had evidently given up. About the same time another was sighted from the masthead; but by changing our course a few points she was kept at a respectful distance. Just after dark we were nearly on top of another before we could change our course. Burning a blue light, the stranger headed for us. As we did not answer her signal, it was repeated, and a minute later she opened fire. The shells passed uncomfortably near, but in a half-hour we lost sight of each other. . . . The fact that we were chased by four cruisers on our first day out proved how effective was the blockade. Upward of fifty vessels were employed at this time outside the port of Wilmington—vessels of all kinds, from the 40-gun frigate to the captured tinplate blockade-runner—a larger number than were ever before employed on like service at one port.

The next few days were uneventful. We stood to the northward and eastward, under easy steam, and spoke several English and foreign vessels, from one of which we got late New York papers. Twenty miles below Long Branch [New Jersey] we made our first prize, the schooner *Sarah A. Boice* of Boston, for Philadelphia in ballast. Her crew and their personal effects were brought on board, and she was scuttled. In all cases the prisoners were allowed to retain a bag of their clothes; nor were they asked for their money, watches, etc. In one case it was reported to me that one of the crew had taken a watch from a prisoner; this being found to be true, it was returned, and the man was punished. The chronometers, charts, and medicine-chests were the only things taken out of the prizes, except such provisions as were necessary.

Standing over toward Fire Island Light, on the Long Island shore, we found seven sail in sight. One ran down toward us, which we recognized at once as a New York pilot-boat. She luffed to under our quarter, launched a small boat, and a few minutes later a large well-dressed man in black, with a high hat, heavy gold watch-guard, a small valise, and a bundle of papers under his arm, stepped over the side. As he did so his eyes glanced up at our flag at the peak, which was lazily unfolding in a light breeze.

"My_____! What is that? What ship is this?" said he.

"The Confederate cruiser *Tallahassee*," I replied.

A more astonished man never stood on deck of vessel. He turned deadly pale, and drops of perspiration broke from every pore; but rapidly bracing himself, he took in the situation, and prepared to make the best of it. He was told that his vessel was a prize, and that I would make a tender of her. He was ordered to go on board, and return with his crew and their personal effects. It was the pilot-boat *James Funk*, No. 22, one of a class of fine weatherly schooners found off New York, from one to two hundred miles out, at all seasons. . . .

I put on board two officers and twenty men, with orders to keep within signal distance. She was very efficient when several sail were in sight, overhauling and bringing alongside vessels, that I might decide upon their fate. The captures of the bark *Bay State* and the brigs *Carrie Estelle* and *A. Richards* followed in quick succession. We had now over forty prisoners and their baggage on board, lumbering up our decks, and it was necessary to make some disposition of them. Toward night No. 22 brought alongside the schooner *Carroll*. She was bonded by the captain, acting for the owners, for ten thousand dollars; and after he had given a written engagement to land the prisoners at New York, they went on board with their effects. . . .

The next victim was another pilot-boat, the *William Bell*, No. 24. My object in capturing these vessels was, if possible, to secure a pilot who could either be paid or coerced to take the ship through Hell Gate into Long Island Sound. It was now near the full moon. It was my intention to run up the harbor just after dark, as I knew the way in by Sandy Hook, then to go on up the East River, setting fire to the shipping on both sides, and when abreast of the navy-yard to open fire, hoping some of our shells might set fire to the buildings and any vessels that might be at the docks, and finally to steam through Hell Gate into the Sound. I knew from the daily papers, which we received only a day or two old, what vessels were in port, and that there was nothing then ready that could oppose us. But no pilot could be found who knew the road, or who was willing to undertake it, and I was forced to abandon the scheme.

From these inquiries arose the report that I would attempt to enter the harbor. Three days were spent between the light-ship and Montauk Point, sometimes within thirty miles of the former —and about twenty prizes were taken. The most important was the packetship *Adriatic*, one thousand tons, from London, with a large and valuable cargo and one hundred and seventy passengers. On account of the latter I was afraid I would have to bond the ship; but fortunately our tender came down before the wind, convoying the bark *Suliote*, and I determined to use her as a cartel after the captain had given bonds for ten thousand dollars. She was laden with coal; but the distance to Sandy Hook was only seventy miles. The passengers were nearly all Germans, and when told that their ship was to be burned were terribly alarmed; and it was some time before they could comprehend that we did not intend to burn them also. Three hours were occupied in transferring them and their effects with our boats. In many cases they insisted upon taking broken china, bird-cages, straw beds, and the most useless articles, leaving their valuables behind. After all were safely on board the *Suliote*, the *Adriatic* was fired and as night came on the burning ship illuminated the waters for miles, making a picture of rare beauty. The breeze was light and tantalizing, so our tender was taken in tow, and we steamed slowly to the eastward toward Nantucket. The neighborhood of New York had been sufficiently worked, and the game was alarmed and scarce.

Rounding South Shoal light-ship, we stood in toward Boston Bay. As the tender proved a drawback to our rapid movements, I determined to destroy her. It was a mistake, for I was authorized by the government to fit out any prize as a cruiser, and this one ought to have been sent along the eastern coast. A number of sail were sighted, but most of them were foreigners; this could be told by the "cut of their jibs." It was not necessary to speak them. A few unimportant captures were made, and then we sighted a large bark. First Lieutenant Ward, the boarding officer, returned, and reported the *Glenarvon*, Captain Watt, a fine new vessel of Thomaston, Maine, from Glasgow with iron. He was ordered to return and secure the nautical instruments, etc., and scuttle her, and bring on board the prisoners. The captain had his wife on board, and as passengers another captain returning home with his wife—an elderly pair. We watched the bark as she slowly settled, strake by strake, until her deck was awash, and then her stern sank gradually out of sight until she was in an upright position, and one mast after another disappeared with all sail set, sinking as quietly as if human hands were lowering her into the depths. Hardly a ripple broke the quiet waters. Her head spars were the last seen. Captain Watt and his wife never took their eyes off their floating home, but side by side, with tears in their eyes, watched her disappear. "Poor fellow," she said afterward; "he has been going to sea for thirty years, and all our savings were in that ship. We were saving for our dear children at home—five of them."

Miserable business is war, ashore or afloat. A brave, true, and gentle woman, at the same time strong in her conviction of what she thought right, was the captain's wife, and she soon won the admiration and respect of all on board. But what shall I say of the passenger and his wife? If I said she was the very reverse of the above, it would not begin to do her justice. She came on board scolding, and left scolding. Her tongue was slung amidships, and never tired. Her poor husband, patient and meek as the patriarch, came in for his full share. Perhaps the surroundings and the salt air acted as an irritant, for I can hardly conceive of this cataract of words poured on a man's head on shore without something desperate happening. . . .

I gave them my cabin; indeed, from the time of leaving Wilmington I had but little use of it. I slept and lived on the bridge or in the chart-room, hardly taking off my clothes for weeks.

We ran along the eastern coast as far as Matinicus, Maine, but overhauled nothing of importance. . . . Steering to the eastward round . . . the western extremity of Nova Scotia, we, of course, had our share of the "ever-brooding, all concealing fog . . . ." Suddenly, one evening, the fog lifted, and we discovered a ship close aboard. Passing under her stern, we read *James Little-field* of Bangor. Hailing the captain, and asking him where from, and where bound, "From Cardiff, with coals for New York," came back as his answer. . . . Lieutenant Ward was sent on board to take charge . . . and keep within one or two cable-lengths of the steamer. As the night closed in the fog became denser than ever, so much so that one end of the vessel could not be seen from the other. . . . For some hours, by blowing our whistle every five minutes, while the ship was ringing a bell, we kept within sound of each other. But the latter gradually grew duller, until we lost it altogether; and I spent an anxious night. . . . But soon after sunrise a rift in the fog, disclosing a small sector of the horizon, showed us the ship some five miles away. Steaming alongside, I determined to take no more risks in the fog. Banking our fires, we passed a hawser from our bows to the ship's quarter, and let her tow us. I held on to the ship, hoping it would become smooth enough to lay the two vessels alongside and take out a supply of coals. . . . The day passed without change in weather or sea, and very reluctantly I was compelled to abandon the hope of free coals, and look to Halifax for a supply. Ordering Lieutenant Ward to scuttle the ship, we left her to be a home for the cod. . . .

After being two or three days without observations and without a departure, to find your port in a thick fog requires a sharp lookout and a constant use of the lead. However, we made a good hit. The first "land" we made was the red head of a fisherman, close under our bows, in a small boat, who . . . in words more forcible than complimentary, warned us against tearing his nets. In answer to our inquiries . . . he offered to pilot the ship in. Accepting his services, and taking his boat in tow, we stood up the harbor. Soon . . . the city of Halifax was in sight.

The harbor of Halifax is well known as safe, commodious, easy of access, and offering many advantages. Coming to anchor, I had my gig manned, and went on board the line-of-battle ship *Duncan*, to call upon Sir James Hope, commanding on this station, and then upon the governor, Sir Richard Graves MacDonald, who received me very kindly, asking me to breakfast next morning, a compliment which I was obliged to decline, owing to the limited time at my disposal. By the Queen's proclamation, the belligerents could use her ports only for twenty-four hours, except in case of distress, and take no supplies, except sufficient to reach the nearest home port. I wanted only coal, and . . . I was able to procure a supply of the best Welsh. . . .

Immediate preparations were made for sea. During the day two or more of the enemy's cruisers were reported off the harbor; indeed, one came in near enough to communicate with the shore. During our stay we had seen late New York papers with accounts of our cruise, and the excitement it had caused on the seaboard. The published reports of most of the prisoners were highly colored and sensational. We were described in anything but complimentary terms. A more blood-thirsty or piratical-looking crew never sailed, according to some narratives.

The run down the coast was uneventful, a few unimportant prizes being made. Many vessels were spoken, but most were foreign. A number were undoubtedly American, but to avoid capture had been registered abroad, and were sailing under other flags. . . . As we approached Wilmington we were reminded, by sighting one or two steamers, that we were again in troubled waters. . . .

The weather was hazy and smoky—so much so that we could not depend on our sights. I therefore ran in toward Masonboro Inlet, about thirty miles to the northward of Fort Fisher, making the land just at dark; then ran into five fathoms, and followed the shore, just outside the breakers curling up on the beach. A sharp lookout was kept, and the crew were at their quarters. The fires were freshened, and watched carefully to avoid smoking or flaming. The chief engineer had orders to get all he could out of her. I knew that one of the blockaders, if not more, would be found close to the shore; and soon one was made out ahead. I tried to pass inside, but found it impossible; the enemy's ship was almost in the surf. A vigilant officer certainly was in command. Our helm was put a-starboard, and we sheered out. At the same time the enemy signaled by flash-lights. I replied by burning a blue light. The signal was repeated by the first and by two others. I replied again by a false fire. Some valuable minutes were gained, but the enemy now appeared satisfied as to our character, and opened fire. We replied with all our battery, directing our guns by the flash of theirs. This was entirely unexpected, for they ceased firing, and began to signal again. Our reply was another broadside, to which they were not slow in responding. The *Tallahassee* was now heading the bar, going fourteen knots. Two or three others joined in the firing, and for some time it was very lively. But, like most night engagements, it was random firing. We were not struck, and the enemy were in more danger from their own fire than from mine.

Soon the Mound loomed up ahead, a welcome sight. Our signal-officer made our number to Fort Fisher, and it was answered. A few minutes later the range lights were set, and by their guidance we safely crossed the bar and anchored close under the fort. The next morning, at daybreak, the blockading fleet was seen lying about five miles off, all in a bunch, evidently discussing the events of the night. At sunrise we hoisted the Confederate flag at the fore, and saluted with twenty-one guns. The fort returned a like number. During the day we crossed the rip, and proceeded up the river to Wilmington. So ended an exciting and eventful cruise of a month. In this time we had made thirty-five captures, about half of which were square-rigged vessels.

The Explosion at City Point

by MORRIS SCHAFF

from *Civil War Papers of the State of Massachusetts,*
Vol. II, 1900

[On July 30, 1864, at 4:55 A.M., Union soldiers exploded the most powerful mine of the war; it had been placed by tunneling under the Confederate earthworks surrounding Petersburg. It was a disastrous failure as a means of attack, but it left a gigantic crater which still remains. A few days later, Confederates in that area set off a smaller and equally unsuccessful mine. On August 11, perhaps in retaliation for the big Petersburg mine, the Confederates used a clockwork bomb to blow up ships, docks, and warehouses at City Point (now Hopewell), Virginia, where Grant had his supply base for what was promising to be a long-drawn-out siege of Petersburg and Richmond.

High above the railroad terminal at the docks stood—and still stands—the beautiful old Eppes Mansion, located at the confluence of the James and Appomattox Rivers. General Grant and his staff had their headquarters' tents and cabins on the grounds of this historic estate, and it was from there that the final Union effort to end the war was to be launched in the spring of 1865. There, too, Lincoln was to come in March, 1865, to discuss peace terms with his military chiefs.

The terrible damage done by the Confederate bomb was quickly repaired, and fresh shipments of arms and ammunition were sent to City Point in time for the spring campaign. Within *a few months the vast Union supply base was again in full operation.*]

ON THE 11TH OF AUGUST [1864] the Confederates blew up the ordnance depot under my charge at City Point, killing over two hundred, wounding many, and fearfully maiming others, besides destroying over $2,000,000 of property.

It is not a matter of any historic interest or value whatever, that I was playing "Seven-up" at the moment of the explosion, yet sometimes the bare facts of an event are most vividly realized and longest remembered through the small details that give them a real human interest. However this may be, on the morning of the explosion Captain . . . Evans of the regulars, came to my office . . . on the bluff . . . perhaps one hundred and fifty yards back from the wharf.

The day was very hot, and knowing that my friend of the regulars was as dry as the rest of them that came down from the lines, I wished to show him the customary and most acceptable hospitality. I went to my demijohn and much to my surprise found it was empty. Evans must have looked especially despondent, for I said, "Come over to Grant's Headquarters; I know where I can get some," having in mind my friend Captain Mason of the 6th Regulars, who commanded Grant's escort. It was only a step, perhaps a hundred yards. When we reached the tent there we found ten or a dozen of Meade's and Grant's staff around a pail two-thirds full of claret punch. Among the rest was Captain John Clitz of the United States Navy. . . .

We had no sooner got there than Clitz, with whom I had had a very exciting game the day before, challenged me, and with Billy Worth . . . for his partner, and Captain Hudson of Grant's staff for mine, we began the game on Captain Mason's bed. I can't be certain how the game would have come out, but I had just captured two tens with a queen . . . when the explosion took place and a 12-lb. solid shot crashed across the bed into Mason's camp mess-chest. Of course there was a sudden stampede. As there was something falling or shells bursting at every instant, I looked up to see what was coming next. The sky looked as it does in the fall of heavy snow flakes. Just then a shell burst immediately over us. In an instant we were all running for dear life. Clitz was the oldest and had complained of rheumatism while we were playing, in fact he had asked me to get him some more claret punch, declaring that it hurt him to walk; yet in the flight he was ahead of us all. Suddenly a piece of the shell came down over my left shoulder. I could have stepped on the hole it made in the ground, but it brought me to my senses, and I at once turned and made my way to the wharf.

From the top of the bluff there lay before me a staggering scene, a mass of overthrown buildings, their timbers tangled into almost impenetrable heaps. In the water were wrecked and sunken barges, while out among the shipping—where were many vessels of all sizes and kinds—there was hurrying back and forth on the decks to weigh anchor, for all seemed to think that something more would happen. I at once went down to the ruined building, a large frame structure six hundred feet long, under the charge of my Sergeant, Harris, an old regular and one of the gentlest and most faithful and honest men I ever knew. I could hear the cries of some of the men, and soon heard Corporal Bradley call out, "For God's sake, Captain, come and help me out." He was pinned down under some heavy timbers with one of his legs crushed.

While engaged in this work the cry was started, "There it goes again!" On looking up I saw that the fire which had started on the wharf had just reached a small pile of ammunition, perhaps ten or fifteen boxes. Knowing, or at least thinking, that I could get to it before it could do any harm, I rushed in and with my army hat beat it out. The amusing part of this was, that an officer, a regular too by the way, was at my side when the cry was started, and when I had put out the fire and looked up, he was tearing up the bluff along with hundreds of others, all running as though they expected to be blown to atoms the next minute. All fear is ignorance; I knew how the ammunition was packed; if I hadn't I should in all probability have been with the rest of them, and possibly in the lead.

The boat or barge, on the deck of which the torpedo was placed, had on board some twenty or thirty thousand rounds of artillery ammunition and in the vicinity of seventy-five or one hundred thousand rounds of small-arms ammunition. Between it and the wharf was a canal boat filled with cavalry saddles and equipment turned in by Sheridan's cavalry a few days before on embarking for Washington, which [had been] threatened by General Early. The explosion sent those old cavalry saddles flying in every direction like so many big-winged bats. One of them struck and killed the lemonade man, the only authorized vender of pop-syrups and lemonade at the depots. He had been with us some time, and was doing a thriving business under a tent-fly, surrounded by mule drivers, white and black, soldiers, civilians, and swarms of flies, when the saddle dashed through the crowd and hit him in the stomach.

Among the flower beds of the garden behind my office one of my clerks fell, with a large piece of his skull torn off by the fuse of a shell that had burst over him. It was the most singular wound I ever saw, in this, that the substance of the brain apparently was not touched, but stood in place, a firm, white convoluted mass.

That night . . . a telegraph order came from Washington to report the names of all the dead. We gathered them together with the aid of a lantern, and then tried to check them off by the pay roll, but as we lifted one by one the coats or whatever covered their faces, to my surprise the foreman . . . said, "I do not know him."

233

The total number killed will never be known. Had the explosion occurred an hour earlier, just before the sailing of the Baltimore boat, when the wharf was crowded, the list of dead would have been . . . much greater. There was a guard . . . detailed to keep all persons from going into the building or on board the boats. . . . A musket was found standing upright in the road, buried to the second band, almost a half mile from the wharf. I have always thought it must have been that of the sentinel . . . for it does not seem possible that any of the rifles in the storehouse could have attained a height such as this one must have reached to gain the necessary velocity to penetrate so deeply. . . .

The true cause [of the explosion] was not known till after the war . . . when there was found among the Confederate archives a drawing of the torpedo and the official report of the Confederate soldier, Captain Maxwell, who with great daring penetrated our lines with it.

The following is an extract from his report:

"I left Richmond on the 26th of July, 1864, to operate with what was known as the 'horological' torpedo against the vessels of Federal forces navigating the James River. Mr. R. K. Dillard . . . was with me. He was well acquainted with the river, and would go anywhere I led, no matter what the danger might be. When we reached Isle of Wight County, on August 2, we heard that an immense supply of stores was being landed at City Point, and at once started for that place intending, if possible, to introduce our machine upon one of the vessels discharging their cargoes.

"We reached City Point before daybreak on August 9, having travelled mostly by night, and crawled upon our knees to pass the picket lines. I had with me an ordinary candle box containing twelve pounds of gunpowder, procured at a country store. In the box was packed a small machine, my own invention, which was arranged by means of a lever to explode a cap at a time indicated by a dial.

"When we got within half a mile of City Point I told Dillard to remain behind while I went forward with my machine. I went out on the wharf loaded with ammunition and various stores for the Federal troops, while on the bank were buildings stored with supplies.

"I sat waiting until I saw the captain of the vessel nearest to me leave his boat. That was my opportunity. I picked up the box of powder and started for the boat. As I reached the edge of the wharf the sentry hailed me. He was a German and could not speak a word of English. He vociferated something at me in German, while I rejoined in broad Scotch. Finally by means of signs I induced him to let me approach the vessel. Just then a Negro appeared at the side of the ship. I gave him the box and told him the captain said put it down below until he came. The man took it without question and carried it down while I went off a little distance.

"In an hour's time the explosion occurred. It was terrific. Its effect was communicated to the other vessel and also to the large building on the wharf, filled with stores, and all were destroyed utterly. I myself was terribly shocked by the explosion, but was not injured permanently. Dillard, my companion was rendered deaf by the explosion, and never recovered from its effects. . . .

"There is one thing only that I regret, and that is, according to the report of the enemy, a party of ladies was killed. Of course, we never intended anything of the kind, not being aware of their presence."

235

Mosby's Greenback Raid

by JOHN H. ALEXANDER
from *Mosby's Men*, 1907

[One of the most picturesque of the Confederate guerrilla leaders in Virginia was John Singleton Mosby, a cavalry fighter whose daring exploits have recently been featured in a television serial. Mosby was a remarkable man whose postwar career as a friend of U. S. Grant, a southern Republican, U. S. Consul at Hong Kong, land agent in Colorado, and assistant attorney for the Department of Justice was almost as interesting as his adventures during the Civil War. He outlived most of his contemporaries and died in 1916.

Mosby had been wounded shortly before the raid described here and was reported to be riding in a buggy when he led his men into action. He was hobbling on a cane when he directed this famous railroad holdup which took place on the Baltimore and Ohio, west of Harpers Ferry on October 14, 1864. Mosby said that he chose a narrow cut for the holdup rather than an open embankment because less risk to the passengers was involved.

Although Mosby refused to share in the cash spoils he did accept a gift of a fine thoroughbred which his men bought from a purse made up from money taken in the raid.]

LATE IN THE EVENING . . . we pulled up in a body of woods where we dismounted and left our horses with a detail, then marched a few hundred yards across a field and reached the railroad at a deep cut. Here we went to work on the track, and soon had one side of it so elevated on fence rails and old ties as to insure the upsetting of the engine when it should come to that point. Then we laid along the bank and waited. . . .

Anticipations of what was certain to happen, and pictures of what might happen, in the next half hour, set my nerves tingling. It is not a pleasant thing to lie calmly under the stars and contemplate the usual contingencies of a straight fight. But the possible horrors of a railroad wreck, and the sufferings of women, children, and, not improbably, the presence of a carload of infantry, took such tangible shapes in my meditations as to give me a very bad half hour.

Presently I heard the train coming, and I hurried around waking up the boys. I then went back to my place and watched and listened to the thumping of my heart. Nearer and louder came the sounds and quicker beat my pulses. Directly the headlight of the engine shot around a curve not far off, and as the engine rushed almost under me, it seemed, my heart well-nigh choked me. And then there was a tremendous thump and the shriek of the steam and the sound of a single shot and then—the deluge.

"Board her, boys!" rang out the Colonel's crisp, steady tones.

That brought me back to sense and braced me. The conductor of the train seemed to take in the situation more promptly than any of us, and never for a moment lost his nerve. He jumped off between his train and us, swinging a lighted lantern, and cried out that he surrendered the train. Down the bank we rushed.

As I ran up the steps on the platform of a coach a tall Ranger was standing with his pistol poked through the door ajar, calling on somebody to surrender. Being short and slim, I slipped under his arm and jumped in. On the first seat sat a soldier with a lady beside him, who, as I stopped, assured me that her "husband was a sick man." Just behind them sat a gentleman, across whose portliness stretched a gold watch chain. He must have noticed that it fascinated my gaze, for he promptly presented it to me, without detaching from it a beautiful gold watch. Of course I could not accept such munificence without some inquiry into the condition of his finances. The generous old man responded to this with the offer of his pocketbook, but I had barely noticed its plump appearance, when a long lank arm reached over my shoulder and appropriated what my modesty might have declined. By this time the boys were crowding into the car. As I moved down the aisle I felt a gentle touch on my arm and a sweet voice asked if I would "protect them." Of course I would, and took my seat between as pretty a pair of cherubs as ever made a fool of a soldier boy. And I stayed there, too, until the looting of the car was completed.

After the looting the cars were to be burnt, but they had to be emptied of certain valuables. First, of course, came the ladies, who were disposed as comfortably as practicable with their baggage which was gathered from the car. You may be sure that my fair protégées received every needed attention, not only from myself but from other gallants whom their beauty attracted. I believe they were the belles of the occasion; and I am sure that they really enjoyed the affair, and doubtless had many stories to relate of their flirtations that night with Mosby's Guerrillas.

The occupants of one car were [German] immigrants who could not understand even enough English to learn how to get out of a fire. They sat immovable under every inducement to "change base." Finally, when the situation was reported to the Colonel, his eye fell on a big bundle of newspapers which had been intercepted, and he ordered that they be set afire and thrown into the car. This gave rise to the only comical feature of the occasion. When the fire brands fell into the aisle, the dumb creatures . . . went tumbling heels over head out of the windows.

We ourselves barely escaped a stampede. Cab Maddux had been left with the horse detail back in the woods. Now Cab was nothing if not enterprising, and as he saw the lights and heard the sounds, he just couldn't stand it. So here he came, rushing across the field. When he came up, it was with some cock-and-bull story about the Yankees coming. Nothing can be more demoralizing to a cavalryman than to be attacked away from his horse, and for a moment or two the situation was more than threatening. The Colonel, however, promptly got control of affairs, and when he satisfied himself that it was a false alarm, maybe Cab didn't get a roasting. It wound up with a threat of that direst of all punishments to a Mosby man—to be sent back to the regular service. . . .

Before the cars were set afire such things as appeared valuable were taken out. As an officer whom West Aldridge had ordered out stepped upon the ground, bearing an innocent looking satchel, Charley Dear courteously relieved him of his baggage. As he parted with it, he charged Charley to be careful with it, as it contained greenbacks. "Greenbacks, greenbacks!" shouted Charley as he made his way toward the Colonel. An investigation revealed a great roll of uncut sheets of the "long green" and Charley's eyes were not the only ones that assumed the dimensions of saucers at the ravishing sight.

About this time West Aldridge came up with a similar fairytale, and substantial exhibits to bring it into the realm of fact. In his final clean-up of a car he noticed a large dark object on the floor between two seats, covered with a handsome gum blanket. There was no response to the investigating kick that he gave it, but the lifting of the blanket revealed a Yankee officer, crouching and clinging to a forlorn hope that he might be overlooked. So tenaciously did he embrace it that West's call on him to come along was unheeded until it was emphasized by the click of his revolver in his ear; and then as Major Ruggles rose to his feet and yielded to his fate, he managed to drop his poncho into the place where he had hidden. He moved off with great reluctance, as one who had left his heart behind him. These peculiarities of behavior recurred to West's mind after he had turned over his prisoner at the

239

car door, and impelled him to return and get that precious poncho. I think he must have been afraid of snakes, for he investigated it again with his foot before picking it up, and found it to be a heavy tin box. As he bore it away it suggested treasure to his excited imagination. . . . Then he sought Colonel Mosby.

"What have you got?" a voice inquired as he was making his way around the crowd.

"Gold; a safe of gold!" he gasped, and his eyes glittered wildly in the star light.

"Come here, boy," and the voice was low and stern and metallic. "You don't have to find Mosby, or tell anybody about this. Let's you and I strike for London with the stuff. . . ." I would not have liked to be the object of the contempt that flashed from his eyes, nor to be the one to whom he hissed back, "And be a thief?" The man to whom he said it was one of the desperadoes of the command, but he only answered, "Well, you are a damned fool!" and stood out of his way as he went on toward Colonel Mosby.

Before this find was published and while the fire and smoke from the burning train were going up . . . Major Ruggles remarked in taunting tones, as he stood on the bank among the boys, that he had contributed upward of two hundred thousand dollars to that fire. "Look here, Major," West replied, and he pulled back the gum and tapped the box with a caressing hand. The Major's countenance fell.

When the contents of the tin box and the satchel were added together they amounted to the handsome sum of over one hundred and sixty thousand dollars. I had as well add here that the next day at Bloomfield they were impartially divided out among the boys who were on that raid, so that each one received about $2,200 in crisp new greenbacks, in uncut sheets of various denominations. My old haversack never bore such contents before; and to tell the truth, my eyes have never fallen upon such a sight since. Some of our prisoners informed us that even a larger amount of money than this, belonging to another paymaster, was missed by us and consumed with the burnt train. Possibly this was true and probably it was said to make us feel bad.

The only man who did not participate in this division was Colonel Mosby himself. No sort of solicitations from his men could induce him to take a share. His emphatic response was that he was fighting for glory, not for spoils. I have always wondered what he took us for. But so sensitive on this point was he, that he would not even permit Mrs. Mosby to accept a purse of gold which the boys subsequently made up and tendered her.

The Confederates Raid Vermont

by JOHN W. HEADLEY
from the Vermont article in
Confederate Operations in Canada and New York, 1906

[One of the most daring raids ever made by the Confederacy was the invasion of Vermont from Canada in October, 1864. Its leader, Bennett H. Young, a twenty-one-year-old cavalryman from Morgan's command, had been captured and imprisoned when Morgan was taken. He escaped and arrived in Canada in the spring of 1864. From there he went by ship to Bermuda and Richmond. He left Richmond bearing a commission as lieutenant in the Confederate Army and a sealed letter from the Secretary of War to Clement C. Clay, the Confederate commissioner in Canada.

Young was then involved in two unsuccessful attempts to release Confederate prisoners of war confined in Northern detention camps. Since he was disappointed by the caliber of men assigned to work with him, he persuaded the Confederate commissioners to let him go to Vermont and pick out a town for attack. He chose St. Albans, which is about fifteen miles south of the Canadian border.

This account of the raid, which was written by the same John W. Headley who was to be one of the men who attempted to burn New York City a few weeks later, is at odds with the known facts on several important points. Headley does not mention the main reason for the raid, which was to rob the St. Albans banks. And he states that the invaders wore Confederate uniforms although many

242

eyewitnesses stated positively that they did not.

Bennett Young lived on until well into the twentieth century and wrote a book about the exploits of the Confederate Partisan Rangers. But he did not include anything about his own adventurous feats during the raid on St. Albans.

He and some of his men were brought to trial in Montreal—after the Canadian government had refused the United States' request for extradition—and were allowed to go free because popular sentiment in Canada was strongly in favor of the Confederate raiders.]

LIEUTENANT YOUNG, after a conference with Mr. Clay, went into Vermont alone and selected St. Albans for an attack which could be made with the twenty reliable men who were now under his command. By arrangement, his men, two and three in a party, went by different routes and trains so as to arrive all together on the night of the 18th of October, 1864. . . . Every man arrived, and each party found rooms at the several hotels, where they remained most of the time. Lieutenant Young and one or two others went out the next forenoon and located the banks and livery stables.

Promptly at 3 o'clock in the afternoon the little command suddenly rallied and formed in the street, with overcoats off and Confederate uniforms on. Each man wore a pair of navy sixes belted on outside. They proclaimed that they took possession of St. Albans in the name of the Confederate States. . . . All the citizens on the street were ordered to go into the square and remain. This was ridiculed by a number of citizens, when the Confederates began to shoot at men who hesitated to go, and one was wounded. The citizens now realized that the exhibition was not a joke.

The Confederates were prepared with fifty four-ounce bottles of Greek Fire each, and while three men went to each bank and secured their money, the others were firing the hotels and other buildings, and securing horses and equipments.

The citizens had been held at bay during the proceedings, which had consumed perhaps three-quarters of an hour. But the city contained about 5,000 inhabitants, and many men began to come into the public square. A number of Federal soldiers appeared among them, and preparations were being made for an attack upon the Confederates, who were now ready to go when a few more horses were equipped.

Suddenly the people began to fire from windows, and three of the Confederates were seriously wounded. A skirmish now ensued, and one citizen was killed. The Confederates dashed their Greek Fire against the houses all about on the square, and began their march to escape, with the citizens and a few soldiers, some in buggies and some on horseback, in pursuit. Lieutenant Young took the road to Shelburne, some eight miles distant, and was beyond reach of the pursuers until at Shelburne he reached a bridge over a river, on which a team was found crossing with a load of hay, for which he was obliged to wait. The pursuers approached, when the Confederates halted and opened fire, at the same time halting the team and turning it upon the bridge set fire to the hay, which fired and destroyed the bridge. The pursuers did not again overtake the Confederates. Lieutenant Young and his men, however, pushed forward and reached the border line of Canada about nine o'clock that night. The party at once donned their citizens' clothing and abandoned the St. Albans horses on the highway. They then dispersed and proceeded on foot into Canada.

The next forenoon Lieutenant Young learned that several of his men had been arrested at Phillipsburg [Quebec]. He at once decided that this must necessarily compel him to give himself up to the authorities and make the cause of his men his own, since he was the commander, and holding a commission and the authority for the raid.

Young stopped at a farm-house, and leaving his revolvers in an adjoining room, he sat at the only fire, which was in the kitchen, to get warm. To his surprise, about twenty-five people from St. Albans, in pursuit of his party, learning that there was a stranger in the house, suddenly rushed in and reached Young before he could get to his pistols, which they secured. They promptly seized him and at once proceeded to beat him with the pistols and with swords.

The American party now started with Young to return to St. Albans. They could have killed him, but doubtless deemed it important to deliver him alive in St. Albans for several reasons. They put Young in an open wagon with two men on each side and one in his rear, all in the wagon! The men were excited and carried their pistols cocked, badgering him with threats to shoot, while they denounced him in unmeasured terms. Young, however, continued to protest against their proceedings, insisting that they were in violation of British neutrality, but they said they did not care a d___n for British law or the British nation. The front gate was some two hundred feet from the house. The road which passed in front of the house led from the United States to Phillipsburg. When they reached the gate to pass out, Young suddenly knocked the men from each side with his arms, seized the reins, and quickly turning the horses, drove toward Phillipsburg. But his captors, who were apparently paralyzed for a moment, soon recovered, and pounced upon him with their pistols and swords. In the midst of the melee, and fortunately for Young, a British officer happened upon the scene. Young told him of his character—that of a Confederate officer on British soil and entitled to protection, that his captors were Americans who proposed to take him without any authority to the United States in violation of British neutrality and in defiance of British law.

The British officer reasoned with the Americans for a time, who were reluctant to listen to argument or to delay their return to St. Albans. The officer, however, told them that others of the raiding party had been arrested and . . . were to be sent to St.

Albans the next day. Young's captors then agreed that the officer should take him ... to Phillipsburg. Here he found five of his comrades under arrest. But it happened that there was no arrangement for the Americans or any one else to carry the prisoners back to St. Albans.

That night Lieutenant Young and his five men were carried to St. Johns, a distance of about twenty miles, and placed in jail. Here a large garrison of British Regulars was stationed, who manifested the warmest friendship for the prisoners. They went so far as to suggest to Lieutenant Young that he and his men might be rescued. They extended every courtesy, and the citizens were likewise friendly and hospitable to the prisoners. Lieutenant Young and his comrades concluded that it would be unwise now to evade the issue and preferred to await their fate in the courts of Canada, since their extradition had been demanded by the Government of the United States.

The Destruction of the Albemarle

by W. B. CUSHING
from *Battles and Leaders of the Civil War*
(VOL. IV), 1884–88

[By 1862 it had been demonstrated that no wooden ship could stand up against an ironclad, yet when Union Naval authorities heard that the Confederates were building a powerful ironclad on the Roanoke River they did not even try to stop them. In April, 1864, the new ironclad ram Albemarle attacked Plymouth, North Carolina, sank the Southfield, and showed that she was in absolute command of the shallow waters of Albemarle Sound. The Union Navy could do nothing against her; its wooden ships were too light to attack the ram, and its ironclads drew too much water to get over the sandbars blocking the entrances to the sound. Two desperate attempts were made in May to get rid of the seemingly impregnable Albemarle. One was by water, when a fleet of double-ended gunboats attacked her; one of them, the Sassacus, actually rammed the giant ship and grappled with her, but was destroyed in the attempt. The other was by land, when five volunteers carried two 100-pound torpedoes across a swamp, transporting them on stretchers and then floating them, guided by swimmers, to the bow of the great ram. But the men were discovered and routed, and the Albemarle remained queen of the bay for the rest of the summer.

Then Lt. William B. Cushing conceived and carried out the plan he describes here. The Confederate captain of the Albemarle, despite the loss of his valuable ship, said of Cushing's bold action

247

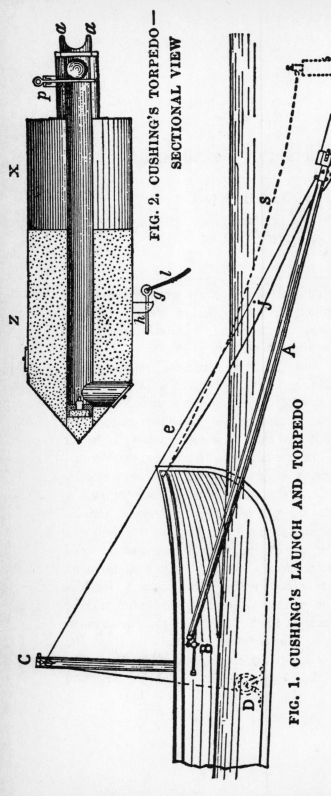

FIG. 1. CUSHING'S LAUNCH AND TORPEDO

FIG. 2. CUSHING'S TORPEDO— SECTIONAL VIEW

A spar A (Fig. 1) was pivoted by a universal joint into bracket B, which was fastened to the outside of the boat. The spar was raised or lowered by halliard e, which passed through a block at the head of the stanchion C, and thence down to a small windlass D. On the end of the spar was a socket, which carried the torpedo. The torpedo was held in place by a small pin g, which passed through a lug h on the lower side of the torpedo, and thence through an inclined plane i, attached to the socket. The lug and pin are shown in Fig. 2. To detach the torpedo, the pin g was pulled, and the torpedo was forced out of the socket by lanyard j, which led from the boat to the head of the socket, passing back of the head

of the torpedo through the lugs a a. A smaller lanyard l, leading to the pin g, was spliced to the lanyard j in such a manner that when the lanyard j was pulled, first the pin and then the torpedo would come out.

The torpedo (Fig. 2) contained an air chamber X and a powder chamber Z. When the torpedo was detached it assumed a vertical position in the water and floated up to the surface. At the top of its central shaft was a grape-shot, held in place by a pin p, to which was attached lanyard s. The pin was a trigger; the lanyard was known as the triggerline. Upon pulling the lanyard the pin came out, the shot fell upon a percussion cap connected to the powder chamber, thus exploding the torpedo.

that "a more gallant thing was not done during the war."

To appreciate fully what Cushing did one must understand how exceedingly complicated the maneuvering of his torpedo launch was. He had to keep the torpedo raised up out of the water until he got the launch over the logboom; then he had to lower it and place it quickly in position. J. R. Soley, writing in 1884, said of Cushing's exploit that: "When it is reflected that Cushing had attached to his person four separate lines: the detaching lanyard, the triggerline, and two lines to direct the movements of the boat, one of which was fastened to the wrist and the other to the ankle of the engineer; that he was also directing the adjustment of the spar by the halliard; that the management of all these lines, requiring as much exactness and delicacy of touch as a surgical operation, where a single error in their employment, even a pull too much or too little, would render the whole expedition abortive, was carried out directly in front of the muzzle of a 100-pounder rifle, under a fire of musketry so hot that several bullets passed through his clothing, and carried out with perfect success, it is safe to say that the naval history of the world affords no other example of such marvelous coolness and professional skill as were shown by Cushing in the destruction of the Albemarle."]

I SUBMITTED in writing two plans. The first was based upon the fact that through a thick swamp the ironclad might be approached to within a few hundred yards, whence India-rubber boats, to be inflated and carried upon men's backs, might transport a boarding-party of a hundred men; in the second plan the offensive force was to be conveyed in two very small low-pressure steamers, each armed with a torpedo and a howitzer. In the latter (which had my preference), I intended that one boat should dash in, while the other stood by to throw canister and renew the attempt if the first should fail. It would also be useful to pick up our men if the attacking boat were disabled. . . .

Finding some boats building [in New York] for picket duty, I selected two, and proceeded to fit them out. They were open launches, about thirty feet in length, with small [steam] engines, and propelled by a screw. A 12-pounder howitzer was fitted to the bow of each, and a boom was rigged out, some fourteen feet in length, swinging by a gooseneck hinge to the bluff of the bow. . . .

Everything being completed, we started to the southward taking the boats through the canals to Chesapeake Bay. My best boat having been lost in going down to Norfolk, I proceeded with the other through the Chesapeake and Albemarle canal. Halfway through, the canal was filled up, but finding a small creek that emptied into it below the obstruction, I endeavored to feel my way through. Encountering a milldam, we waited for high water, and ran the launch over it; below she grounded, but I got a flatboat, and, taking out gun and coal, succeeded in two days in getting her through. Passing with but seven men through the canal, where for thirty miles there was no guard or Union inhabitant, I reached the sound, and ran before a gale of wind to Roanoke Island.

In the middle of the night I steamed off into the darkness, and in the morning was out of sight. Fifty miles up the sound I found the [Union] fleet anchored off the mouth of the river, and awaiting the ram's appearance. Here, for the first time, I disclosed to my officers and men our object, and told them that they were at liberty to go or not, as they pleased. These, seven in number, all volunteered. . . .

The Roanoke River is a stream averaging 150 yards in width, and quite deep. Eight miles from the mouth was the town of Plymouth, where the ram was moored. Several thousand [Confederate] soldiers occupied town and forts, and held both banks of the stream. A mile below the ram was the wreck of the *Southfield*, with hurricane deck above water, and on this a guard was stationed. Thus it seemed impossible to surprise them, or to attack with hope of success.

Impossibilities are for the timid: we determined to overcome all obstacles. On the night of the 27th of October we entered the river, taking in tow a small cutter with a few men, whose duty was to dash aboard the wreck of the *Southfield* at the first hail, and prevent a [signal] rocket from being ignited.

We passed within thirty feet of the pickets without discovery and neared the vessel [the *Albemarle*]. I now thought that it might be better to board her, and "take her alive," having in the two boats twenty men well armed with revolvers, cutlasses, and hand-grenades. To be sure, there were ten times our number on the ship and thousands near by; but a surprise is everything, and I thought if her fasts were cut at the instant of boarding, we might overcome those on board, take her into the stream, and use her iron sides to protect us afterward from the forts. Knowing the town, I concluded to land at the lower wharf, creep around, and suddenly dash aboard from the bank; but just as I was sheering in close to the wharf, a hail came, sharp and quick, from the ironclad, and in an instant was repeated.

I at once directed the cutter to cast off, and go down to capture the guard left in our rear, and, ordering all steam, went at the dark mountain of iron in front of us. A heavy fire was at once opened upon us, not only from the ship, but from men stationed on the shore. This did not disable us, and we neared them rapidly. A large fire now blazed upon the bank, and by its light I discovered the unfortunate fact that there was a circle of logs [chained together] around the *Albemarle*, boomed well out from her side, with the very intention of preventing the action of torpedoes. To examine them more closely, I ran alongside until amidships, received the enemy's fire, and sheered off for the purpose of turning, a hundred yards away, and going at the booms squarely, at right angles, trusting to their having been long enough in the water to have become slimy—in which case my boat, under full headway, would bump up against them and slip over into the pen with the ram. This was my only chance of success, and once over the obstruction my boat would never get out again. As I turned, the whole back of my coat was torn out by buckshot, and the sole of my shoe was carried away. The fire was very severe.

In a lull of the firing, the captain hailed us, again demanding what boat it was. All my men gave comical answers, and mine was a dose of canister from the howitzer. In another instant we had struck the logs and were over, with headway nearly gone, slowly forging up under the enemy's quarterport. Ten feet from us the muzzle of a rifle gun [an 8-inch cannon] looked into our faces, and every word of command on board was distinctly heard.

My clothing was perforated with bullets as I stood in the bow, the heel-jigger in my right hand and the exploding-line in the left. We were near enough then, and I ordered the boom lowered until the forward motion of the launch carried the torpedo under the ram's overhang. A strong pull of the detaching-line, a moment's waiting for the torpedo to rise under the hull, and I hauled in the left hand, just cut by a bullet.

The explosion took place at the same instant that 100 pounds of grape, at 10 feet range, crashed among us, and the dense mass of water thrown out by the torpedo came down with choking weight upon us.

Twice refusing to surrender, I commanded the men to save themselves; and, throwing off sword, revolver, shoes, and coat, struck out from my disabled and sinking boat into the river. It was cold. . . and the water chilled the blood, while the whole surface of the stream was plowed up by grape and musketry, and my nearest friends, the fleet, were twelve miles away; but anything was better than to fall into rebel hands, so I swam for the opposite shore. As I neared it a man, one of my crew, gave a great gurgling yell and went down.

The rebels were out in boats, picking up my men; and one of the boats, attracted by the sound, pulled in my direction. I heard my own name mentioned, but was not seen. I now struck out down the stream, and was soon far enough away again to attempt landing. This time, as I struggled to reach the bank, I heard a groan in the river behind me, and, although very much exhausted, concluded to turn and give all the aid in my power to the officer or seaman who had bravely shared the danger with me. . . .

Nearing the swimmer, it proved to be Acting Master's Mate Woodman, who said that he could swim no longer. Knocking his cap from his head, I used my right arm to sustain him, and ordered him to strike out. For ten minutes at least, I think he managed to keep afloat, when, his physical force being completely gone, he sank like a stone.

Again alone upon the water, I directed my course toward the town side of the river, not making much headway, as my strokes were now very feeble, my clothes being soaked and heavy, and little chop-seas splashing with choking persistence into my mouth every time I gasped for breath. Still, there was a determination not to sink, a will not to give up; and I kept up a sort of mechanical motion long after my bodily force was expended. At last, and not a moment too soon, I touched the soft mud, and in the excitement of the first shock I half raised my body and made one step forward; then fell, and remained half in the mud and half in the water until daylight, unable even to crawl on hands and knees, nearly frozen, with my brain in a whirl, but with one thing strong in me—the fixed determination to escape.

As day dawned I found myself in a point of swamp that enters the suburbs of Plymouth, and not forty yards from one of the forts. The sun came out bright and warm. . . . Its light showed me the town swarming with soldiers and sailors, who moved about excitedly, as if angry at some sudden shock. It was a source of satisfaction to me to know that I had pulled the wire that set all these figures moving, but as I had no desire of being discovered my first object was to get into a dry fringe of rushes that edged the swamp;

but to do this required me to pass over thirty or forty feet of open ground, right under the eye of a sentinel who walked the parapet.

Watching until he turned for a moment, I made a dash to cross the space, but was only half-way over when he again turned, and forced me to drop down right between two paths, and almost entirely unshielded. Perhaps I was unobserved because of the mud that covered me and made me blend with the earth; at all events the soldier continued his tramp for some time while I, flat on my back, lay awaiting another chance for action. Soon a party of four men came down the path at my right, two of them being officers, and passed so close to me as almost to tread upon my arm. They were conversing upon the events of the previous night, and were wondering how it was done. . . . This proved to me the necessity of regaining the swamp, which I did by sinking my heels and elbows into the earth and forcing my body, inch by inch, toward it. For five hours then, with bare feet, head, and hands, I made my way where I venture to say none ever did before, until I came at last to a clear place, where I might rest upon solid ground.

The cypress swamp was a network of thorns and briers that cut into the flesh at every step like knives; frequently, when the soft mire would not bear my weight, I was forced to throw my body upon it at length, and haul myself along by the arms. Hands and feet were raw when I reached the clearing, and yet my difficulties were but commenced. A working-party of soldiers was in the opening, engaged in sinking some schooners in the river to obstruct the channel. I passed twenty yards in their rear through a corn furrow, and gained some woods below. Here I encountered a Negro, and after serving out to him twenty dollars in greenbacks and some texts of Scripture . . . I had confidence enough in his fidelity to send him into town for news of the ram.

When he returned, and there was no longer doubt that she had gone down, I went on again, and plunged into a swamp so thick that I had only the sun for a guide and could not see ten feet in advance. About 2 o'clock in the afternoon I came out from the dense mass of reeds upon the bank of one of the deep, narrow streams that abound there, and right opposite to the only road in the vicinity. It seemed providential, for, thirty yards above or below, I never should have seen the road, and might have struggled on until, worn out and starved, I should find a never-to-be-discovered grave. As it was, my fortune had led me to where a picket party of seven soldiers were posted, having a little flat-bottomed, square-ended skiff toggled to the root of a cypress-tree that squirmed like a snake in the inky water. Watching them until they went back a few yards to eat, I crept into the stream and swam over, keeping the big tree between myself and them, and making for the skiff. Gaining the bank, I quietly cast loose the boat and floated behind it some thirty yards around the first bend, where I got in and paddled away as only a man could whose liberty was at stake.

Hour after hour I paddled, never ceasing for a moment, first on one side, then on the other, while sunshine passed into twilight and that was swallowed up in thick darkness, only relieved by the few faint star rays that penetrated the heavy swamp curtain on either side. At last I reached the mouth of the Roanoke, and found the open sound before me. My frail boat could not have lived in the ordinary sea there, but it chanced to be very calm, leaving only a slight swell, which was, however, sufficient to influence my boat, so that I was forced to paddle all upon one side to keep her on the intended course.

After steering by a star for perhaps two hours for where I thought the fleet might be, I at length discovered one of the vessels, and after a long time got within hail. My "Ship ahoy!" was given with the last of my strength, and I fell powerless, with a splash, into the water in the bottom of my boat, and awaited results. I had paddled every minute for ten successive hours, and for four my body had been asleep, with the exception of my arms and brain.

255

The picket-vessel, *Valley City*, upon hearing the hail, at once got under way, at the same time lowering boats and taking precaution against torpedoes. It was some time before they would pick me up, being convinced that I was the rebel conductor of an infernal machine, and that Lieutenant Cushing had died the night before. At last I was on board, had imbibed a little brandy and water, and was on my way to the flag-ship.

As soon as it became known that I had returned, rockets were thrown up and all hands were called to cheer ship; and when I announced success, all the commanding officers were summoned on board to deliberate upon a plan of attack. In the morning I was well again in every way, with the exception of hands and feet, and had the pleasure of exchanging shots with the batteries that I had inspected the day before.

The Confederates Try to Burn
New York City

by JOHN W. HEADLEY

from "Burning of New York,"

in *Confederate Operations in Canada and New York,* 1906

[When the plot to terrorize Chicago on Election Day failed, the
Confederates assigned to strike at New York had to remain quiet
because 10,000 troops were guarding the city. Union authorities,
remembering the Draft Riots and the more recent desperate attempts made by the Confederates on Northern soil, were taking
no chances.

The small group of plotters, headed by Robert M. Martin
and John W. Headley, both of whom had ridden with Morgan's
raiders, bided their time. A new date of November 25 was set.
But working against them was a creature who had so many aliases
that it is hard to pin him down to any one name. He is best known
as Richard Montgomery. He was operating as a double spy for
both the North and the South and had the complete confidence
of the authorities on both sides. He hoodwinked Assistant Secretary of War Charles A. Dana so successfully that Dana wrote a
laudatory article about this double spy as late as 1891, although
he did not mention his name. Montgomery's true identity was
established later by piecing together two long known but never
before associated clues. When David Homer Bates' Lincoln in
the Telegraph Office was published in 1907, page 82 indicated that

Montgomery's identity had been revealed during the Lincoln Conspirators' Trial. On page 26 of the Pitman edition of the trial testimony it is made clear that Dana's trusted agent was Richard Montgomery. Yet this man was a professional perjurer who was a close associate of that even greater perjurer, Charles A. Dunham, alias Sanford Conover. Conover proved to be such a bold—and stupid—liar that he almost wrecked the Government's case against the Lincoln Conspirators in May, 1865. But that was later in Montgomery's career. The information he gave Dana about the plot to burn New York in November, 1864, was correct. Perhaps he felt that he could afford to supply correct information about the plot at this time because rumors about it were already in circulation. At just about the same date (November 1), the American consul at Halifax sent word to Seward warning him that the Confederates would set fire "to the principal cities in the Northern states on the day of the Presidential election." Since newspapers in Richmond had been openly predicting that the cities of the North would soon be in ashes, the Federal Government sensibly took precautions. Martin and Headley's little group were shadowed by detectives who watched every move they made.

The inside story of the Confederate plot to burn New York was told in 1906 by John W. Headley. And he named names. He revealed the fact that he got bottles of Greek Fire from a local chemist because a Captain E. Longuemare had made all the necessary arrangements. He also told how W. L. McDonald, New York piano merchant, helped the Confederates escape.]

I FOUND the place . . . in a basement on the west side of Washington Place. The heavy-built old man I met wore a long beard. . . . All I had to do was to tell him that Captain Longmire [Longuemare] had sent me for his valise. He handed it over the counter without saying a word. I turned and departed with the same silence. The leather valise was about two and a half feet long and heavy. I had to change hands every ten steps to carry it. No carriage was in sight. I had not expected the valise to be so heavy. But I reached the City Hall Square with it safely and boarded a street car which started there for Central Park, going up [the] Bowery. . . .

The car was crowded and I had to put the valise in front of me on the floor in the passway, as the seats ran full length on each side of the car. I soon began to smell a peculiar odor—a little like rotten eggs—and I noticed the passengers were conscious of the same presence. But I sat unconcerned until my getting-off place was reached, when I took up the valise and went out. I heard a passenger say as I alighted, "There must be something dead in that valise."

When I lugged it into our cottage the boys were waiting and glad of my safe return. I was given the key with the valise and opened it at once with some curiosity to investigate the contents. None of the party knew anything about Greek Fire, except that the moment it was exposed to the air it would blaze and burn everything it touched. We found it to be a liquid resembling water. It was put up in four-ounce bottles securely sealed. There were twelve dozen bottles in the valise. We were now ready to create a sensation in New York. It had been agreed that our fires would be started in the hotels, so as to do the greatest damage in the business district on Broadway. The eight members of our party had each taken a room at three or four hotels. In doing this we would buy a black glazed satchel for $1.00 and put an overcoat in it for baggage. The room at each hotel was used enough to show that it was being occupied. In leaving, of course, the overcoat would be worn and the satchel left behind empty.

It was agreed that our operations should begin promptly at 8 o'clock P.M., so that the guests of hotels might all escape, as we did not want to destroy any lives.

We separated to meet at the same place the next evening at

6 o'clock, and then, as Captain [Robert Cobb] Kennedy remarked to me, "We'll make a spoon or spoil a horn."

. . . At 6 o'clock promptly on the evening of November 25, 1864, our party met in our cottage headquarters, two failing to report.

The bottles of Greek Fire having been wrapped in paper were put in our coat pockets. Each man took ten bottles. It was agreed that after our operations were over we should secrete ourselves and meet here the next night at 6 o'clock to compare notes and agree on further plans.

I had rooms at the Astor House, City Hotel, Everett House, and the United States Hotel. Colonel [Robert M.] Martin occupied rooms at the Hoffman, Fifth Avenue, St. Denis, and two others. Lieutenant Ashbrook was at the St. Nicholas, La Farge, and several others. Altogether nineteen hotels were fired. . . .

I reached the Astor House at 7:20 o'clock, got my key, and went to my room in the top story. It was the lower corner front room on Broadway. After lighting the gas jet I hung the bedclothes loosely on the headboard and piled the chairs, drawers of the bureau, and washstand on the bed. Then stuffed some newspapers about among the mass and poured a bottle of turpentine over it all. I concluded to unlock my door and fix the key on the outside, as I might have to get out in a hurry, for I did not know whether the Greek Fire would make a noise or not. I opened a bottle carefully and quickly, and spilled it on the pile of rubbish. It blazed up instantly and the whole bed seemed to be in flames before I could get out. I locked the door and walked down the hall and stairway to the office, which was fairly crowded with people. I left the key at the office as usual. . . .

Across at the City Hotel I proceeded in the same manner. Then in going down to the Everett House I looked over at my room in the Astor House. A bright light appeared within but there were no indications below of any alarm. After getting through at the Everett House I started to the United States Hotel, when the fire bells began to ring up town. I got through at the United States Hotel without trouble, but in leaving my key the clerk, I thought, looked at me a little curiously. It occurred to me that it had been discovered that my satchel had no baggage in it and that perhaps the clerk had it in mind to mention the fact.

As I came back to Broadway it seemed that a hundred bells were ringing, great crowds were gathering on the street, and there was general consternation. I concluded to go and see how my fires were doing. There was no panic at the Astor House, but to my surprise a great crowd was pouring out of Barnum's Museum nearly opposite the Astor. It was now a quarter after nine o'clock by the City Hall tower clock.

Presently the alarm came from the City Hotel and the Everett. The surging crowds were frantic. But the greatest panic was at Barnum's Museum. People were coming out and down ladders from the second and third floor windows and the manager was crying out for help to get his animals out. It looked like people were getting hurt running over each other in the stampede, and still I could not help some astonishment for I did not suppose there was a fire in the Museum.

In accordance with our plan, I went down Broadway and turned across to the North River Wharf. The vessels and barges of every description were lying along close together and not more than twenty yards from the street. I picked dark spots to stand in, and jerked a bottle in six different places. They were ablaze before I left. One had struck a barge of baled hay and made a big fire. There were wild scenes here the last time I looked back. I started straight for the City Hall.

There was still a crowd around the Astor House and everywhere, but I edged through and crossed over to the City Hall, where I caught a car just starting up town. I got off . . . opposite the Metropolitan Hotel to go across and see how Ashbrook and

Harrington had succeeded. After walking half a square I observed a man walking ahead of me and recognized him. It was Captain Kennedy. I closed up behind him and slapped him on the shoulder. He squatted and began to draw his pistol, but I laughed and he knew me. He laughed and said he ought to shoot me for giving him such a scare.

We soon related to each other our experience. Kennedy said that after he touched off his hotels he concluded to go down to Barnum's Museum and stay until something turned up, but had only been there a few minutes when alarms began to ring all over the city. He decided to go out, and coming down the stairway, it happened to be clear at a turn and the idea occurred to him that there would be fun to start a scare. He broke a bottle of Greek Fire, he said, on the edge of a step like he would crack an egg. It blazed up and he got out to witness the result. He had been down there in the crowd ever since, and the fires at the Astor House and the City Hotel had both been put out. But he had listened to the talk of the people and heard the opinion expressed generally that Rebels were in the city to destroy it. He thought our presence must be known. Harrington had broken a bottle in the Metropolitan Theater at 8 o'clock, just after he fired the Metropolitan Hotel adjoining; and Ashbrook had done likewise in Niblo's Garden Theater adjoining the La Farge Hotel.

We went into the crowd on Broadway and stopped at those places to see what had happened. There was the wildest excitement imaginable. There was all sorts of talk about hanging the Rebels to lamp posts or burning them at the stake. Still we discovered that all was surmise apparently. So far as we could learn the programme had been carried out, but it appeared that all had made a failure. It semed to us that there was something wrong with our Greek Fire.

All had observed that the fires had been put out in all the places as easily as any ordinary fire. We came to the conclusion that Longmire and his manufacturing chemist had put up a job on us after it was found that we could not be dissuaded from our purpose.

Martin and I got together as agreed and found lodging about 2 o'clock. We did not awake until 10 o'clock next day. We went into a restaurant on Broadway near Twelfth Street for breakfast. It was crowded, but everyone was reading a newspaper. After giving our order we got the *Herald, World, Tribune,* and *Times,* and to our surprise the entire front pages were given up to sensational accounts of the attempt to burn the city. It was plainly pointed out that rebels were at the head of the incendiary work, and quite a list of names was given of parties who had been arrested. All our fictitious names registered at the different hotels were given and interviews with the clerks described us all. The clerk of the United States Hotel especially gave a minute description of my personal appearance, clothing, manners, and actions. He said I did not eat a meal at the hotel, though I had been there two days as a guest, and had nothing in my black satchel.

It was stated in the papers that the authorities had a full knowledge of the plot and the ring-leaders would be captured during the day. One paper said the baggage of two of them had been secured, and all avenues of escape being guarded, the villains were sure to be caught, the detectives having a full knowledge of the Rebels and their haunts.

As soon as we finished breakfast we slipped out and took a car [up the] Bowery . . . for Central Park. Here we loafed, and read the afternoon papers, which indicated that they had some knowledge of our crowd, although from arrests that had been made we thought the authorities were on a cold trail.

We left the park at 4 o'clock in the afternoon to go down town and get supper and see what appeared in the extra editions which were being issued. As we reached Union Square, Martin suggested that he would get out at McDonald's piano store and

263

see about our baggage, while I would go on and order supper at a favorite restaurant on Fourteenth Street, by the time he arrived. The car was halted in front of McDonald's; Martin got off and started in—there being two steps to ascend from the pavement to the entrance, which was a vestibule. I noticed Miss Katie McDonald, the daughter of our friend, standing at a front window looking out, and the moment she saw Colonel Martin she shuddered, and putting her hand, palm outward, before her face motioned him away. Martin saw the warning and turned instantly, running to overtake our car. I halted it and he came in, looking pale. He sat down without saying a word but looked back casually.

When we reached the restaurant he told me that he saw a big crowd in McDonald's store, just as Miss McDonald gave him the sign and a look of horror. The last issue of the *Evening Post* gave such particulars as to almost designate our crowd. The account said two had been arrested and the police were after the others, with every prospect of securing the whole party. It stated that the plot of these Rebels had been divulged to the authorities a month before by a man from Canada, but on condition that he was to receive one hundred thousand dollars for his information. The authorities at Washington were willing to pay the price provided the man could prove in any way that his story was true. It appeared so ridiculous that the authorities did not want to part with the money unless they received straight goods. They finally agreed that the Rebels should be pointed out to detectives, who would follow us and investigate the case, and, if the story was genuine, the money would be paid. It stated that the detectives had been going with us all over the city and related how we had spent our time. But they had finally abandoned us as a lot of well-behaved young men who seemed to be simply enjoying ourselves, and they had never been able to trace us to any of the places where we would be supposed to go if we had any connection with the New York "Sons of Liberty" who were under surveillance. . . .

Colonel Martin and I decided . . . that we had better meet our companions and arrange a plan to get out of New York and back into Canada. At 6 o'clock we reached our cottage, and soon to our delight the other boys put in an appearance. All had calculated that some of the others had surely been arrested. All approved the suggestions that we had better escape from the city at once if possible. We found that a train left on the New York Central Railroad at 11 o'clock P.M., and that the sleepers were open for passengers at 9 o'clock. After discussing a number of plans it was decided that we would . . . get in that sleeper the moment it was opened. As I remember now only two of the party had secured their baggage.

Our first trouble developed when we came to buy tickets. However, we went direct from the cottage to the depot and found that tickets could be bought at 8 o'clock. Two of the party who had boarded on a secluded street and were not well known in Toronto ventured to buy the tickets and succeeded. We slipped into the sleeping-car at 9 o'clock. We believed anyhow that all the policemen could not have a knowledge of us and our greatest fear was from detectives. We retired at once in our berths, but did not undress, and kept a close watch out the windows until the time of departure. When the train backed into the station and back to the sleeper there was a great crowd about the station and a number of men . . . we felt sure were detectives. They scrutinized every passenger that entered the train. We had examined the rear of our car and found a way to get out in case of a fight and a chase.

Colonel Martin had said to me that in case they came on to search for us . . . we would fight [it] out, with a chance to get mixed in the crowd and escape back into the city. I supposed he had told the others the same plan.

But to our great relief the train pulled out on time. Still, we had a fear that a force might be on board to search the train before we reached any outside stations. However, we lay in waiting for more than an hour, when we felt safe and undressed for much-needed rest and sleep.

We could only get tickets to Albany, which was the destination of this train. The next day was Sunday and no trains ran from Albany to Niagara. . . . We arrived at Albany about 6 o'clock Sunday morning and scattered among the hotels, where we spent the day in our rooms. In the evening we took a sleeper on the through train and crossed over the Suspension Bridge into Canada before morning. We arrived at Toronto in the afternoon. That night Colonel Martin and I gave a full account of our operations in New York City to Colonel Jacob Thompson, upon whose orders the enterprise had been undertaken.

[It may only have been a coincidence, but while the Confederates were busy trying to set New York City on fire, an actor who was to achieve world-wide notoriety a few months later was playing the part of Marc Anthony in Shakespeare's Julius Caesar. This was at the Winter Garden next door to the LaFarge House, one of the hotels the Confederates tried to burn. The young actor, who was performing on the stage in company with his two older brothers for the first and only time, was John Wilkes Booth. And Booth had only recently been in Canada. When he was killed, a bill of exchange on a Montreal bank, dated October 27, 1864, was found on his body.

One of the Confederates who took part in the plot to burn New York paid for his actions with his life. This was Robert Cobb Kennedy, who was later arrested in Michigan while trying to get from Canada to Richmond. He was imprisoned in Fort Lafayette in New York Harbor and was sentenced to be hanged there at noon on March 25, 1865. At dawn that morning he made a confession in which he said: "*I know that I am to be hung for setting fire to Barnum's Museum, but that was only a joke. I had no idea of doing it. I had been drinking . . . and just to scare the people, I emptied a bottle of phosphorus on the floor.*" Six hours later, he was dead.

And one month before this, on February 24, Kennedy's fellow secret agent, John Yates Beall, who had tried to capture the U.S.S. Michigan on Lake Erie, had been hanged on Governor's Island for helping Headley and Martin try to wreck a train near Buffalo.]

1865

THE WINTER OF 1864-65 WAS A SEVERE ONE WITH MUCH SNOW AND heavy rain. Lee's veterans shivered with cold in the trenches around Petersburg and Richmond while Grant was concentrating all his efforts on bringing huge supplies of arms and ammunition to City Point, Virginia, for his spring campaign.

The Thirteenth Amendment to the Constitution, which was intended to abolish slavery, was passed by the House and the Senate and was to get the necessary approval of three-fourths of the Northern states before the year was out. Meanwhile, the Confederacy, desperately short of manpower, was planning to use slaves as soldiers.

Sherman started north through the Carolinas, heading toward Grant. A peace conference, held at Hampton Roads on February 3, came to nothing, and the Confederacy, numbed and reeling, waited for the end which was already in sight.

After being inaugurated for a second term on March 4,

Lincoln went to City Point, to join Grant. On March 27 and 28, a high-level policy meeting was held; during it Lincoln gave Grant, Sherman, and Admiral Porter his ideas about the peace terms he wanted to offer the Confederates.

Grant's great army began its whirlwind campaign on March 29. Its infantry broke the Confederate lines around Petersburg and Richmond, causing those cities to be abandoned on April 2. Jefferson Davis and his Cabinet fled to the Deep South, while the remnants of Lee's shattered army began their last march, heading west toward Appomattox Court House.

The Confederacy was beaten even before the year 1865 began. Its frantic effort to strike back at the North by the many secret missions carried out in the autumn of 1864 was actually its last gasp. Its stunned people watched General Joseph E. Johnston surrender what was left of the Confederate forces that had stood between Sherman and Grant. Then, during the negotiations for this surrender on generous terms proposed by Sherman, came the shock of the Lincoln assassination. Hysteria and hatred spoiled any chance for an amicable settlement of the war.

The fighting, except for a last-minute encounter in Texas, was over. But, unaware of what was happening at home, the raider Shenandoah was roaming around the Pacific Ocean, seeking Yankee ships to destroy. Hers was the last official secret mission of the war. Not until she got the news from a British ship and set sail for England, where she surrendered to the British authorities on November 6, was the American Civil War brought to a close.

One other secret naval action in 1865, a seemingly minor one, may have been fraught with more significance than appears on the surface. There had been a number of Confederate attempts to seize ships by putting armed men aboard, disguised as innocent-looking civilian passengers, who, at a prearranged signal, would hold up the captain and take over the vessel. One such case, a particularly interesting one, occurred early in the war when a band of Confederates boarded the steamer Saint Nicholas at Baltimore. Their leader, Colonel Richard Thomas (alias Zarvona) was brought to the ship disguised as a heavily veiled, ailing French woman. With him came a milliner's trunk filled with arms and ammunition. Shortly before 1:00 A.M. on June 29, 1861, the Confederates captured the ship and sailed her out into Chesapeake Bay where they took two Northern vessels as prizes of war and ran the Saint Nicholas up the Rappahannock to sell her to their government for $45,000.

On the return journey Thomas ran into trouble. A woman lighthouse-keeper recognized him by a scar on his face when he and his men landed at Point Lookout in a small boat. Then, by coincidence, two police officers who had been sent down the Bay to make some arrests were on the steamer Saint Mary with the prisoners they had taken. Thomas was unlucky enough to be on the same steamer. On the way to Baltimore, one of the police officers found out from the passengers that Thomas and his crew were on board. He ordered the captain to stop at Fort McHenry. When Thomas saw that the ship was about to make an unschedued landing there, he drew a pistol and gathered his men around him to try to prevent the steamer from approaching the fort. But it was too late, soldiers were rushing to the landing in force, and there was a good chance that the guns of the fort might be used on the Saint Mary, since it was evident from the commotion on her deck that something was wrong.

Thomas and his men scattered to hide in remote parts of the ship. When a company of infantrymen came aboard, they quickly discovered and arrested all the invaders except Thomas. It took them an hour and a half to locate him. This redoubtable raider with the scarred face must have been very small, for he was eventually found hidden away in a bureau drawer in the ladies' cabin.

A truly strange secret naval mission, the purpose of which has never been fully explained, took place on April 4, 1865, after Richmond had fallen. A band of Confederates, disguised as local wood-choppers, captured the Baltimore steamer Harriet De Ford, put the passengers ashore, ran the ship down Chesapeake Bay, and then, after hearing the great cannon salute at Washington celebrating the fall of Richmond, decided to strip and burn the steamer. At the time many people believed that the ship was captured in order to take Jefferson Davis to the Bahamas.

Several documents in the National Archives hint at another possible explanation for the seizure of the Harriet De Ford. One of the Booth conspirators (Atzerodt), soon after his arrest said that Booth's chief aide, John Harrison Surratt, had told him that they were to have a vessel available to take them through the blockade. The fact that Booth lay concealed near the shores of the Potomac River from April 16 to April 21 tends to make one believe that he was waiting to be picked up by a ship—or by a smaller boat that would take him to a ship. More possible confirmation can be found in several other documents in the Archives, which show that Booth, some time after November 18, 1864, ordered his theatrical costumes, prompt books, and other personal property to be sent from Canada to the Bahamas. The schooner bearing his baggage was detained for legal reasons at Rimouski, a small town on the St. Lawrence. Booth's effects, along with other cargo, were sold at auction for the benefit of the salvors.

All this, of course, may be purely coincidental. No one, unfortunately, has made a careful investigation of the remarkable ease with which ships from Canada could ply between their home ports and various places in the Caribbean and the Confederacy. One of them, a yacht named the Octavia, was at City Point when Lincoln and Admiral Porter decided to visit Richmond on April 4, 1865, only two days after the city was evacuated. This mysterious private yacht attempted to follow the Presidential flotilla up the James until Porter ordered her to turn back. What she was doing in those waters is still not known.

The year 1865, so far as the Civil War was concerned, was a year of endings, the close of an era, and the beginning of a new age. Many of the men who had risked their lives in its secret missions lived to see the United States become a unified world power.

Capturing a Confederate Guerrilla Leader

by HARRY GILMOR
from *Four Years in the Saddle*, 1866

[Starting out before dawn on February 4, 1865, a contingent of three hundred Federal cavalrymen under the command of Lieutenant Colonel E. W. Whitaker rode through the bitter cold and falling snow toward Moorefield, a small town in the Shenandoah Mountains west of the valley. With them was Major Harry H. Young, Sheridan's fabulous chief of scouts. Two spies had brought them word that Major Harry W. Gilmor, one of the Confederacy's ablest guerrilla leaders, was in Moorefield. He had been wounded during the previous autumn and had only recently returned to active service. Gilmor had had many narrow escapes, the narrowest of which was when he had been hit by a rifle bullet directly over the heart. He was saved by a pack of playing cards in his breast pocket. The bullet had gone through all the cards except the one nearest his body. It was the ace of spades.

Gilmor had joined Turner Ashby's Partisan Rangers early in the war and was soon given a command of his own. He and his men had worked in the upper part of the Shenandoah Valley. In February, 1864, they held up a train near Harpers Ferry, and when Jubal Early made his famous raid on Washington in July of that year, Gilmor went ahead of the invaders to the outskirts of his native Baltimore. There he and his troopers had fired a wooden railroad bridge by running a burning train on it. Later he was with McCausland when Confederate raiders burned Chambersburg, Pennsylvania, after having been refused the $100,000 ransom demanded for sparing the town.

The Federal Government had good reason to want Harry Gilmor dead or alive. Colonel Whitaker's official report tells how the Confederate guerrilla leader was taken by surprise early in the morning of February 5 while he was still asleep: "I left a detachment . . . to search the town . . . and turned . . . down the South Fork, Major Young taking the advance, when, as it had become light enough, I discovered several of the enemy mounted and rapidly moving across the fields and hills on our right flank, taking the same direction as my column. On communicating the fact to the scouts a lively race set in. . . . The houses on the banks of the fork were being hastily searched . . . when the large number of horses in the stable next the road to Mr. Randolph's house, three miles from Moorefield, excited much suspicion; and as Major Young asked the colored woman sternly 'what soldiers were in the house?' she at once replied, 'Major Gilmor is upstairs.' Major Young immediately surrounded the house. . . ."]

THE DOOR suddenly opened, and five men entered with drawn pistols, and, although dressed as Confederates, I saw at a glance what they were. But it was too late for a fight, for they had seized my pistols, lying on a chair under my uniform. "Are you Colonel Gilmor?" said one of them. I did not answer at first; I was glancing around to see if there was any chance of escape. My attention was arrested by feeling the muzzle of a pistol against my head, and hearing the question repeated.

"Yes; and who in the devil's name are you?"

"Major Young, of General Sheridan's staff."

"All right. I suppose you want me to go with you?"

"I shall be happy to have your company to Winchester, as

General Sheridan wishes to consult you about some important military affairs. . . ."

Seeing one of his men going through my pockets, I flung him aside, when the major ordered them in the most peremptory manner not to touch a thing belonging to me.

I delayed as much as I could, hoping my men would make a diversion in my favor, but the major desired me every few minutes to "be lively," and seemed to be rather uneasy. From the window I saw two hundred cavalry drawn up on the other side of the river near by. I was hurried to the back yard, where I found my black mare already saddled and waiting for me. My dog was also there, and wanted to follow, but, knowing he would be confiscated, . . . I sternly ordered him back to the house, as if he belonged to the establishment.

I mounted my black mare, while my cousin [Hoffman Gilmor] was put on an old country horse. We rode across the fork, where I was introduced by Major Young to Colonel Whittington [E. W. Whitaker], commanding the cavalry. Just at this moment three of my men made a gallant dash from the other side of the stream. The first bullet from them whistled near my head, but I could not resist giving them a cheer, and shouting out, "Give them the devil, boys!" Some one poked a cocked pistol into my face, with the words "Hush up, or I'll blow your brains out!" But, knowing the speaker had the fear of Major Young before his eyes, I continued to cheer the brave boys as loud as I could. The whole column was thrown into confusion, and I firmly believe that if my own little battalion could have been at hand, they would have recaptured me. Major Young, however, told me afterward that he would have killed me rather than let me be retaken. The colonel wheeled the column . . . and moved off toward Moorefield.

I had not gone half a mile before Major Young thought it best to put me on a more indifferent horse, saying, "Colonel, I can not trust you on such a splendid animal, for you know that you will leave us if you get the smallest chance." He was right, for I was already on the look-out for a break in the fence. . . .

My feelings can not be imagined as I passed through Moore-field, and saw the ladies run out into the street—some of them weeping—to bid me good-by, and express their sorrow for my situation. I tried to be cheerful, but it was hard to bear.

We took the river road to Romney, to get on the Northwest-ern Turnpike to Winchester. . . . I rode at the head of the column with Colonel Whittington, while some other prisoners were kept in the centre by the provost guard. . . .

Night came on soon after leaving Romney, and, though the weather was intensely cold, and the horses very tired, we pushed on six or seven miles farther, when we halted for an hour to re-fresh both man and horse. . . . Then we continued on our way to Winchester.

The night was so very cold that most of us had to dismount and walk. In passing through the mountain, I watched closely for an opportunity of breaking away and plunging down the rugged hill side; but four men were constantly near me with pistols drawn and cocked, and no chance appeared until we got within two or three miles of Big Capon River. Here Major Young asked the colonel to turn me over to him, and let him push rapidly ahead to Winchester; but the colonel refused, and the major, becoming angry, took all his men, the scouts, off with him to Winchester. These were the only men I cared for, and I felt certain now of making my escape.

We were then some distance ahead of the main column, and when Young and his men left us there were none in sight except the colonel and his orderly, the surgeon, H———, and myself. We halted, and the orderly was sent back to hurry up a fresh guard for me. The doctor and H——— were on their horses, while the colonel and I were standing in the road in advance of them. The place, too, was a good one, on the side of a small mountain, and I made up my mind to seize the colonel before he could draw his pistol, throw him down, and make my escape. I was about three paces from him when I formed this plan, had moved up closer to carry it into effect, and was just about to make the spring, when I was seized with an unaccountable fit of trembling and could not move. It was not fear, for although the colonel was even a larger man than myself, powerfully made, and apparently a cool head, I knew that my success was certain; for who could stand such a sudden shock as he would certainly have received? I had been standing some time, and was very cold, but I never trembled like that except when I had an ague-chill. I can not account for it; all I know is, that to keep him from noticing it, and not dreaming that any of the scouts would return, I put my hand on H____'s horse, and at length quieted my nerves, when suddenly up dashed four scouts. The snow was so deep they gave no sound of their approach. They had been sent back by Major Young for my guard. My heart sank within me; but I determined not to enter Winchester without making a strong effort to escape.

We went on to Big Capon, where the colonel camped for the night, and where we found Major Young waiting anxiously for us. He told me afterward that he did not expect to see me again; he feared I would have escaped before his scouts could get back.

We quartered in the house of a gentleman named Beall, whose son had served with me. It was about 11 P.M., when, after a good supper, we all lay down on the floor round the fire. Major Young, with five or six of his men, were in the rooms, besides the colonel, surgeon, one sentinel, H____, and myself. One of the scouts, who had deserted my command some time before, sat in a chair between my head and the door, with a cocked pistol in his hand. He was a consummate scoundrel and murderous villain, and told me that he was anxious for a chance to shoot me. The room was about 14 x 15, having a door in front, one opening upon a back porch, another into our host's chamber, and another into

I know not where. I soon discovered that all of the party were very sleepy. The scouts had been drinking freely. . . . I determined that I would not sleep a wink, but watch my chance.

I had drawn off my boots, placed them on the rounds of a chair-back to rest my head upon. We were much crowded together, and the colonel lay close by my side. On the other side was the door leading to the right, which I saw was locked. In less than an hour every man was snoring loudly, including the sentry at the back door, and the scout who sat at my head with his pistol in his lap. The host was inside the circle of feet, standing before the fire, quietly scrutinizing each sleeper. I made a slight motion to attract his attention, that he might see I was awake. He looked fixedly at me. I made signs to him that I should try to escape, and pointed to the chamber door in an inquiring manner, to know if I could get out in that way. He became very pale, knowing the peril he would be in should he assist in my escape; nor did he know that I was what I represented myself to be, as personally I was a stranger.

After closely scrutinizing all the sleepers, he moved toward the chamber door, stepping carefully over them; and, though he made no sign whatever, I thought I could see, by the look he gave me from his door, that he was willing to help me. This silent parley had lasted full an hour and a half, and I was becoming very anxious to make the effort, for I knew that the colonel intended to march before daylight. I sat up, and, after quietly looking around me, began to remove my boots from the chair, when one of the heavy steel spurs caught in the round and made some noise, at which the sentry at the back door raised his head, but was evidently not much aroused; and I, after some remark about the coldness of the weather, pulled on my boots, unfastened the spurs, and laid down again, pretending to sleep. In ten minutes the sentry was snoring louder than ever, and now, thought I, surely success will attend me; but just then the colonel turned over, and, in changing his position, let one knee fall across my leg. Thinking he might not be very sound asleep, I would not move till I heard him snore; then, when I tried to get free, he awoke, so I had to lie still and pretend I had merely turned in my sleep. The colonel was soon fast asleep again, and I once more thought my chance was good, when the door opened, and in walked the colonel's orderly, who took his stand by the fire, and did not wink his eye until at daylight we were all called up to breakfast. Poor H——, too, was anxious for my escape, and twice got the orderly to go out at the back door with him for water, to give me a chance.

We reached Winchester about noon, when I was separated from the other prisoners and taken to a small room in the hotel, destitute of furniture except a chair and the frame of an old bedstead. It was severely cold, but I was allowed no fire. Two sentinels, kept in the room, were instructed by the lieutenant to shoot me if I passed a line chalked on the floor.

The lieutenant gave me a pair of his own blankets, or I should have had none, for I gave mine to H——. I asked the provost marshal for something to lie upon, but he sent, instead, handcuffs. A number were brought before a pair of the "ruffles," as they called them, was found to fit, and, for the first time, I found myself in irons. I asked by whose authority I was subjected to this indignity, and was told that it was by order of General Sheridan. I knew it was useless to appeal to him, and so spent an hour in cursing the crew, and wound up by flinging in a few lively epithets at the head of the guard, rather ungenerously, for it seems they were ordered to hold no conversation with me, and consequently could not reply. One of the scouts . . . a decent, brave man, brought me every day a glass of toddy; but, apart from this, I had only common army rations. I was allowed to see no one, although several ladies went to Sheridan and begged . . . to visit me.

So I remained here until the third day after my coming. . . . Ironed hand and foot—for they had also put shackles upon me— and exposed to excessive cold, my sufferings were severe. I shall not soon forget those two days and three nights, nor shall I soon forget or forgive this inhuman treatment; and I then resolved that, when exchanged and once more free, I would iron every Federal officer that fell into my hands—a vow I prefer to think I should never have carried out.

On the morning of the third day Major Young informed me that I was to be taken to some other prison, but he would not tell me where. The irons being removed, I found about twenty-five cavalrymen ready to escort me to Stevenson's Depot, where I was to take the cars for Harpers Ferry. Major Young had seven or eight of his scouts with him, and informed me that they would accompany me to the fort where I was to be confined. I guessed at once that Fort Warren was to be my prison, and, not long after, the major confirmed my suspicion. From first to last, he was as kind to me as it was possible for him to be, but, at the same time, he watched me like a hawk, and was always ready to draw his revolver. He told me frankly that he would not trust me far, for he knew I would take desperate chances to escape. He did not iron me, as he had been ordered, nor did he ask me for my parole of honor, but I did not make a movement that was not quickly seen.

On arriving at Harpers Ferry, we had some difficulty in getting through the crowd assembled to meet us, and at one time it looked rather squally, for they threatened me with violence. Major Young, perfectly cool, waved them aside with his revolver at full cock, and whispered to me, in the event of an attack, to take one of his pistols and shoot right and left. "They will have," said he, "to walk over my dead body before they touch you." The cowardly scoundrels made a good deal of noise, but, finding they made no impression, began to slink off, when a tall, vulgar-looking lieutenant of artillery, somewhat intoxicated, cried out at the top of his voice, "I say, Gilmor, where is the watch some of your dammed thieves stole from me on the Philadelphia train?"

Without deigning to utter a syllable, Major Young gave him a powerful blow across the mouth with the barrel of his pistol, which knocked him from the low platform. The fellow got up, with the blood streaming out, and slunk off without another word. This stopped all talk of taking me away from Major Young.

When we arrived at the Relay House, nine miles from Baltimore, Major Wiegel, the provost marshal, came into the car and announced himself, saying he had thought proper to do so, because there might be some excitement in the city upon our arrival at the depot.

I told Major Wiegel that I was in charge of Major Young, and that I had no doubt he would find the means to protect me in such an event. Here Major Young joined in, and said, "I will protect you at the hazard of my life; and, Major Gilmor, you shall have arms with which to protect yourself in case of attack;" and added, laughingly, "I would enjoy a small-sized skirmish amazingly. I think that you and I could whip a small crowd ourselves."

Major Wiegel then informed us that he had ordered a guard to be drawn up at the depot. I assured him I felt not the slightest uneasiness on the subject, being confident I was in no danger, or, if so, that the means were ample for my protection.

At Major Wiegel's suggestion, we left the car from the side opposite to that generally used, and, before I could interfere, he had thrown his cloak over my shoulders, and replaced my hat with his own. He then led the way outside the depot to his office.

[Harry Gilmor spent the rest of the war in Fort Warren in Boston Harbor. He was released in July, 1865, and became police commissioner of Baltimore from 1874 to 1879. He died in 1883 at the age of forty-five, his life cut short by the wound he had received during his active fighting days.

Harry Young, after fighting all the way through to Appomattox, was killed in Mexico soon after the war.]

Lee Sends His Last Message
to Jefferson Davis

by JOHN S. WISE
from *The End of an Era*, 1899

[When Grant's massive attack broke the Confederate lines around Petersburg and Richmond and those two cities had to be evacuated on April 2, 1865, the Confederacy had only a week of existence left. Lee's closely pursued armies raced toward Appomattox, while Jefferson Davis and his Cabinet fled southward, making Danville, Virginia, their first temporary stopping place.

When Davis wanted to communicate with Lee, the man selected to undertake this last secret official mission on land for the Confederacy was nineteen-year-old John S. Wise, son of Henry Alexander Wise, who had been the governor of Virginia from 1856 to 1860.

Young John Wise was descended from an aristocratic Virginia family which had settled in that state in 1635. He had been educated at the Virginia Military Institute, and as a cadet had taken part in the battle of New Market on May 15, 1864. He also saw service in the heavily entrenched area around Petersburg.

His book, The End of an Era, from which this account is taken, gives an intimate picture of life among the more affluent families of antebellum Virginia. Most of the leaders of the Confederacy were known personally to Wise, for his father had not only been governor but was also a general in the army. During his visit to Lee, young Wise had an opportunity to spend some time with his father.

Supplies supposed to be sent to the starving Confederates at Amelia Court House had not arrived, and Lee's telegram asking for rations to be shipped to Burkeville had been intercepted at Jetersville by Sheridan's troopers. Harry Young sent four of his best scouts down the line with copies of the message to transmit telegrams in the hope of inducing the supply train to enter the area so they could capture the badly needed rations for their own use.]

MANY MESSAGES came from Mr. Davis at Danville, inquiring for news from General Lee. Shortly after General [H. H.] Walker reported that the wires were cut at Jetersville, another message came fom Mr. Davis. He asked if General Walker had a trusted man or officer who, if supplied with an engine, would venture down the road toward Burkeville, endeavor to communicate with General Lee, ascertain from him his situation and future plans, and report to the president. I was present when this telegram arrived. By good luck, other and older officers were absent. The suspense and inactivity of the past three days had been unendurable, and I volunteered gladly for the service. At first, General Walker said that I was too young; but after considering the matter, he ordered me to hold myself in readiness, and notified Mr. Davis that he had the man he wanted, and requested him to send the engine. The engine, with tender and a baggage car, arrived about 8:00 P.M.

General Walker summoned me to headquarters, and gave me my final instructions. Taking the map, he showed me that in all probability the enemy had forced General Lee westward from Burkeville, and that there was danger of finding the Union troops already there. I was to proceed very slowly and cautiously. If the enemy was not in Burkeville, I must use my judgment whether to switch my train on the Southside [Rail] Road and run westward, or to leave the car and take a horse. If the enemy had reached Burkeville, as he feared, I was to run back to a station called Meherrin, return the engine, secure a horse, and endeavor to reach General Lee.

"The reason that I suspect the presence of the enemy at Burkeville," said he, "is that this evening, after a long silence, we have received several telegrams purporting to come from General Lee, urging the forwarding of stores to that point. From the language used, I am satisfied that it is a trick to capture the trains. But I may be mistaken. You must be careful to ascertain the facts before you get too close to the place. Do not allow yourself to be captured."

The general was not a demonstrative man. He gave me an order which Mr. Davis had signed in blank, in which my name was inserted by General Walker, setting forth that, as special messenger of the President, I was authorized to impress all necessary men, horses, and provisions to carry out my instructions. He accompanied me to the train, and remarked that he had determined to try me, as I seemed so anxious to go; that it was a delicate and dangerous mission, and that its success depended upon my quickness, ability to judge of situations as they arose, and powers of endurance. He ordered the engineer, a young, strong fellow, to place himself implicitly under my command. I threw a pair of blankets into the car, shook hands cordially with the general, buttoned my papers in my breast pocket, and told the engineer to start. I did not see General Walker again for more than twenty years.

I carried no arms except a navy revolver at my hip, with some loose cartridges in my haversack. The night was chilly, still, and overcast. The moon struggled out now and then from watery clouds. We had no headlights, nor any light in the car. It seemed to me that our train was the noisiest I had ever heard. The track was badly worn and very rough. In many places it had been bolstered up with beams of wood faced with strap iron, and we were compelled to move slowly. The stations were deserted. We had to put on our own wood and water. I lay down to rest, but nervousness banished sleep. The solitude of the car became unbearable. When we stopped at a water-tank, I swung down from the car and clambered up to the engine. Knowing that we might have to reverse it suddenly, I ordered the engineer to cut loose the baggage car and leave it behind. This proved to be a wise precaution.

About two o'clock, we reached Meherrin Station, twelve miles south of Burkeville. It was dark, and the station was deserted. I succeeded in getting an answer from an old man in a house near by, after hammering a long time upon the door. He had heard us, but he was afraid to reply.

"Have you heard anything from Lee's army?" I asked.

"Naw, nothin' at all. I heerd he was at Amelia Cote House yesterday."

"Have you heard of or seen any Yankees hereabouts?"

"None here yit. I heerd there was some at Green Bay yesterday, but they had done gone back."

"Back where?"

"I dunno. Back to Grant's army, I reckin."

"Where is Grant's army?"

"Gord knows. It 'pears to me like it's everywhar."

"Are there any Yankees at Burkeville?"

"I dunno. I see a man come by here late last evenin', and he said he come from Burkeville; so I reckin there weren't none thar when he lef', but whether they is come sence, I can't say."

I determined to push on. When we reached Green Bay, eight miles from Burkeville, the place was dark and deserted. There was nobody from whom we could get information. A whippoorwill in the swamp added to the oppressive silence all about. Moving onward, we discovered, as we cautiously approached a turn in the road near Burkeville, the reflection of lights against the

285

low-hanging clouds. Evidently, somebody was ahead, and somebody was building fires. Were these reflections from the camp-fires of Lee's or of Grant's army, or of any army at all? On our right, concealing us from the village and the village from us, was a body of pine woods. Not until we turned the angle of these woods could we see anything. I was standing by the engineer. We were both uncertain what to do. At first, I thought I would get down and investigate; but I reflected that I should lose much time in getting back to the engine, whereas, if I pushed boldly forward until we were discovered, I should be safe if those who saw us were friends, and able to retreat rapidly if they were enemies.

"Go ahead!" I said to the engineer.

"What, lieutenant? Ain't you afraid they are Yankees? If they are, we're goners," said he hesitatingly.

"Go ahead!" I repeated; and in two minutes more we were at the curve, with the strong glare of many fires lighting up our engine. What a sight! Lines of men were heaving at the rails by the light of fires built for working. The fires and working parties crossed our route to westward, showing that the latter were devoting their attention to the Southside Road. In the excitement of the moment, I thought they were destroying the track. In fact, as I afterward learned, they were merely changing the gauge of the rails. Grant, with that wonderful power he possessed of doing everything at once, was already altering the railroad gauge so as to fetch provisions up to his army. The enemy was not only in Burkeville, but he had been there all day, and was thus following up his occupation of the place. Lee must be to the north or to the west . . . either upon or trying to reach the Southside Railroad, which led to Lynchburg. All these things I thought out a little later, but not just at that moment. A blazing meteor would not have astonished our foes more than the sight of our locomotive. They had not heard our approach, amid the noise and confusion of their own work. They had no picket out in our direction, for this was their rear. In an instant, a number of troopers rushed for their horses and came galloping down upon us. They were but two or three hundred yards away.

"Reverse the engine!" I said to the engineer. He seemed paralyzed. I drew my pistol.

"It's no use, lieutenant. They'll kill us before we get under away," and he fumbled with his lever.

"Reverse, or you're a dead man!" I shouted, clapping the muzzle of my pistol behind his ear. He heaved at the lever; the engine began to move, but how slowly! The troopers were coming on. We heard them cry, "Surrender!" The engine was quickening her beats. They saw that we were running, and they opened fire on us. We lay down flat, and let the locomotive go. The fireman on the tender was in an exposed position, and seemed to be endeavoring to burrow in the coal. A shot broke a window above us. Presently the firing ceased. Two or three of the foremost of the cavalrymen had tumbled into a cattle-guard, in their reckless pursuit. We were safe now, except that the engine and tender were in momentary danger of jumping the rotten track.

When we were well out of harm's way, the engineer, with whom I had been on very friendly terms till this last episode, turned to me and asked, with a grieved look, "Lieutenant, would you have blowed my brains out sure 'nuff, if I hadn't done what you tole me?"

"I would that," I replied, not much disposed to talk; for I was thinking, and thinking hard, what next to do.

"Well," said he, with a sigh, as with a greasy rag he gave a fresh rub to a piece of machinery, "All I've got to say is, I don't want to travel with you no mo'."

"You'll not have to travel far," I rejoined. "I'll get off at Meherrin, and you can go back."

"What!" exclaimed he. "You goin' to get off there in the dark by yourself, with no hoss, and right in the middle of the Yankees?

"Durn my skin if I'd do it for Jeff Davis hisself!"

Upon our arrival at Meherrin, I wrote a few lines to General Walker, describing the position of the enemy, and telling him that I hoped to reach General Lee near High Bridge . . . and that I would communicate with him further when I could.

It was a lonesome feeling that came over me when the engine went southward, leaving me alone and in the dark at Meherrin. The chill of daybreak was coming on, when I stepped out briskly upon a road leading northward. I knew that every minute counted, and that there was no hope of securing a horse in that vicinity. I think that I walked three or four miles. Day broke and the sun rose before I came to an opening. A kind Providence must have guided my steps, for at the very first house I reached, a pretty mare stood at the horse-rack saddled and bridled, as if waiting for me. The house was in a grove by the roadside. I found a hospitable reception, and was invited to breakfast. My night's work had made me ravenous. My host was past military age, but he seemed dazed at the prospect of falling into the hands of the enemy. I learned from him that Sheridan's cavalry had advanced nearly to his place the day before. We ate breakfast almost in silence. At the table I found Sergeant Wilkins, of the Black Walnut Troop, from Halifax County. He had been on "horse furlough." Confederate cavalrymen supplied their own horses, and his horse furlough meant that his horse had broken down, that he had been home to replace it, and that he was now returning to duty with another beast. His mare was beautiful and fresh—the very animal that I needed. When I told him that I must take his horse, he laughed, as if I were joking; then he positively refused; but finally, when I showed the sign manual of Jefferson Davis, he yielded. . . .It was perhaps fortunate for Sergeant Wilkins that he was obliged to go home again, for his cavalry command was engaged heavily that day, and every day thereafter, until the surrender at Appomattox.

On the morning of April 6, mounted upon as fine a mare

as there was in the Confederacy, I sallied forth in search of General Lee. I started northward for the Southside Railroad. It was not long before I heard cannon to the northeast. Thinking that the sounds came from the enemy in the rear of Lee, I endeavored to bear sufficiently westward to avoid Union forces. Seeing no sign of either army, I was going along leisurely, when a noise behind me attracted my attention. Turning in my saddle, I saw at a distance of several hundred yards the heads of a cavalry command coming from the east, and turning out of a cross-road that I had passed into the road that I was traveling. They saw me, and pretended to give chase; but their horses were jaded, and my mare was fresh and swift. The few shots they fired went wide of us, and I galloped out of range quickly and safely. My filly, after her spin, was mettlesome, and as I held her in hand, I chuckled to think how easy it was to keep out of harm's way on such a beast.

But this was not to be my easy day. I was rapidly approaching another road, which came into my road from the east. I saw another column of Union cavalry filing into my road, and going in the same direction I was going. . . . I could not ride forward: I should have come upon the rear of their column. I could not turn back: the cavalry force behind was not a quarter of a mile away. I stopped, thus disclosing who I was. Several of them made a dart for me; several more took shots with their carbines; and once more the little mare and I were dashing off, this time through the woods to the west. . . .

I resolved now to get out of the way, for it was very evident that I was trying to reach General Lee by riding across the advance columns of Sheridan, who was on Lee's flank. Going at a merry pace, just when my heart was ceasing to jump and I was congratulating myself upon a lucky escape, I was "struck flat aback," as sailors say. From behind a large oak a keen, racy-looking fellow stepped forth, and, leveling his cavalry carbine, called "Halt!" He was not ten feet away.

Halt I did. It is all over now, thought I, for I did not doubt that he was a Jesse scout. (That was the name applied by us to Union scouts who disguised themselves in our uniform.) He looked too neat and clean for one of our men. The words "I surrender" were on my lips, when he asked, "Who are you?" I had half a mind to lie about it, but I gave my true name and rank. "What the devil are you doing here, then?" he exclaimed, his whole manner changing. I told him. "If that is so," said he, lowering his gun, to my great relief, "I must help to get you out. The Yankees are all around us. Come on." He led the way rapidly to where his own horse was tied behind some cedar bushes, and, mounting, bade me follow him. He knew the woods well. As we rode along, I ventured to inquire who he was. "Curtis," said he, "one of General Rooney Lee's scouts. . . ."

After telling him of my adventure, I added: "You gave me a great fright. I thought you were a Yankee, sure, and came near telling you that I was one."

"It is well you did not. I am taking no prisoners on this trip," he rejoined, tapping the butt of his carbine significantly.

"There they go," said he, as we came to an opening and saw the Union cavalry winding down a red-clay road to the north of us, traveling parallel with our own route. "We must hurry, or they'll reach the Flat Creek ford ahead of us. Fitz Lee is somewhere near here, and there'll be fun when he sees them. There are not many of them, and they are pressing too far ahead of their main column."

After a sharp ride through the forest, we came to a wooded hill overlooking the ford of Flat Creek, a stream which runs northward, entering the Appomattox near High Bridge.

"Wait here a moment," said Curtis. "Let me ride out and see if we are safe." Going on to a point where he could reconnoitre, he turned back, rose in his stirrups, waved his hand, and crying, "Come on, quickly!" galloped down the hill to the ford.

I followed; but he had not accurately calculated the distance. The head of the column of Union cavalry was in sight when he beckoned to me and made his dash. They saw him and started toward him. As I was considerably behind him, they were much nearer to me than to him. He crossed safely; but the stream was deep, and by the time I was in the middle, my little mare doing her best with the water up to her chest, the Yankees were in easy range, making it uncomfortable for me. The bullets were splashing in the water all around me. I threw myself off the saddle, and, nestling close under the mare's shoulder, I reached the other side unharmed. Curtis and a number of pickets stationed at the ford stood by me manfully. The road beyond the ford ran into a deep gully and made a turn. Behind the protection of this turn, Curtis and the pickets opened fire upon the advancing cavalry, and held them in check until I was safely over. When my horse trotted up with me, wet as a drowned rat, it was time for us all to move on rapidly. . . .

Curtis advised me to go to Farmville, where I would be beyond the chance of encountering more Union cavalry, and then to work eastward toward General Lee. . . . About a mile from Farmville, I found myself to the west of a line of battle of infantry, formed on a line running north and south, moving toward the town. Not doubting they were Union troops, I galloped off again, and when I entered Farmville I did not hesitate to inform the commandant that the Yankees were approaching.

The news created quite a panic. Artillery was put in position and preparations were made to resist, when it was discovered that the troops I had seen were a reserve regiment of our own, falling back in line of battle to a position near the town. I kept very quiet when I heard men all about me swearing that any cowardly panic-stricken fool who would set such a report afloat ought to be lynched.

I had now very nearly joined our army, which was coming

291

directly toward me. Early in the afternoon, the advance of our troops appeared. . . . Eastward . . . a heavy fire opened, and continued for an hour or more. As I afterward learned, Fitz Lee had collided with my cavalry friends of the morning, and, seeing his advantage, had availed himself of it by attacking them fiercely. To the north, about four o'clock, a tremendous fire of artillery and musketry began, and continued until dark. I was riding towards this firing, with my back to Farmville. Very heavy detonations of artillery were followed . . . by crashes of musketry. It was the battle of Sailors' Creek. . . .

It was long after nightfall when the firing ceased. We had not then learned the particulars, but it was easy to see that the contest had gone against us. The enemy had . . . stampeded the remnant of Pickett's division, broken our lines, captured six general officers, including Generals Ewell and Custis Lee, and burned a large part of our wagon trains. As evening came on, the road was filled with wagons, artillery, and bodies of men, hurrying without organization and in a state of panic toward Farmville. I met two general officers, of high rank and great distinction, who seemed utterly demoralized, and they declared that all was lost. That portion of the army which was still unconquered was falling back with its face to the foe, and bivouacked with its right and left flanks resting upon the Appomattox to cover the crossings to the north side, near Farmville. Upon reaching our lines, I found the divisions of Field and Mahone presenting an unbroken and defiant front. Passing from camp to camp in search of General Lee, I encountered General Mahone, who told me where to find General Lee. He said that the enemy had "knocked hell out of Pickett." "But," he added savagely, "my fellows are all right. We are just waiting for 'em." And so they were. When the army surrendered, three days later, Mahone's division was in better fighting trim and surrendered more muskets than any other division of Lee's army.

It was past midnight when I found General Lee. He was

in an open field north of Rice's Station and east of the High Bridge. A camp-fire of fence-rails was burning low. Colonel Charles Marshall sat in an ambulance, with a lantern and a lap-desk. He was preparing orders at the dictation of General Lee, who stood near, with one hand resting on a wheel and one foot upon the end of a log, watching intently the dying embers as he spoke in a low tone to his amanuensis.

Touching my cap as I rode up, I inquired, "General Lee?"

"Yes," he replied quietly, and I dismounted and explained my mission. He examined my autograph order from Mr. Davis, and questioned me closely concerning the route by which I had come. He seemed especially interested in my report of the position of the enemy at Burkeville and westward, to the south of his army. Then, with a long sigh, he said: "I hardly think it is necessary to prepare written dispatches in reply. They may be captured. The enemy's cavalry is already flanking us to the south and west. You seem capable of bearing a verbal response. You may say to Mr. Davis that, as he knows, my original purpose was to adhere to the line of the Danville [Rail] Road. I have been unable to do so, and am now endeavoring to hold the Southside [Rail] Road as I retire in the direction of Lynchburg."

"Have you any objective point, general—any place where you contemplate making a stand?" I ventured timidly.

"No," said he slowly and sadly, "no; I shall have to be governed by each day's developments." Then, with a touch of resentment, and raising his voice, he added, "A few more Sailors' Creeks and it will all be over—ended—just as I have expected it would end from the first."

I was astonished at the frankness of this avowal to one so insignificant as I. It made a deep and lasting impression on me. It gave me an insight into the character of General Lee which all the books ever written about him could never give. It elevated him in my opinion more than anything else he ever said or did. It revealed him as a man who had sacrificed everything to perform a conscientious duty against his judgment. . . .

After another pause, during which, although he spoke not a word and gave not a sign, I could discern a great struggle within him, he turned to me and said: "You must be very tired, my son. You have had an exciting day. Go rest yourself, and report to me at Farmville at sunrise. I may determine to send a written dispatch."

[*Young John Wise stayed with the retreating Confederate Army that night. He met his father General Henry A. Wise and then in the morning went to see General Lee again.*]

General Lee . . . wrote upon a piece of paper a few words to the effect that he had talked with me, and that I would make a verbal report. If occasion arose, he would give further advices. "This," said he, "you will deliver to the President. I fear to write, lest you be captured, for those people are already several miles above Farmville. You must keep on the north side to a ford eight miles above here, and be careful about crossing even there." He always referred to the enemy as "those people." Then he bade me adieu. . . .

As I rode along in search of the ford to which General Lee had directed me, I felt that I was in the midst of the wreck of that immortal army which, until now, I had believed to be invincible.

It was about eight o'clock in the evening of Saturday, April 8, 1865, when the hoofs of my horse resounded on the bridge which spans the Roanoke at Danville. I do not recall the exact distance traversed that day, but it was enough for man and beast.

The lights of Danville were a welcome sight. The town was crowded with people, the result of the recent influx from Richmond. Riding up Main Street to the principal hotel, I learned

that President Davis was domiciled at the house of Major Suther-
lin . . . near the crest of a steep hill. As I approached, I saw that
it was brilliantly illuminated. A sentry at the yard gate challenged
me. I announced my name, rank, and mission, and was admitted.
At the door, a colored man, whom I recognized as the body servant
of the President, received me. In a few moments, Burton Harrison
appeared, giving me a kindly greeting, and saying that the President
and his Cabinet were then holding a session in the dining-room,
and desired me to enter and make my report. I laughed, drew
forth the short note of General Lee to the President, and remarked
that my dispatches were for the most part oral.

I felt rather embarrassed by such a distinguished audience,
but Mr. Davis soon put me at ease. . . . I was the first person who
had brought him any direct news from General Lee since his departure from Richmond.

Those present, as I remember them, were, besides the President and Burton Harrison, Mr. Benjamin, General Breckinridge,
Secretary Mallory, Secretary Reagan, perhaps General Bragg, and
several others whom I did not know, or do not recall. They sat
around a large dining-table, and I stood at the end opposite Mr.
Davis. He was exceedingly considerate, requested me to make my
report, which I did as briefly as possible, and then asked me a
number of questions. When he had done examining me, several
others of the party made inquiries. One thing I remember vividly.
Somebody inquired how many efficient troops I thought General
Lee had left. I was prepared for this question to the extent of having tried to conjecture. In doing so, I had assumed that at the time
he started from Petersburg he had nearly one hundred thousand
men. That was the popular impression. With this in my mind as
a basic figure, I believed that his army had dwindled to one third
of its number when it left Petersburg; and so I ventured the
opinion that he might still have thirty thousand effective men, although I was cautious enough to add that Mahone's and Field's

divisions were the only two that I had seen which seemed to be intact and to have preserved their organization. When I said thirty thousand, I thought I detected a smile of sad incredulity on several faces; and I have often wondered since how much that statement detracted from the weight attached to my report in other respects.

One question I answered as I felt. "Do you think General Lee will be able to reach a point of safety with his army?"

"I regret to say, no. From what I saw and heard, I am satisfied that General Lee must surrender. It may be that he has done so to-day. In my opinion, Mr. President, it is only a question of a few days at furthest, and, if I may be permitted to add a word, I think the sooner the better; for, after seeing what I have seen of the two armies, I believe the result is inevitable, and postponing the day means only the useless effusion of noble, gallant blood."

I am sure none of them had heard such a plain statement of this unwelcome truth before. I remember the expression of face— almost a shudder—with which what I said was received. I saw that, however convinced they might be of the truth of it, it was not a popular speech to make.

The Last of the Confederate Cruisers

by JOHN THOMSON MASON
from *Century Magazine*, August, 1898

[On June 19, 1864, the famous Confederate raider, the Alabama, was sunk in a naval battle off the coast of France by the U.S. Kearsarge. The Confederate commissioners in England hastened to replace her and succeeded in making a deal with the owners of the Glasgow-built Sea King, a fast ship 227 feet long, of 1,160 tons, heavily planked with teak. Because of her extra-sturdy hull, which could withstand the pressure of ice floes, it was decided to send her into the northern Pacific to prey upon New England whaling ships there.

The story of the Shenandoah (as she was renamed) during her cruise around the world and her continuing to raid Yankee shipping long after the war had ended, is one of the most picturesque adventure tales of the Civil War. Several books have been written about her, and more will doubtless appear as additional details of her historic voyage come to light.

The account given here was written by a midshipman who accompanied the ship on the entire voyage. Since the captain and other officers had published their accounts before his, he had the advantage of being able to make use of the information they had supplied. There is much more to the story of the Shenandoah, however, than was made public in the accounts published in the nineteenth century. The ship's log, which is now in the possession of the Chicago Historical Society, and private diaries and day-by-day records kept by various members of the Shenandoah's company show that everything was not as smooth sailing as her officers implied. There were several drunken sprees, for instance, when stores of liquor were confiscated, and some of the crew apparently tried to force their attentions on wives of the whaling-ship captains who had been taken prisoner. Worst of all was the near-mutiny which flared up when a decision had to be made about the final destination for the long voyage. Opinion, even among the officers, was by no means unanimous that a 17,000-mile run to Liverpool should be made when the friendly ports of Melbourne and Capetown were much closer.

Nor does Mason say anything about the daring plot to capture San Francisco with its rich stores of gold, a seemingly madcap scheme that was seriously proposed by Captain Waddell during the last stages of the voyage. Only one U.S. naval ship, the ironclad Saginaw, was stationed in San Francisco Bay, and Waddell thought it possible to seize her by a surprise night attack and then threaten the city with the captured warship's heavy guns.

This idea was abandoned in favor of taking the Shenandoah to Liverpool and surrendering her to the British authorities there. When her flag was run down the mast on November 6, 1865, in that English seaport, the last fighting unit of the Confederacy went out of existence. The flag used during the voyage is now in the Confederate Museum in Richmond. The Shenandoah was sold to the Sultan of Zanzibar to be used as his private yacht. She was wrecked in a hurricane a few years later, was refloated, sent to Bombay for repairs, and then was—perhaps deliberately—sent to the bottom by her German captain while on the way back to Zanzibar.]

ON OCTOBER 1, 1864, a number of Confederate naval officers, who had been . . . waiting orders in England and France, received instructions from Commodore Samuel Barron, the senior officer in

Europe . . . to proceed at once to Liverpool, and report for duty to Captain James D. Bulloch, the Confederate naval agent there. I was fortunate enough to be one of those officers, having been sent to Europe more than a year before to join the *Alexandria,* then building at Liverpool, which was seized by the English government before her completion.

Upon our arrival at Liverpool, we were instructed to procure an outfit for a two years' cruise as quickly as possible, to have our trunks packed in wooden cases so they might have the appearance of ordinary merchandise, and to send them on board the steamer *Laurel* at Clarence Basin. Nothing was told us of the destination of the *Laurel;* but if questioned by any one, we were to say that we were going home. . . .

Twenty-three officers and about a dozen picked men, the latter being the remnant of the crew of the *Alabama,* which had been kept together for such an occasion, met at the rendezvous, and were soon carried on board the *Laurel,* then lying in the river; and before daylight the next morning the *Laurel* weighed anchor and went to sea. . . . The *Laurel* was a small steamer owned by the Confederate government and used afterward as a blockade-runner. She cleared for Matamoras [Mexico], via Nassau, but her real destination was the Madeira Islands, where she was to rendezvous with the *Sea King,* afterward [named] the *Shenandoah,* the latter having sailed from London the same day we left Liverpool. In addition to the "passengers" I have mentioned, the *Laurel* had on board the guns, gun-carriages, ammunition, and all the other equipment and stores of a warlike nature intended for the *Shenandoah.* Five days of rapid steaming, with fine weather and a smooth sea, brought us to Madeira, where we anchored in the beautiful harbor of Funchal, to await the arrival of our consort, whose movements had not been so rapid as ours.

The *Sea King* had been purchased in London by an English merchant engaged in the shipping-trade. She was loaded with coal and assorted merchandise, the latter being provisions and stores of a non-warlike character intended for the cruise. She was supplied with a crew and officers from the English merchant service, and cleared for Bombay and other ports in the East Indies on a cruise not to exceed two years. She was an ordinary merchant vessel of the kind usually sent on such a voyage. None of her officers or crew, with the exception of the captain, who had received some hints, suspected for a moment that the ship was bound on any other voyage than the one named in the shipping articles. In short, there was nothing about the vessel, officers, crew, or cargo to excite the suspicions of the most watchful, and the result was that she left her dock without difficulty or detention. At the moment of starting, however, Lieutenant William C. Whittle, who was to be the executive officer of the *Shenandoah*, was put on board as a passenger, under an assumed name. As soon as the ship was fairly outside of English jurisdiction, Mr. Whittle made himself known to Captain Corbet of the *Sea King*, showed his authority from the owner to purchase the vessel, took charge of her, and immediately shaped her course for the Madeira Islands, where she arrived a few days later than the *Laurel*. The *Sea King* did not come into the harbor, but signaled the *Laurel*, and we went out at once and joined her. The two vessels were run under the lee of Desertas Island, an uninhabited rock, where they were anchored alongside, and the guns, ammunition, and other stores on the *Laurel* were transferred to the decks of the *Sea King* as rapidly as possible.

Captain Corbet had with him a crew of forty or more, and we had hoped that most, if not all, of them would be only too glad to join us; but in this we were grievously disappointed. . . . Only a few firemen and coal-heavers remained with us; and when ready for sea, instead of a crew of one hundred and fifty men, which would have been our proper complement, we could muster only nineteen, all told, including those in the fire-room, the cook, and a cabin-boy. . . .

300

On the evening of the 19th of October, just eleven days after the two vessels left England, we parted company with the *Laurel* . . . and the cruise of the *Shenandoah* began. Short-handed we most certainly were; but as the officers, including the captain and doctors, numbered twenty-four, we had, with our crew of nineteen, forty-three souls on board; and as we were all in the best of spirits, able and willing to do any kind of work required of us, we were not so badly off, after all.

The *Shenandoah* was a full-rigged ship of excellent sailing qualities. She carried a cloud of canvas, having cross-jack, royal studding-sails, jib-topsail, and all the "high-fliers." She had rolling topsail-yards, which were of great assistance to us in shortening sail in the early days of the cruise, when sailors were so scarce. She was of the class of vessels known as "auxiliary screws," having a propeller that could be hoisted out of the water when not in use, and a funnel that shut down, like a telescope, flush with the ship's rail. Her engines were small, the steaming apparatus being intended for use only in calm weather, and she could not steam much more than eight knots an hour under the most favorable conditions. She was a fast sailer, however, and on more than one occasion during our cruise her log showed seventeen knots.

The armament, which was mounted under many difficulties during the first few days after leaving Madeira, consisted of six guns—two rifled 32-pounders forward, and four 8-inch shell-guns amidships. There were also two little brass "pop-guns" on the poop-deck, which the *Sea King* had carried as a merchantman. . . .

It would be difficult to describe the condition of the *Shenandoah*'s decks and of the ship generally at the start. The stores from the *Laurel* had been simply thrown on board, and lay about in hopeless confusion. The heavy guns and gun-carriages, in huge boxes, so lumbered up the deck that it was almost impossible to move, much less work the ship. The vessel was new and strange to us all, and the stores put on board her at London were stowed without any expectation of their being used during the voyage, so that everything had to be overhauled. The officers and men were divided into gangs, and went to work with a will. Fortunately for us, the weather continued fine, and in the course of ten days we had things in pretty good shape—port-holes cut and guns mounted and secured, magazines built and ammunition safely stored, the fore and after holds carefully re-stowed, and everything snug for the voyage.

Meantime the ship was heading to the southward, the object of the cruise being to destroy the American whaling fleet, more particularly that in the North Pacific Ocean and the Arctic Sea. On October 29, ten days after the cruise began, when about fifteen degrees north of the equator, we captured our first prize, the bark *Alina* of Searsport, Maine, bound from England to Buenos Ayres, and loaded with railroad iron. Vessel and cargo were valued at $95,000. All neutral ports being closed to us, and our own closely blockaded, we had no alternative but to destroy her; so, the vessel and cargo being appraised and condemned as prize by a drumhead prize court, the *Alina* was scuttled within an hour after her capture. We took nothing from the prize but her ensign and chronometer, the officers and crew of the prize being allowed to take their personal effects, or baggage, with them when sent on board the *Shenandoah* as prisoners. We made it a rule from the start that there should be no pillaging of the captured vessels. If we needed stores for the ship's use, we took them, but our sailors were never allowed to plunder on their own account. The *Alina* had a crew of nine men, six of whom joined us at once, and were a most welcome addition to our slender ship's company.

During the next few weeks we were in the track of vessels crossing the equator, and made a number of captures. . . . From each of these prizes we received recruits for our ship's company; in some cases all hands volunteered, with the exception of the officers.

By the latter part of November we were pretty well to the southward, and early in December we entered the whaling-grounds of the South Atlantic. We did not stop to cruise here, as our principal field of operations was to be in the North Pacific and the Arctic. In passing, however, we picked up one whaler, the bark *Edward* of New Bedford, with a good-sized whale alongside, which the crew were busily engaged in cutting up and drying out. We were now quite near the island of Tristan da Cunha, an out-of-the-way place inhabited by some forty people, mostly English and Americans, who very seldom saw any one from the outside world, no vessels stopping there, except an occasional whaler to get fresh water and provisions. Having burned our prize, we ran into Falmouth Bay, the harbor of this little island, and put ashore the officers and crew of the *Edward*, and got from the inhabitants of the island some fresh meat, for which we gave in exchange flour that we had taken from the prize. This island was the first land we had seen since leaving Madeira, but we did not drop anchor, and no one was allowed to go ashore. On the 7th of December we took our departure from Tristan da Cunha, and shaped our course around the Cape of Good Hope for Australia. The day after leaving Tristan da Cunha we discovered that the coupling-band of our propeller-shaft had been damaged seriously, thus rendering our steaming apparatus useless for the time being. But as our main reliance in fast traveling was upon the sails, this accident caused us no delay. We got the propeller upon deck, however, and in the course of a few weeks the engineers repaired the injury as well as it was possible to do it at sea. In the meantime we continued our course under sail with fair winds and fine weather, which lasted until Christmas, when we encountered a very severe gale of wind, which continued for several days, and did us considerable damage.

Late in the afternoon of the 29th of December . . . in the middle of the Indian Ocean, we very unexpectedly captured the bark *Delphine* of Bangor, Maine. The gale of the previous few days had scarcely abated, and the sea was running very high, when the *Delphine* came up astern of us. We were under reefed topsails, with propeller up and fires out, and the bark was under a good press of canvas, and to windward of us, so that we were very much afraid she would give us the slip before we could make sail. But the captain of the *Delphine* had no suspicions, taking us for an Englishman, and ran close up to us for the purpose of exchanging signals. The *Shenandoah* was then hauled close up to the wind, and the bark passed under our stern, leaving us to windward, when we at once fired a blank cartridge from one of our little guns. The *Delphine* at first paid no attention to this, but kept her sails full, and gained on us rapidly. We then cleared away the two forward guns, and prepared to give her a rifle-shot; but before we were ready for this she hauled up her mainsail and hove to. Captain Nicholls of the *Delphine* was of course greatly chagrined at the manner in which he had been caught; and when informed that his vessel was to be destroyed, he declared that his wife, whom he had with him, was a delicate and nervous woman, and that it would be as much as her life was worth to bring her from one ship to the other in such rough weather. Captain Nicholls pleaded so earnestly that Captain Waddell was much moved, and thought seriously of letting the bark go under bonds. At this juncture the first lieutenant suggested that the surgeon be sent off to see Mrs. Nicholls. Dr. Lining, upon his return, reported that she was a person of robust health and strong nerves, and that there was not the slightest cause for apprehension on her account. We had taken two stanch whale-boats from the *Edward*, and these were found very useful in transferring the crew of the *Delphine* in the high sea that was running. We brought all hands off safely, hoisting Mrs. Nicholls and the stewardess on board in a boatswain's chair; but it was nearly midnight before we got the bark on fire and resumed our course. The prisoners from the *Delphine* remained with us until we reached Australia. Captain Nicholls and his wife were taken into the ward-room mess and were given quarters in the starboard cabin. Mrs. Nicholls was a handsome woman, and after the first few days she was quite gracious, and would sit in the ward-room and chat with the officers and play checkers and backgammon with us. Captain Nicholls, however, was very melancholy, and refused to be comforted. One of the officers endeavored to rally him by saying: "Now, captain, just suppose that on the morning of the day you came up with us you had altered your course only a quarter of a point; we should not have seen you, and you would never have been captured." Captain Nicholls turned on him with a grim smile, and retorted: "That shows how much you know about it. That is just what troubles me; I did alter my course that very morning exactly a quarter of a point, and that was the only reason I was captured."

On January 25, 1865, we made the land of Australia. About noon we took on board a pilot, and in the afternoon of the same day we were safely anchored in Hobson's Bay, the port of Melbourne. We had expected to spend only a few days here, but the week of steaming just before reaching port, with the damage to our shaft sustained in the South Atlantic, and imperfectly repaired, had been productive of serious results. A diver who was sent down to examine the stern bearings reported the injury so great that it would be necessary to dock the vessel in order to make the necessary repairs. Thus our stay in Melbourne became a matter of weeks instead of days.

On the morning of February 18 we weighed anchor and went to sea. Our crew of thirty-odd men had suffered somewhat from desertions at Melbourne, so that we were still deplorably shorthanded; and although we had applications enough to man our ship twice over, we were compelled to decline all overtures to enlist men while in British waters. When the ship was fairly outside of English jurisdiction, however, it soon became known that there were a number of strangers on board; and when these "stowaways" were mustered on deck they numbered forty-two, about twice the number of our own crew—men of all nations, kindred, and tongues. Among them was the captain of an English steamer lying at Melbourne when we left, who had thrown up his command to come on board of us, and who was made captain's clerk. . . .

On the twenty-first day of June we entered Bering Sea, and crossed the 180th meridian of longitude. . . . The sight of large pieces of "fat-lean," or whale meat, floating in the water warned us that whalers were at work near by, and very soon afterward we came up with several.

The week which followed was the busiest of the cruise. Not a day passed without our making one or more captures. In all we took twenty-five whale-ships, which, with the exception of three or four, were burned. Some disposition had to be made of the prisoners, and as we could not put them ashore in those frozen regions, we were obliged to bond one vessel in every six or seven, in order to dispose of the crews of the others. One of the vessels which we bonded was in charge of a woman, the wife of the captain, who had died at sea. Occasionally, when the weather was fine and we had more prisoners than we could conveniently accommodate on board, we put them astern in whale-boats for the day. On one occasion we had twenty-four of these loaded boats towing astern.

Our last capture was made on the 28th of June, on which day we took eleven vessels. Nine of them were fired, and were all burning at the same time within a few miles of one another. One of these eleven vessels had been caught in an ice-floe, and was so badly injured that her captain had determined to abandon her, preparatory to which there was a sale of all the movables on board, which the other vessels had assembled to attend. Most of these were at anchor near the injured vessel, and hence we captured them all with but little trouble.

The captain of one of these vessels showed fight. He mounted the poop-deck of his ship, armed with a bomb-gun used in killing whales, and threatened to fire into the boat which was about to board him. The officer in charge of the boat, however, disregarded this threat, and pulled to the gangway and went on board with his crew. When the flag was about to be hauled down, another scene of the same sort was enacted; but by this time the boarding party had discovered that the belligerent captain had been celebrating the occasion, and was royally drunk. He was taken in charge after some resistance, and refusing to leave his ship, had to be lowered into the boat with a block and tackle. Several of the ships, when they saw what was going on slipped their cables, and steered, some for the shore to get within the marine league, and some for the ice-floes; but as the wind was light, and we had steam up, we very soon had them all in hand.

We were now in Bering Strait, and the next morning entered the Arctic Ocean, where we encountered heavy floes of ice, and the navigation was very dangerous. There was every reason to believe that a number of whalers had passed into the Arctic ahead of us, and we hoped to come up with them; but the captain was afraid to venture very far, the ice being so heavy; and after a day spent in the Arctic, we turned and steered to the southward. On the 5th of July we passed out of Bering Sea into the open Pacific, and saw the last of the ice-floes.

For the next month nothing occurred to break the monotony of ordinary sea life on the *Shenandoah*. We were steering to the southward to get into the track of the China traders and the Pacific mail-steamers. By the end of the month, we were in the desired cruising-ground, and on the 2d of August we overhauled and spoke the English bark *Barracouta*, from whom we received news of the collapse of the Confederate government. While in the Arctic Ocean we had received, [on June 22] from the *William Thompson*, one of the captured whalers, California papers of

April 22, giving an account of the assassination of Mr. Lincoln and the evacuation of Richmond [and the surrender of Lee]; but the same papers contained the proclamation of Mr. Davis, issued from Danville, saying that the war would be prosecuted with renewed vigor. We had hoped all along that the disaster might not be as bad as these accounts stated; but the *Barracouta* had left San Francisco on July 20, and it was impossible to doubt the correctness of the news she gave us, and yet so strong had been our faith that it seemed incredible to us.

The important question now arose as to what was the proper disposition to be made of the *Shenandoah*. . . . Immediately after parting company with the *Barracouta*, the guns of the *Shenandoah* were dismounted and sent below into the hold for ballast; the portholes, which were of our own construction, were boarded up again; and all the small arms and warlike appliances were stowed away between decks. We kept the ship under sail most of the time, with propeller up and smokestack "reefed," saving the little fuel that remained for condensing fresh water for the use of the ship's company, and for any other emergency that might arise. . . .

On the 5th of November, 1865, we reached England, anchoring in the Mersey on the morning of the 6th, and the cruise of the *Shenandoah* ended, the vessel being surrendered to the English authorities. When we took on board the pilot, the first question we asked him was about the war in America, as we had been hoping against hope that there might be some mistake about the news we had received in the Pacific. This called forth an amusing cartoon from *Punch*, representing the *Shenandoah*, with Captain Waddell, astride of one of his guns, shouting through a huge trumpet to a pilot-boat in the distance: "Is Queen Anne dead?"

308

Codes and Ciphers
in the Civil War

THE ART OF SECRET WRITING IS VERY OLD, SO OLD THAT A DEVICE
used by the Spartans 2,500 years ago embodied the basic principle
for one of the most important ciphers of the American Civil War.
This operated as follows: a general going to the front was given
a cylindrical staff called a "skytale," a duplicate of which was kept
at Sparta. When a secret message was to be sent, a narrow strip
of parchment was wound slantwise around the home staff so the
edges just met. Then the words were written across the wound-up
parchment. The strip was removed and sent to the front, where
it was wound on the other staff. The letters automatically fell
into place so the wording could easily be read. If the messenger
was captured the individual letters, seemingly placed at random
down the long strip, would make no sense.

Even older, perhaps, than the skytale, is the simple substitution cipher in which one letter is represented by another letter,
figure, or symbol. Julius Caesar used such a cipher. His method

was merely to move four letters down the alphabet; A then became D, B became E, and so forth.

After the fall of the Roman Empire interest in cryptography dwindled and was not revived until the Renaissance. In the sixteenth and seventeenth centuries the foundations for more advanced methods were laid down by such innovators as Trithemius, Porta, Vigenère, Cardan, and Rossignol.

Porta was probably the first to devise a cipher in which the use of a key word or phrase made the message more difficult to read because—unlike a simple substitution cipher—the replacement symbol for each letter kept changing constantly. His method was published in 1563; Vigenère improved upon it in 1587. The Vigenère Tableau, or Vicksburg Code as the Confederates called it, is so easy to construct that a spy can reproduce the working square from memory. And the key can also be short enough to memorize, although a longer phrase is better. No incriminating documents will then be found on the spy if the message is intercepted. The table on page 312 shows the Vigenère with instructions on its use written by A. J. Myer, Chief Signal Officer of the Union Army.

Post-Renaissance interest in cryptography lasted more than a century; then there was another long period of inactivity during which the old methods were continued without much change or improvement. Napoleon believed that secret communications were more suitable for diplomatic purposes than for military use because of the time required for enciphering and deciphering a message. Early in the nineteenth century, however, a remarkable revival of interest took place. In 1819 Rees's Cyclopaedia carried a long, well-illustrated historical survey of the subject, written by William Blair. Even more important was the invention of the electric telegraph in the late 1830's. The telegraph required letter substitution, and Samuel B. Morse was working on his primitive new device and on a numerical code for it in 1836.

The first Morse Code was very different from the simplified one used today. It should never have been called a code in the first place, for it was really a cipher. In a code a complete word or phrase is replaced by a single meaningless word; whereas a cipher is an interchange of individual symbols for each letter, sometimes through several intermediate shifts. Code words may also be enciphered in order to make the message more difficult to read.

Codes and ciphers were very much in the public mind during the late 1830's and the early 1840's while the telegraph was still a novelty. The earliest message was transmitted by Morse in 1837 over 1,700 feet of wire; then a forty-mile demonstration was made in 1844 from Washington to Baltimore.

It was at this time that a strange young Virginian, whose inventive mind created the detective story and the modern short story, turned his attention to secret writing. Edgar Allan Poe's articles on the subject appeared between 1839 and 1841. It was he who first pronounced the famous dictum "that human ingenuity cannot construct a cipher which human ingenuity cannot resolve."

Poe put his cryptographic learning to good use in one of his most famous short stories, "The Gold-Bug," which was published in 1843. In this he showed how any simple substitution cipher can be solved by using the frequency of letter occurrence as a means for revealing the hidden message. This story, which reached a much wider audience than the same author's analytical writings on cryptography, made the simple substitution cipher known to every literate person in America nearly twenty years before the Civil War. But Poe's own interests went far beyond anything as elementary as the substitution cipher.

In his articles on cryptography he described a new way to read a "skytale" message by slipping part of the wound-up strip down a cone until the correct diameter of the original staff was

ABCDEFGHIJKLMNOPQRSTUVWXYZ

A	a b c d e f g h i j k l m n o p q r s t u v w x y z
B	b c d e f g h i j k l m n o p q r s t u v w x y z a
C	c d e f g h i j k l m n o p q r s t u v w x y z a b
D	d e f g h i j k l m n o p q r s t u v w x y z a b c
E	e f g h i j k l m n o p q r s t u v w x y z a b c d
F	f g h i j k l m n o p q r s t u v w x y z a b c d e
G	g h i j k l m n o p q r s t u v w x y z a b c d e f
H	h i j k l m n o p q r s t u v w x y z a b c d e f g
I	i j k l m n o p q r s t u v w x y z a b c d e f g h
J	j k l m n o p q r s t u v w x y z a b c d e f g h i
K	k l m n o p q r s t u v w x y z a b c d e f g h i j
L	l m n o p q r s t u v w x y z a b c d e f g h i j k
M	m n o p q r s t u v w x y z a b c d e f g h i j k l
N	n o p q r s t u v w x y z a b c d e f g h i j k l m
O	o p q r s t u v w x y z a b c d e f g h i j k l m n
P	p q r s t u v w x y z a b c d e f g h i j k l m n o
Q	q r s t u v w x y z a b c d e f g h i j k l m n o p
R	r s t u v w x y z a b c d e f g h i j k l m n o p q
S	s t u v w x y z a b c d e f g h i j k l m n o p q r
T	t u v w x y z a b c d e f g h i j k l m n o p q r s
U	u v w x y z a b c d e f g h i j k l m n o p q r s t
V	v w x y z a b c d e f g h i j k l m n o p q r s t u
W	w x y z a b c d e f g h i j k l m n o p q r s t u v
X	x y z a b c d e f g h i j k l m n o p q r s t u v w
Y	y z a b c d e f g h i j k l m n o p q r s t u v w x
Z	z a b c d e f g h i j k l m n o p q r s t u v w x y

Under each letter of the message to be sent write the letters of the key word, repeating it as often as the number of letters in each sentence of the message requires, and always commencing a new sentence with the first letter of the key word. Find in the table the first letter of the message perpendicularly under the letter A; then find the first letter of the key word horizontally opposite A. The letter at the intersection of the horizontal and perpendicular columns, starting from the two letters thus found, will be the cipher-letter to be written in place of the true letter. The same process is required for each letter, until the message becomes complete.

To interpret such a cipher the process must be reversed. Write as before the letters—the letters of the key word under those of the cipher; take the first letter of the key word in the table opposite *A*, and trace down that column till the first letter of the cipher is found; the letter opposite this, and perpendicularly under *A*, will be the first letter of the message; and so on until the message is complete.

The key word being "complete victory" to encipher the message "the army will move to-night," writing under the letters of the message the correspondent letters of repetitions of "complete victory," we have:

```
The army will move tonight
Com plet evic tory complet
```

Taking *T* at the side of the table and *C* at the top, and following the columns in which they are to their intersection, we find the letter *V*. Record this as the first letter of the cipher message. Then take *H* at the side and *O* at the top; we find at the intersection *V*. Record this as second letter of the cipher. Taking *E* at the side and *M* at the top, we have at the intersection the letter *Q* as third letter of the cipher. The word "the" is thus in cipher "v v q," and is so written. The words of the whole message enciphered in the same manner become

```
vvq-pcqr-adtn-fcmc-vczxrlm
```

To decipher this cipher; writing under the letters the correspondent letters of the key word, we have

```
vvq-pcqr-adtn-fcmc-vczxrlm
Com-plet evic tory complet
```

Finding the letter *C* at the top of the table, and tracing down that column to the letter *V*, we find opposite this letter, at the side of table, and perpendicularly under the letter *A*, the letter *T*. Record this as the first letter of message. Find next the letter *O* at top of table; trace down the column to the letter *V*, and opposite this, at the side of the table, is *H*, the second letter of the message. Find *M* at the top of the table; trace down the column to *Q*, and at the side is the letter *E*. The word "the" is then found. By such process repeated, the whole cipher is interpreted.

found. He also told how to make cipher disks, grilles, and book and dictionary codes. And he dealt with the general principles of solving a keyed cipher, showing that it could be done without even bothering to try to find the key. In fact, Poe may be said to be the founder of American cryptography. Many a young soldier in both armies during the Civil War used his works as their guide. There was not much else of American origin they could get.

At the beginning of the Civil War, the Signal Corps of the United States consisted of one man, Major Albert J. Myer. Two of his best students had gone over to the Confederates with whom they were to achieve greater eminence than the man who had taught them all they knew about field signaling. They were J. E. B. Stuart and E. P. Alexander.

The Signal Corps had to deal constantly with ciphers because messages could be sent by two flags—or by torches at night—only by substituting numerical combinations for letters. Myer was greatly interested in cryptography. Even in the first edition of his book, A Manual of Signals, which was hastily printed on an Army press in 1864, he devoted nine pages to a reprint of an article from Harper's Weekly on "Curiosities of Cipher." His book is the pioneer American official text on secret writing. In the second edition (1866) he described various methods for transferring letters of the alphabet into signals that can be sent by flags, lights, sounds, etc., and then expanded the section on cryptograms to sixty pages. He also printed illustrations of the Vigenère Tableau, various ciphering instruments, and tells how to make book and dictionary codes. Then in order to show that practically anything can be used to convey a secret message, he prints a pictographic cipher based on what he calls "ludicrous sketches of little figures of men."

A similar device was used by Conan Doyle in his Sherlock

Holmes story "The Adventure of the Dancing Men." Doyle is said to have gotten the idea for his grotesque cipher from the Carbonari, an early nineteenth-century Italian secret society, but he may very well have seen Myer's book.

1. A message in the original cipher as shown in Myer's *Manual of Signals*

2. The cipher used in "The Adventure of the Dancing Men"

Myer also describes briefly what he calls "Route Ciphers," which are actually codes, for they involve complete words. (William R. Plum deals with this type of cipher at length in his book, The Military Telegraph During the Civil War.) Route Ciphers were the most commonly used method of secret writing employed by the Union Army. Basically this method was similar to the ancient skytale. It was invented by Anson Stager, a telegraph company superintendent who created it for McClellan's use early in the war. The message was written in a number of columns of so many words each, which were read up or down

315

in order to scramble the meaning. The key was given by a pre-arranged first word that informed the receiver how many columns of how many words read in what order were required to restore the original message. This simple method proved to be very effective because the Confederates had had practically no training in cryptography. After struggling with the apparently indecipherable scrambled words, the Confederates would print the coded messages in their newspapers in the hope that one of their readers might find a solution. But Poe was dead, and no one in the South could decode the captured documents.

The Confederates used the Vigenère for military dispatches and came up with all kinds of elaborate combination ciphers for secret service messages. One of these used six different alphabetical substitutions in one message, yet the men in the Union telegraph room were able to read it without knowing the key.

Myer also discusses the book or dictionary code which Poe had described earlier. Myer suggested that all the words in two copies of a dictionary (one for the sender and one for the receiver) be numbered consecutively so a message can be sent by simply substituting a number for the desired word. This was a time-saving improvement over the previously used method of listing page, column, and line. Many references to dictionary codes appear in Civil War literature, notably in the Official Records of the Navy. General Abner Doubleday said in his book on Fort Sumter (page 24) that he was able to correspond secretly with his brother in the North because they each had a copy of the same dictionary.

Since the Vigenère Tableau was widely used by the Confederates, Union Signal Corps men were often faced with the necessity of breaking an enciphered message without knowing the key. By sheer bull-dogged persistence they would try to break the cipher by guessing at the key word or phrase. They would use popular phrases, Confederate patriotic sayings, or place and personal names, until they sometimes hammered their way through

This apparently simple cipher was not so simple to decipher as may seem. Here, for instance, is the message as sent:

> I send shall can me you doing? daylight move spare one provisions enemy at all Jones thousand the the attack my is cavalry all are shall artillery very four and what and to-night sick thousand infantry.

The scrambled words obviously make no sense as they are arranged. But with the message went a code word telling how to rearrange them—in this case in columns six words wide and six lines deep. The message then reads:

	1	2	3	4	5	6
1	I	send	shall	can	me	you
2	doing?	daylight	move	spare	one	provisions
3	enemy	at	all	Jones	thousand	the
4	the	attack	my	is	cavalry	all
5	are	shall	artillery	very	four	and
6	what	and	to-night	sick	thousand	infantry

The code word also indicated how to read the message—in this instance by going *up* the first column, *down* the third, *up* the second, *down* the fifth, *up* the sixth, and *down* the fourth. The last four words in column 4 (Jones is very sick) are nulls put in to fill up space and deceive the would-be reader. The message then reads:

> What are the enemy doing? I shall move all my artillery to-night and shall attack at daylight. Send me one thousand cavalry, four thousand infantry, and all the provisions you can spare.

to a solution. In one instance they succeeded because they tried using the names of Confederate generals as key words.

Oddly enough, however, a systematic way of breaking the Vigenère without knowing the key had been published abroad in 1863 by a German major named F. W. Kasiski. His method made use of recurring two or three-letter combinations and had other novelties. Apparently no one in the United States bothered to find out what was happening in cryptanalysis in other countries, so the war was over before the new Kasiski system became known here.

In an emergency situation there was often no time for enciphering a message before sending it. On such occasions, resort was hurriedly made to such simple devices as merely writing out the words backward. Toward the very end of the war an ingenious Union telegrapher improved on this by not only sending the message backward but in garbled phonetic spelling. One of Lincoln's most important telegrams was dispatched in this form:

CITY POINT, VA., 8:30 A.M., APRIL 3, 1865

TINKER, WAR DEPARTMENT: A LINCOLN ITS IN FUME A IN HYMN TO START I ARMY TREATING THERE POSSIBLE IF OF CUT TOO FORWARD PUSHING IS HE IS SO ALL RICHMOND AUNT CONFIDE IS ANDY EVACUATED PETERSBURG REPORTS GRANT MORNING THIS WASHINGTON SECRETARY WAR.

It needs no translation; if read rapidly backwards the intent comes through.

Other means of secret communication were also used during the Civil War. The want-ad columns of newspapers became a regular medium for the exchange of underground information. An advertisement offering so many acres of farm land for sale could provide an opportunity to inform Richmond (via the New York Herald) how many pounds sterling were being transferred from secret service funds in Canada to England. Arrivals and departures of spies and agents could be announced (to those who understood) by advertising agreed-upon aliases. Practically any kind of information could be transmitted in this way, for the whole art of secret communication depends upon having prearranged a key to unlock the hidden meaning.

A document in the National Archives indicates that the Confederates were even making use of the new science of photography to smuggle messages out of Canada. The words were written as small as possible—but not enciphered—and the message was then reduced photographically until the letters were so tiny that they could be made out only by using a very powerful glass. This miniature photograph (a forerunner of microfilm) was then hidden inside a metal button sewed onto a coat worn by a British subject who was about to enter the United States.

Codes and ciphers run all through the Civil War. Most of the disguised messages dealing with underground activities were intended to be destroyed as soon as their contents were noted and acted upon. It is amazing that we have as many examples of them as we do.

The national tragedy that came at the very end of the Civil War also involved cryptography, for at least two puzzling ciphers are connected with the Lincoln assassination. The first is a letter introduced as evidence by the Government during the trial of the conspirators. This mysterious document, dated "Washington, April 15, '65," and signed "No. Five" was supposedly found floating in the water near Morehead City, North Carolina. Its substitution cipher was so easy that the pile driver who found it was able to translate it with the aid of a local amateur. What it says might be important if there was any reason to believe that it is an authentic message from one of the conspirators, but the circumstances surrounding its finding and its too simple cipher make it seem more like a fraud.

Among the objects left by Booth in a trunk in his Washington hotel was a printed copy of the Vigenère Tableau (with an extra alphabet beginning "ZABC, etc." to complicate the message). The Government used this to try to implicate the leaders of the Confederacy in the assassination plot. They introduced as evidence a Vigenère cipher reel which had been found in Judah P. Benjamin's office when Richmond fell. Then they attempted to show that this necessarily meant that the Confederate government had been giving Booth instructions in cipher as to how to go about killing Lincoln. But no one bothered to mention the fact that the standard Vigenère on the cipher reel was not identical with the more complicated one found in Booth's trunk.

Everyone in the War Department who was familiar with cryptography knew that the Vigenère was the customary Confederate cipher and that for a Confederate agent (which Booth was known to have been) to possess a copy of a variation of it meant no more than if a telegraph operator was captured with a copy of the Morse code. Hundreds—and perhaps thousands— of people were using the Vigenère. But the Government was desperately seeking evidence against the Confederate leaders so they took advantage of the atmosphere of mystery which has always surrounded cryptography and used it to confuse the public and the press. This shabby trick gained nothing, for the leaders of the Confederacy eventually had to be let go for lack of evidence.

It is only fitting that what was probably the last official cipher message of the Confederacy was written in the Vigenère. This was a brief note from Jefferson Davis dated April 24, 1865, at Charlotte, North Carolina, and sent to his secretary, Burton H. Harrison, at Chester, South Carolina. It read: "The hostile government reject the proposed settlement, and order active operations to be resumed in forty-eight hours from noon today." By a curious coincidence, the key words needed to decipher this communication were "Come Retribution."